Land in the American West

PRIVATE CLAIMS AND THE COMMON GOOD

Land in the American West

PRIVATE CLAIMS
AND THE COMMON GOOD

EDITED BY

William G. Robbins

James C. Foster

UNIVERSITY OF WASHINGTON PRESS

Seattle and London

TO THE MEMORY AND SPIRIT OF TOM McCALL

OREGON'S PUBLIC CONSCIENCE

ISBN 0-295-98020-6

The paper used in this publication is acid-free and recycled from 10 percent post-
consumer and at least 50 percent pre-consumer waste. It meets the minimum
requirements of American National Standard for Information Sciences—
Permanence of Paper for Printed Library Materials,
ANSI Z39.48-1984 ⊗ ♻

Contents

v

Contents

Preface

"Land" and "the West" figure prominently among the ideas that fire Americans' imaginations and fuel American controversies. Throughout the nation's history the two concepts have merged essentially into a single, pervasive passion: opportunity. French writer and politician Alexis de Tocqueville spoke of Americans' restlessness, of our "bootless chase of that complete felicity" that forever escapes us.[1] From the seventeenth century on, restless westward migration in search of free land and a new beginning has defined that American chase. From the outset this chase has also spawned disputes. Violent clashes between indigenous peoples and European immigrants regularly (and tragically) occurred until near the end of the nineteenth century. More recently, clashes between indigenous groups and European Americans continue to be played out in federal courts. Struggles between fence-building ranchers and open-range grazers occasionally resulted in bloodshed. Long-standing encounters between environmentalists (once conservationists) and miners, loggers, and developers continue into the modern day. The Sagebrush Rebellion and the Wise-Use movement are merely the latest chapters in ongoing conflicts over western lands.

A salient dimension of all of these disputes is the tension between private claims and the common good. The Preamble of the U.S. Constitution reflects this fundamental tension. In 1787 the framers declared their intentions to "secure the Blessings of Liberty to ourselves and our posterity" and to "promote the general Welfare." Much of American history can be explained in terms of various efforts to reconcile these uneasy social goals. This is particularly true of history in the American West. In a region where millions of acres are federally owned, individual property rights and public interest often are at odds. When it comes to public lands, many would define the public interest as merely the sum of private property rights. But others counter that private use is antithetical to sustaining Americans' shared inheritance.

What does it mean to "own" land? To "own" a forest? To "own" a river? Where does a "right to property" inhere? What obligations do landowners have to future generations? Do the current struggles over land use call for a new concept of property? Such conflicts can appear to be intractable. As U.S. Supreme Court Justice John Paul Stevens framed the clash in a recent decision involving a controversy generated by a western land dispute:

> We assume respondents have no desire to harm either the red-cockaded woodpecker or the spotted owl; they merely wish to continue logging activities that would be entirely proper if not prohibited by the [Endangered Species Act]. On the other hand, we must assume . . . that those activities will have the effect, even though unintended, of detrimentally changing the natural habitat of both listed species and that, as a consequence, members of those species will be killed or injured.[2]

Disputes such as these were the subject of a three-day symposium in January 1997 at Oregon State University titled "Land in the American West: Private Claims and the Common Good." At that conference several hundred people gathered to listen, to reflect on, and to discuss topics related to land use in the western United States. A stimulating mix of plenary sessions, break-out sessions, and luncheon speakers provided appealing venues. An engaging group of presenters, drawn from numerous disciplines and reflecting various perspectives, inspired lively conversations. Three prominent writers—William Kittredge, Craig Lesley, and Kathleen Dean Moore—offered an evening of literary readings, titled "Writers and Western Landscapes." The purpose of the symposium was to contribute to ongoing discussion about the history and present condition of land use in the western United States. The conference organizers envisioned the gathering as a way for some of the country's leading minds to intervene in continuing dialogue about land and property-related issues. These conference proceedings hold the promise of generating further creative discourse over land in the American West. This collection of essays consists of papers or remarks presented at the conference that have been revised for publication.

JAMES C. FOSTER

NOTES

1. Alexis de Tocqueville, *Democracy in America,* ed. Phillips Bradley, 2 vols. (New York: Vintage, 1954), 2: 145.

2. *Babbitt v Sweet Home Chapter of Communities for a Great Oregon,* 515 U.S. 687, 697 (1995).

Acknowledgments

The debts we accumulated along the way to producing this book begin with the valuable assistance of our Oregon State University colleagues who helped plan the symposium, select the speakers whose contributions appear in this volume, and organize conference logistics. We extend our special thanks to David J. Brooks, J. Boone Kauffman, Kathleen Dean Moore, and Joe B. Stevens. We also are grateful to the two major sponsors of the event: the College of Liberal Arts at Oregon State University (and Dean Kay Schaffer), and the Oregon Council for the Humanities (and its former director, Richard Lewis). The Thomas Hart and Mary Jones Horning Endowment in the Humanities and the Jackson Foundation provided generous financial support. Oregon State University's departments of English and Philosophy and its Center for the Humanities also contributed financial resources to the symposium. Julidta Tarver, Managing Editor at the University of Washington Press, was an early and enthusiastic supporter of this book project and has lent her expertise to seeing it into print. And finally, our grateful appreciation to Mecila Cross of the Dean's Office at Oregon State who patiently handled the finances and logistics of the "Land in the American West" conference, put the several manuscript files on one composite disk, and efficiently tended to telephone and correspondence details.

Land in the American West

PRIVATE CLAIMS AND THE COMMON GOOD

INTRODUCTION

In Search of Western Lands

WILLIAM G. ROBBINS

The postponement of outgrowing the romantic metaphor of frontier, of unspoiled mountain backdrop, of rustic cabin in the sun, of
being left alone, of feeling like the land will continue to endure our
assaults on it, is almost too seductive to resist.

—Eric Torso

"If Hollywood wanted to capture the emotional center of Western history," historian Patricia Nelson Limerick observed, "its movies
would be about real estate"—that is, about drawing lines and creating borders. A good contemporary beginning might be the neighborhood
of Peace Cove, Oregon, a rural greenscape of nurseries and berry patches
along the meandering Willamette River about twenty or so miles up-
stream from Portland. The neighborhood earned headlines in the Portland *Oregonian* in early 1997, when Hollywood Video millionaire Mark
Wattles asked for a variance from Oregon's land-use laws to build a fifty-
thousand-square-foot home on prime farmland along the river. When
Wattles purchased the thirty-plus-acre rhubarb farm two years earlier, the
land carried an agricultural exemption that limited property taxes to $545
a year. The title included a farm-management plan, limiting to one acre a
potential home and landscaping area. Wattles—who acknowledged, "I
have a lot of money. I don't know what to do with all the money I have"—
received a green light from county planners in mid-1996 to build and
landscape up to eight acres of the rich farmland along the riverfront.[1]

The monster home—which includes an eight-thousand-square-foot
basketball court and a four-thousand-square-foot swimming pool—has
placed Oregon's pacesetting land-use planning system at some risk. Gov-

ernor Tom McCall (1967–75), who signed the Oregon plan into law in May 1973, had urged the legislature to put a stop to "the unfettered despoiling" of the state. "Sagebrush subdivision, coastal 'condomania' and the ravenous rampage of suburbia in the Willamette Valley," he said, threatened to mock the state's reputation as an environmental model. The groundbreaking measure required every Oregon city and county to draft comprehensive land-use planning structures that would adhere to certain state-mandated guidelines.[2]

The Wattles case suggests that land issues in Oregon and elsewhere in the American West continue to resonate with historical questions framed by the tensions between private claims, opportunity, and pursuit of the main chance with concerns for the larger common good. Since the inception of the American republic, the constitutional guarantees to individual liberty and freedom of opportunity have clashed with similar constitutional promises to guarantee the rights of aboriginal people and to promote the general welfare of all citizens. Because much of the territory of the American West was annexed and peopled by the expanding U.S. empire since the mid-nineteenth century, the more significant of those disputes have centered in the vast area of the trans-Mississippi West. With its sizable federal lands, the presence of most of the country's Indian reservations, and its still extensive natural–resource base, the American West has been the focus of the more contentious disputes involving private claims and the common good.

The struggle for control over western land has often been violent and tumultuous. The greatest violence, of course, took place between the Euro-American newcomers and indigenous peoples. The Euro-Americans gradually wrested control of the region through a series of military campaigns and forced treaties that often confined native peoples to inferior lands. Although the Indian wars were over by the 1870s, violent clashes over western land continued in the form of range wars between cattle barons (who saw the Great Plains as a vast commons to enter and occupy) and homesteading, fence-building farmers (who wanted exclusive property rights to limited acreages). Because millions of acres of mineral, timber, and grazing lands—as well as appropriation rights to water—are federally owned, the public's interest and individual property claims have often clashed.[3] The Sagebrush Rebellion of the late 1970s and the early 1980s and the Wise-Use movement of more recent years redefined access to public lands as an inherent property right and an expression of individual liberty.[4] By contrast, those who opposed singular claims to public land argued that the invocation of exclusive private rights violated the general belief that the public commons was to be shared equally among all citizens.

Despite the romance that continues to infuse many stories about the American West, the region cannot be reduced to a simple morality tale, an uncomplicated place with a linear narrative about the courage and hard work of pioneering people who made the land hospitable and fruitful. That version of the "settling" of the West is terribly flawed because it refuses to acknowledge the presence of others who already inhabited the region. It fails to recognize that from the Native American perspective, the region's history is little more than a chronicle of white "settlers" coveting Indian land and their subsequent effort to exterminate, dispossess, and remove the native population.[5] Once the federal government had established control over the region, it pursued policies that progressively limited native sovereignty and opened the former Indian lands to the play of market forces.

That process of subjugating and removing Native Americans was apparent throughout the American West after the Civil War, when the region became strategically important to the nation's rapidly industrializing economy. To the dramatically expanding productive power of the United States, the West provided an investment arena for surplus capital, a source of raw materials for the industrial sectors, and a seemingly vast vacant lot to enter and occupy. Railroad building, the introduction of large livestock herds, mining activity, bonanza farming enterprises, and speculation in town sites attracted both the shrewd and the gullible from the eastern United States and from across the ocean. French political scientist Emile Boutmy remarked that the most "striking and peculiar characteristic" of late-nineteenth-century American society was its commercial character: "It is not so much a democracy as a huge commercial company for the discovery, cultivation, and capitalization of its enormous territory."[6]

As such, the American West held material attractions that awakened interest, especially among British and European investors looking for potentially lucrative arenas for their surplus capital. Often invested in railroad construction or other infrastructure improvements, transatlantic financing provided the critical opening wedge for further economic expansion.[7] Capital invested in internal improvements thus provided the necessary infrastructure that made possible the later expansion of the western economy. Investments in the first rail lines to extend beyond the Mississippi coincided with the effort to control and confine Native Americans of the Plains, effectively ending their pastoral and communitarian mode of existence and opening millions of acres of grazing land to the livestock industry.[8]

The federal government heavily subsidized the newly emerging property relations in the West through a series of costly military garrisons to ensure that the recently "pacified" tribes remained confined to reservations. The government further served as the interlocutor in ascribing legal attachments to western lands recently freed to market forces, and the government administered and distributed land as private property in the form of enormous grants to railroads, in low-cost leases to mining companies, and in individual claims to settlers.[9] The work of distributing land was an additional expense, borne by the national treasury, but with the principal end of placing land at market and transferring legal title to the private sector. There is little doubt about the ultimate objective and purpose of the federal government's disposal of the public domain (at least until the late nineteenth century). The Land Ordinance of 1785 clearly stated that lands ceded by the original states to the federal government and those purchased from Indian tribes "shall be disposed of."[10]

Historian John Opie has observed that the great land ordinances of the 1780s "put sovereign territory on the market"—a principle that was later confirmed under the Constitution through the recognition of private property. Writer James Oliver Robertson has contended that "land meant agriculture, crops, surpluses, rents, food in the belly, and riches; it meant place and position, status and power, security and continuity." Although the desire to acquire land may have involved all social classes, in the long run the larger capital enterprises were better equipped to buy out or push aside small holders when such actions were critical to their interests. Those enterprises were the primary forces in directing the course of capitalist development in the West. The realities of the "opening of the West" to the yeoman ideal thus took an ironic turn: in Alan Trachtenberg's words, "Incorporation took swift possession of the garden, mocking those who lived by the hopes of cultural myth."[11]

The western territorial and state land office business—much of it rife with charges of misconduct—was a significant service provided largely free of charge to the expanding network of capitalist legal relations. Federal and state officials charged with overseeing the process were important links in carrying out land policy. Beyond the world of government agencies, investors organized a variety of land-stock companies and fueled a series of land-speculation frenzies. The federal government, as Malcolm J. Rohrbough has shown, substantially aided the transfer (both legal and illegal) of public lands to the private sector. "The management of the public domain," he points out, "lay at the center of life on the frontier." Until late in the nineteenth century, therefore, the function of federal land policy was the orderly distribution of public lands to private ownership. Land, after all, was the great temptation to those who conceived of property, security, and status in terms of landed real estate.[12]

Perhaps the greatest service to would-be financiers and investors in western land enterprises was the U.S. Army reconnaissance and exploring expeditions of the Corps of Topographical Engineers, including the great railroad surveys of the 1850s. The engineers engaged in several fact-finding expeditions, the best known of which were those led by John C. Fremont. According to William H. Goetzmann, Fremont's travels through the Rocky Mountains and the Far West between 1841 and 1845 "helped point out the value of Oregon and California to Congress." The later boundary and reconnaissance surveys in the northern and southern West during and after the war with Mexico provided an "incalculable service to the nation as it acted as a vanguard of settlement, . . .clearing away the Indian barrier and laying out the lines of communication." Those federally funded undertakings provided the first reputable scientific geographic knowledge of the West: its complex system of rivers, valleys, and mountains and its expansive and awe-inspiring basins and plateaus.[13]

These explorations provided real and practical information to an expanding U.S. empire, to potential investors in western land, and to those parties interested in the prospects for actual settlement. The completion of the first transcontinental railroad in 1869—brought into being with a sizable federal land grant and with an infusion of federally guaranteed bonds—closed time and space across North America's western interior.[14] That extraordinary technological boost to land travel vastly extended the geographic reach of investment capital and further boosted speculation in western lands, town sites, and additional interior railroad networks. As such, western lands became qualitatively more valuable by virtue of their relative proximity to markets.[15] In brief, through its federal surveys and its policies of disposal and management, the federal government was the great facilitator of western economic growth. Its work in exploring and mapping, preserving public order, and selling and leasing land directed the course of change in the West.

With extensive land, mineral, and timber resources in the continent's vast interior, the United States had at hand the material requirements for unparalleled growth in productive power. As the United States moved toward core status among the world's industrial nations, it stood at an auspicious moment in modern history: the onset of an era that Henry R. Luce would later call "The American Century." Indeed, its wealth of natural resources made the country almost an empire in itself. That natural abundance, geographer John Agnew has argued, was enormous—large quantities of all of the major minerals required for industrialization, vast acreages of rich agricultural soils extending across the central and western portions of the continent, and immense stands of timber to provide a broad range of wood products.[16] To unleash those tremendous productive forces, a consensus of sorts emerged among the nation's economic and political elites that promoted close ties between the requirements of the private sector and the articulation of those circumstances in public policy.

The effects of that expansive, relatively unrestrained, and innovative capitalism were especially apparent in the American West, where special opportunities for capital abounded. Because of its vast wealth in geographic space and natural resources, there were few structural and institutional restraints to slow the pace of the region's integration into national and international economic relationships. Restrained only by distance, a sometimes spare labor force, and a still developing transportation infrastructure, there were few restrictions to market forces in the West. Before even minimal regulations came to the western ranges, cattlemen and sheepherders grazed their animals at will on public, territorial, and Indian lands, treating those classes of land as vast, free spaces, as an opportunity that promised profits to those willing to take the chance.[17]

Of course, the play of the market on the western ranges ultimately proved to be an economic and environmental disaster, when too many operators with too many animals overgrazed too many ranges. Disaster struck during the winter storms of 1886–87, the infamous "big die-up," when the great blizzard devastated western herds. In the following years, the cattle industry went through a restructuring because of market conditions and legal challenges to the unlimited and free use of the public domain. The latter represented a more aggressive invocation of the principles of republican landownership and, in effect, changes in capitalist property relations. The new age of the ranch-cattle business represented the end of the grand pastoral style of the range-cattle industry and the assertion of exclusive ownership of specific parcels of land. This restructuring also paralleled the onset of a frenzied scramble by settler-farmers to take up land in much of the old cattle kingdom and a continuation of market-induced disruptions that persist to the present.[18]

Writer Kevin Starr once remarked that the American West has been the "testing ground for the national experience," a region of metaphor and symbol, the place that provided rationale and definition for a larger sense of national purpose.[19] The special attributes of that mythical West were possibility and opportunity, a place where human perseverance and effort could effect the good society, where the promise of freedom and abundance burned bright with hope. Wallace Stegner captured that mythical geography of the mind in a "vagrant's vision of beatitude," a cryptic paraphrasing of Harry McClintock's 1928 hobo ballad: "a place where the bulldogs have rubber teeth and the cinder dicks are blind and policemen have to tip their hats, where there's a lake of stew and whiskey too, where the handouts grow on bushes and the hens lay soft-boiled eggs."[20]

One can read earlier expressions of those sentiments in Richard Henry Dana's assessment of his visit to coastal California in 1835: "In the hands of an enterprising people, what a country this might be." But reality in nineteenth-century California, especially for common people, proved to be quite different from McClintock's hobo vision. If an argument can be made for a feudal landed tradition in the United States, it rests with the great Mexican land-grant system that remained largely intact (although under different ownership) after the conquest of 1848. What is fascinating about California is the manner in which those inherited land grants became the social and economic base for the new power structure that emerged in later decades. Book dealer and publisher Hubert Howe Bancroft pointed to the inequitable distribution of the old Mexican grants as the state's particular evil. Although the Southern Pacific Railroad held great influence in California, "more formidable," Bancroft contended, "is land monopoly."[21]

As the American population pressed westward in the second half of the nineteenth century, the federal government's land policy played a significant part in shaping the social matrix of the emerging agricultural communities. "To a greater or lesser extent," Carey McWilliams has argued in *California, The Great Exception*, every western state "experienced the leavening effect" of the government's "free or 'cheap' land policy . . . that is, every state except California." The state's finest agricultural lands, including properties deeded by Mexico to a few hundred owners, experienced a period of frenzied speculation after the conquest. The enormous holdings eventually fell into the hands of San Francisco and Sacramento capitalists who had successfully manipulated state and federal laws to their advantage. California's large agribusiness ownership patterns of today, therefore, mirror the past—a consequence of the early landed estates that date to the Mexican period.[22]

The business activities of Henry Miller, an immigrant butcher who came to San Francisco in 1850, provide an appropriate case study of California's newly emerging landownership pattern. After forming a partnership with Charles Lux, Miller took advantage of distressed owners of Mexican land grants and began piecing together an enormous land and cattle empire. Miller and Lux were equally adept at finding loopholes in American land law, including the use of dummy entrymen, which provided easy and cheap access to land. The firm ultimately acquired nearly one million acres and controlled at least ten times that amount. "Many of these holdings," historian M. Catherine Miller has observed, "survived intact into the twentieth century" and became California's massive corporate farms. As late as the 1970s, the firm of Miller & Lux still ranked among the top twenty-five largest landowners in California.[23]

The capitalist mode of agricultural production came to California in a series of waves: the hide and tallow trade of the Spanish and Mexican period; the great livestock boom from the conquest of 1848 to 1870; the growth and domination of bonanza wheat farming into the 1890s; and finally the growing speculation in potentially irrigable land and greater diversification in crop production. But through all of those shifts one transcendent reality remained: monopolization in landownership. As

early as 1871, Henry George referred to California as "a country of planta-
tions and estates." Twentieth-century writers see little in the state's landownership patterns to alter that judgment. According to McWilliams,
California never experienced the small family-farm tradition. More recently, Donald Pisani has observed that California has been "the great exception" in American agriculture, characterized by "wealthy, nonresident
land barons and migratory farm laborers or tenants."[24]

Similar conditions prevailed elsewhere in the former Spanish/Mexican
empire. Anglo capitalists who came to New Mexico with the arrival of
the railroad during the 1880s saw the territory's vast open spaces as opportunity, the chance to turn what they considered unoccupied land to profitable advantage. Aided by the U.S. Congress, which declared most of the
old Hispanic land grants part of the public domain, Anglo homesteaders,
railroad companies, and the federal government turned the Hispanic vil-
lagers' common land into private ownerships. The result was an enormous
Hispanic loss of land, severe constraints on their access to formerly common land, and continued friction to the present day. Writer John Nichols
brilliantly illustrates the struggle for access to those former communally
shared places in his 1987 novel *The Milagro Beanfield War*. In the end,
with their assumptions of communal use and sharing, the Spanish/Mexi-
can grants prove ill-suited to the ruthless and competitive rigors of the
new order.[25]

But according to Devon G. Pena, a protest leader among Hispanic
farmers in Colorado's San Luis Valley, the real war continues. The farmers, longtime residents of the area, are locked in a dispute with Zachary
Taylor, a North Carolina timber baron and descendant of the Mexican
War general of same name. Taylor, who owns 121 square miles of the
Sangre de Cristo Mountains above the valley, is liquidating his high-
altitude timber estate, much to the chagrin of Hispanic valley farmers,
who value the mountains because of the moisture they store for summer
irrigation. For more than a century Hispanics have used the present "Taylor Ranch" as a commons for hunting, grazing, and a place to gather fire-
wood. Although many of the farmers can trace their residence in the
valley to seven generations, they are pessimistic about the future: "Without the uplands, the lowlands can't exist," said local resident Maria Mon-
dragon Valdez in a recent *New York Times* article. The ownership of most
of the Sangre de Cristo chain by outside millionaires, such as Taylor and

media magnate Ted Turner, presents a direct threat to Hispanic liveli-hoods.[26]

It is nearly impossible to understand the politics of early U.S. history without the ownership of land as a primary part of that narrative. For more than a century the nation's land policy was singularly obsessed with transferring ownership to private hands. Opie has asserted that for much of its existence, the federal government's General Land Office "stood as the nation's long-term direct promoter of *privatization*"—that is, until market forces of a different kind redirected federal land policy from dis-posal to permanent management in the late nineteenth century. Al-though the new program was to be carried out "in the people's interests," Patricia Nelson Limerick has asked, "Which people? Which interest?" Historical questions about property and ownership, she observes, were wrapped around some unwieldy objects: (1) pelts, hides, and wildlife in general; (2) rights to valuable minerals; (3) grazing rights and "property" in grass; (4) access to timber (and not necessarily the land itself) and transportation routes, especially railroads; and (5) control of water or "owning" priority to a certain amount of water.[27]

Nowhere have those political questions and struggles created more controversy than on the public lands. Because the U.S. government failed to transfer all of the region's public lands to the private sector, the western states hold an anomalous relationship to federal authority in comparison with their eastern counterparts. Excluding Hawaii, the federal govern-ment controls more than 50 percent of the twelve states from the Rocky Mountains westward; in some states the federal presence is huge. Alaska leads the list of those states in which federal, state, and native lands make up most of the state. Among the political units in the lower forty-eight states, Nevada ranks at the top, with the federal government controlling approximately 86 percent of the state; Idaho (64 percent), Utah (62 per-cent), Wyoming (51 percent), and Oregon (50 percent) follow. In these and other public land states in the American West, the Forest Service, the Bureau of Land Management, the National Park Service, and to a lesser degree the Army Corps of Engineers and the Bureau of Reclamation touch every facet of western life.[28]

The role of the federal government has washed across almost every as-pect of western life and continues to do so. When Nye County, Nevada, commissioner Dick Carver climbed aboard his D-7 Caterpillar bulldozer on July 4, 1994, to reopen a closed national forest road, he rekindled long-standing historical questions involving federal lands in the West: (1) who has access; (2) who determines how the land should be used; (3) what are the proper boundaries between the public and private sectors; and (4) what are the constitutional issues at stake. For Carver and other supporters of the county-supremacy movement, Nye County resistance represented an effort to assert the county's ownership over federal lands within its jurisdiction and to reclaim what the county deemed as a loss of sovereignty over land-use decision making.[29]

But the county-supremacy movement represents much more. As powerful new social forces have been brought to bear on federal lands in the past two decades, the region's long-standing industries—mining, grazing, and timber extraction—have come under increasing attack. That changing social context has blurred the old distinctions between public and private and the ready access of the latter to the former. New federal legislation—such as the Endangered Species Act and the Clean Water Acts and other measures to protect land, water, and air—have increasingly limited extractive activity and challenged the prerogatives of the region's formerly dominant productive forces. But the environmental costs of sacrificing federal lands in the name of economic development have become an issue for public debate in the late twentieth century only with the emergence of growing national awareness of the amenity values of public lands.[30]

In his effort to assert a private right to public lands, commissioner Carver is a throwback to the early days of federal stewardship, when the development of western resources was the highest priority of public land managers, a time when federal bureaucrats worked closely with extractive corporations in formulating policy. The objective of Progressive Era management of public lands was the efficient and scientific development of timber, mineral, and water resources.[31] But in the decades after World War II, the growing prosperity of metropolitan areas in the West ushered in a new era of contested politics centered on public lands. Greater numbers of urban residents began to appreciate the federal estate for values other than resource extraction, hence the showdown with Carver and others who feel that traditional rights to the public domain are being sharply circumscribed.[32]

The Sagebrush Rebellion of the late 1970s and early 1980s, the more recent Wise-Use movement, and the county-supremacy phenomenon represent little more than new lyrics to a very old tune. Frustrated with the federal government's increasing air, water, and land regulations since the 1970s, and the growing influence of urban-based environmental organizations in shaping federal policy, longtime residents of the rural West have protested to sustain the health of their communities and to protect their jobs. They believe their future livelihoods will be secured if the federal government were to cede public lands to the states. Although there are powerful corporate players involved in these disputes, working ranchers and blue-collar loggers have captured most of the public's attention. Questions regarding access to public lands, historian Richard White has argued, "were but part of a much larger and more complicated struggle between an ascendant metropolitan West and a declining rural West."[33] Under those contentious circumstances, workers in rural communities have often served as pawns for distant investors seeking legitimacy through the support of local constituents.

Nowhere has that encounter been waged with more bitterness and legal conflict than in the forests of the Pacific Northwest. Three decades ago the region's public and private forests were valued chiefly for their production of wood fiber, the vital resource that drove so much of the Northwest's economy. Today timber companies and the U.S. Forest Service still treasure the public forests for their material resources. On the one hand, private landowners believe that they hold rights to their own forest lands and should be excluded from any form of regulation. On the other hand, environmental organizations insist that the larger citizenry has a vested public interest in the management of private timberlands. Biologist Daniel B. Botkin suggests that the controversy over Pacific Northwest timberlands raises basic questions about the public's interest in sustaining the ecological health of the region's forests.[34]

Because of the controversies over public and private lands in the United States, environmental historian Donald Worster believes that the nation is moving by fits and starts through a second conservation revolution. The first revolution led to the establishment of the great public reserves—the "inventing of the American commons." The second revolution, according to Worster, is the "ecologizing" of both public and private land use in the United States. The public is increasingly looking at land "as an interconnected, interdependent community of living organisms." Nancy Langston's study of the Blue Mountains in northeastern Oregon uses historical examples to underscore Worster's argument. Langston points to the difficulties of imposing different sets of land-use practices where federal and private lands are intimately connected. In the Blue Mountains, private landowners and federal managers have found that activities on one ownership affect adjacent ownerships. "One piece of land," she observes, "is never separate from another."[35]

Even if there is a growing cultural preference to treat landscapes as interdependent living organisms, powerful forces are at work in the rural West that threaten all land-use practices. Changing demographic patterns in almost every western state during the past decade are intensifying land-use and property-rights issues. The thirteen westernmost states (including Alaska and Hawaii) grew at a faster rate (9.1 percent) than any other region in the country between 1990 and 1995. Equally important, U.S. Census Bureau estimates show that most rural counties in the West during this period grew in population after years of steady decline. This dramatic reversal in the rural West can be attributed to a variety of social factors: (1) "white flight" from perceived urban problems; (2) retirees seeking the quiet of low-tax rural environments; and (3) footloose "telecommuters" desiring immediate access to skiing, hiking, and the great outdoors.[36] Rising land values and property taxes, clashes between traditional rural practices and the lifestyles of the newcomers, and increased tensions over environmental issues have accompanied those changes.

For example, seventy-one-year-old Lamar Crandall knew the Old West had died when he needed a police escort to herd his cattle to summer pasture. The Springville, Utah, native and his sons Craig and Calvin run Crandall Farms, Inc., a cattle and grain business with access to 14,200 acres of private land and leases to another 12,000 acres of state and federal lands. The Crandall operation is running up against the West's booming high-tech, service, and tourist industries—interest groups that place a very different value on mountains, forests, and open spaces. The Crandall ranch, at the edge of busy Interstate 15 and a few miles south of Provo, is slowly being ringed by subdivisions, as Springville's orchards and fields give way to houses and pavement. The Crandalls' greatest concern, however, is maintaining access to the land they have used (but do not own) for generations. With a growing number of outdoor enthusiasts clamoring for more room to recreate on federal lands, the Crandalls have found their traditional grazing rights on public lands increasingly restricted.[37]

Terry DeFreese, a new resident of a Springville subdivision and a computer programmer who uses his three weeks of vacation to camp, hunt, and fish, has compassion for his neighbors, the Crandalls. He understands why ranchers, loggers, and miners are opposed to locking up the entire state in wilderness, but DeFreese points to a new reality: "We're the majority. It's not fair, but we are the majority." In Utah's prime agricultural areas like Springville, DeFreese and his fellow newcomers have consumed nearly one million acres of the state's twelve million acres of choice farmland in the last two decades. Booth Walentine, director of the Utah Farm Bureau, laments the situation and predicts rising food prices in local supermarkets. But he opposes government intrusion in the way of land-use restrictions and state programs to purchase development rights to farmland: "The only way transferable property rights will work is if someone can get a direct line to Solomon. We believe very strongly that despite the disruptive problems it creates, the market system is still the best allocator of resources."[38]

Therein rests the dilemma and the centerpiece to the great contemporary debate about land in the American West: the historical and persisting tension between private claims and the common good. Issues involving property rights on both public and private lands have become increasingly complex as the new millennium approaches. Livability, urban encroachment on farm and forest lands, grazing rights on state and public lands, deteriorating habitat for spawning salmon, and the appropriate management of the national forests are issues that resonate with historical antecedents. Those who promote property rights and argue that the uninhibited play of the market can resolve these questions do not have history on their side. Private ownership, unrestricted use of land, and the unregulated market have been disastrous for many communities. Those circumstances have also had severe environmental implications.[39] One must remember that property rights restrictions and market regulations are not recent, secretly hatched government conspiracies; rather, they were developed over time as fairly popular actions in the public's interest.

"We do not need to deconstruct regulation," economist William Ashworth has contended, "but to reconstruct it. We need a new regulatory paradigm." The free-market approach to private and public lands—as a viable mechanism to serve the common good—provides an intriguing model in theory, but in practice the strategy is terribly flawed.[40] Clear water, unpolluted air, viable ecosystems, and free access to majestic scenery require collective public initiative and should not be left to individual choice. The sprawling subdivisions around Springville, Utah, and Mark Wattles's efforts to buy his way around Oregon's land-use regulations are only two examples of the play of private money on the western landscape. Both public and private lands in the American West are contested terrain. In the interests of the greater common good, ways to protect the public's stake in the future should be sought.

The words of Montana writer William Kittredge provide an appropriate closing to this introduction: "Don't get me wrong. The West is big enough to hold a lot more people. But they can live sweet lives only if Westerners are willing to control the ways we grow and to stop regarding urban planners as fascists or socialists or both."[41]

NOTES

The source of the epigraph used at the beginning of the introduction is Eric Torso, "When Property Becomes Peril," *Northern Lights* 22 (winter 1996): 24.

1. Patricia Nelson Limerick, *The Legacy of Conquest: The Unbroken Past of the American West* (New York: W. W. Norton, 1987), 55; and *Oregonian*, January 23, 1997.

2. Gerrit Knaap, "Land Use Politics in Oregon," in *Planning the Oregon Way: A Twenty-Year Evaluation*, ed. Carl Abbott, Deborah Howe, and Sy Adler (Corvallis: Oregon State University Press, 1994), 3–9.

3. I am indebted to my colleagues James Foster and Kathleen Dean Moore for this discussion.

4. For more on the Sagebrush Rebellion, see R. McGreggor Cawley, *Federal Land, Western Anger: The Sagebrush Rebellion and Environmental Politics* (Lawrence: University Press of Kansas, 1993).

5. This argument is adapted in part from William G. Robbins, "The Indian Question in Western Oregon: The Making of a Colonial People," in *Experiences in a Promised Land: Essays in Pacific Northwest History*, ed. G. Thomas Edwards and Carlos A. Schwantes (Seattle: University of Washington Press, 1986), 51–67.

6. Emile Boutmy, quoted in William Cronon, *Nature's Metropolis: Chicago and the Great West* (New York: W. W. Norton, 1991), 53–54.

7. Douglas C. North, "International Capital Flows and the Development of the American West," *Journal of Economic History* 16 (1965): 495, 500; E. J. Hobsbawm, *The Age of Capital, 1848–1875* (New York: New American Library, 1984), 27–28; and Oscar O. Winther, "Promoting the American West in England, 1865–1890," *Journal of Economic History* 7 (1956): 513.

8. For a general discussion of the imperial aspects of this westward expansion, see Donald Meinig, *The Shaping of America: A Geographical Perspective on Five Hundred Years of History*, vol. 2, *Continental America: 1800–1867* (New Haven, Conn.: Yale University Press, 1993).

9. Limerick, *Legacy of Conquest*, 82–83; and Steve Talbot, *Roots of Oppression: The American Indian Question* (New York: International Publishers, 1981), 34–35.

10. John Opie, *The Law of the Land: Two Hundred Years of American Farmland Policy* (Lincoln: University of Nebraska Press, 1987), 25–27.

11. Ibid.; James Oliver Robertson, *American Myth, American Reality* (New York: Hill and Wang, 1980), 40; and Alan Trachtenberg, *The Incorporation of America: Culture and Society in the Gilded Age* (New York: Hill and Wang, 1982), 22.

12. Malcolm J. Rohrbough, *The Land Office Business: The Settlement and Administration of American Public Lands, 1789–1837* (New York: Oxford University Press, 1968), xi–xii, 299–301; Cawley, *Federal Land, Western Anger*, 16; and Robertson, *American Myth, American Reality*, 48. Also see Gerald D. Nash, "Bureaucracy and Reform in the West: Notes on the Influence of a Neglected Interest Group," *Western Historical Quarterly* 2 (1971): 293–304. In other works Nash has observed that carrying out land policy in California "was vitiated by corruption" and loosely drafted legislation. See Nash, "The California State Land Office, 1858–1898," *Huntington Library Quarterly* 27 (1964): 347.

13. William H. Goetzmann, *Army Exploration in the American West, 1803–1863* (1959; reprint, Austin: University of Texas Press, 1991), 65, 261–62, 295, 305; and Goetzmann, *Exploration and Empire: The Explorer and the Scientist in the Winning of the West* (New York: W. W. Norton, 1966), 281, 316–17.

14. For the influence of railroads in transforming time and space, see William Cronon, *Nature's Metropolis: Chicago and the Great West* (New York: W. W. Norton, 1991), 74–80.

15. Trachtenberg, *Incorporation of America*, 20; and John A. Agnew, *The United States in the World Economy: A Regional Geography* (Cambridge: Cambridge University Press, 1987), 3. For the point about land as a qualitative productive factor, see North, "International Capital Flows," 493.

16. Agnew, *United States in the World Economy*, 49.

17. Rodman W. Paul, *The Far West and the Great Plains in Transition, 1859–1900* (New York: Harper and Row, 1988), 200–202; and Robert G. Athearn, *High Country Empire: The High Plains and the Rockies* (1960; reprint, Lincoln: University of Nebraska Press, 1965), 142–44.

18. Paul, *Far West and the Great Plains*, 203–5; and Carl Abbott, Stephen J. Leonard, and David McComb, *Colorado: History of the Centennial State* (Boulder: Colorado Associated University Press, 1982), 168–69. For more on the influence of disruptive market forces on the Great Plains, see Donald Worster, *Dust Bowl: The Southern Plains in the 1930s* (New York: Oxford University Press, 1979), 83; and Barrington Moore Jr., *Social Origins of Dictatorship and Democracy: Lord and Peasant in the Making of the Modern World* (Boston: Beacon Press, 1966), 133.

19. Kevin Starr, "A Response: Moving beyond the Turner Thesis," *Proceedings of the American Antiquarian Society* 101, pt. 1 (1991): 125.

20. Wallace Stegner, *Where the Bluebird Sings to the Lemonade Springs* (New York: Random House, 1992), xxi.

21. Richard Henry Dana, quoted in Kevin Starr, *Americans and the California Dream, 1850–1915* (New York: Oxford University Press, 1973), 41. Hubert Howe Bancroft, *History of California,* 7 vols. (San Francisco: History Book Company, 1890), 7: 35.

22. Carey McWilliams, *California, The Great Exception* (1949; reprint, Santa Barbara, Calif.: Peregrine Smith, 1979), 89–90; Donald Worster, *Rivers of Empire: Water, Aridity, and the Growth of the American West* (New York: Pantheon, 1985), 98–99; and Nash, "California State Land Office," 348, 356.

23. M. Catherine Miller, *Flooding the Courtrooms: Law and Water in the West* (Lincoln: University of Nebraska Press, 1993), 2–4.

24. Raymond F. Dasmann, *The Destruction of California* (New York: Macmillan, 1965), 61–69, 120–22; Worster, *Rivers of Empire*, 99–100; Henry George, quoted in McWilliams, *California, The Great Exception*, 99–100; and Donald Pisani, *From Family Farm to Agribusiness: The Irrigation Crusade in California and the West, 1850–1931* (Berkeley: University of California Press, 1984).

25. John Nichols, *The Milagro Beanfield War* (New York: Ballantine, 1987);

and Sarah Deutsch, *No Separate Refuge: Culture, Class, and Gender on an Anglo-Hispanic Frontier in the American Southwest, 1880–1940* (New York: Oxford University Press, 1987), 19–22.

26. *New York Times*, March 25, 1994.

27. Opie, *Law of the Land*, 21, 57, 60; and Limerick, *Legacy of Conquest*, 70–72.

28. Richard White, *"It's Your Misfortune and None of My Own": A New History of the American West* (Norman: University of Oklahoma Press, 1991), 137; Clyde A. Milner II, "Introduction," in *The Oxford History of the American West*, ed. Clyde A. Milner II, Carol A. O'Connor, and Martha A. Sandweiss (New York: Oxford University Press, 1994), 6; and Michael P. Malone and Richard W. Etulain, *The American West: A Twentieth-Century History* (Lincoln: University of Nebraska Press, 1989), 221.

29. Erik Larson, "Unrest in the West," *Time*, October 23, 1994, pp. 52–67.

30. Ibid.; and Carl Abbott, "The Federal Presence," in *The Oxford History of the American West*, ed. Milner, O'Connor, and Sandweiss, 469–71.

31. Cawley, *Federal Land, Western Anger*, 16. For the classic study posing this argument, see Samuel Hays, *Conservation and the Gospel of Efficiency* (Cambridge: Harvard University Press, 1959).

32. See Cawley, *Federal Land, Western Anger*, 18.

33. White, *"It's Your Misfortune and None of My Own,"* 571.

34. Daniel B. Botkin, *Our Natural History: The Lessons of Lewis and Clark* (New York: Grosset, Putnam, 1995), 23–31.

35. Donald Worster, *The Wealth of Nature: Environmental History and the Ecological Imagination* (New York: Oxford University Press, 1993), 107; and Nancy Langston, *Forest Dreams, Forest Nightmares: The Paradox of Old Growth in the Inland West* (Seattle: University of Washington Press, 1995), 41.

36. *Oregonian*, June 29, 1996.

37. *Gazette-Times* (Corvallis), June 30, 1996.

38. Ibid.; and *Oregonian*, July 7, 1997.

39. See, for example, the discussion in Worster, *Wealth of Nature*, 57–59.

40. William Ashworth, *The Economy of Nature: Rethinking the Connections between Ecology and Economics* (Boston: Houghton Mifflin, 1995), 56–57.

41. William Kittredge, *New York Times*, January 10, 1997.

PART I
THREE PERSPECTIVES
ON PROPERTY RIGHTS

Private Property and the Public Interest

Land in the American Idea

DANIEL W. BROMLEY

R ecent incidents indicate that private land-use practices are increasingly seen as important by the general public. After the inaugural Earth Day in 1970, environmental concerns tended to focus on air and water pollution. More recently, however, as the concern for endangered species has intensified, the general public's attention and scrutiny has shifted to land-use practices. Controversies over endangered species—northern spotted owls, red-cockaded woodpeckers, and other plants and animals—illustrate just how central land-use debates have become. The U.S. Supreme Court's 1995 decision in *Babbitt v. Sweet Home Chapter of Communities for a Great Oregon* brought this issue close to those who own land.[1] In other words, over the years the locus of contention in environmental policy has shifted.

The first generation of environmentalism focused on dirty industries, automobile emissions, and the runoff of topsoil and agricultural chemicals. In the second generation, however, behaviors on private land are suddenly in the public glare. This scrutiny has not been pleasant for the parties involved. Small wonder: The roots of the sanctity of private land run both deep and wide in America. The dominant issue in contemporary environmental policy concerns the collective interest in private land. Some may regard this idea as a contradiction in terms; therein lie the seeds of much current discontent. The problem may be rephrased as being a conflict of private and public values with respect to land and how the land is used.

On the one hand, there are those who believe that the owner is the ultimate source of authority with respect to private land use. Adherents to this position cite the "takings" clause of the Fifth Amendment to the U.S. Constitution in which "just compensation" is required for taking private property for public use or benefit. On the other hand, there are those who believe that landowners may sustain the current extent of their property interest in land only at the forbearance of others in the polity. Adherents to this position cite a series of U.S. Supreme Court decisions in which the determination of the extent of the property interest resides with the general public; that is, collective determination of acceptable behavior on private land indeed finds support under the Constitution.

Both sides of this debate have recently engaged in some spirited skirmishes, one manifestation being the introduction of a "property rights" clause in the Congressional Republican's "Contract with America" in 1994. Although this particular legislative initiative failed to gain much support at the national level, several states passed laws mandating compensation to private landowners when public action reduces property values by a specified amount. But these regulatory actions cannot constitute a "takings" under the Constitution.[2] Therefore, when regulations—for whatever reason—constrain a landowner from committing antisocial acts, there is no Constitutional basis upon which the government must be made to compensate the party so constrained. This view is evident in the *Babbitt v. Sweet Home* decision, which shows that the U.S. Supreme Court holds a similar opinion.[3] Other cases reveal a similar perspective about the collective interest in private property.[4] Not surprisingly, several cases have resulted in decisions showing the other side of this matter.[5]

For those who believe that they know precisely the content of property rights in land, this seeming inconsistency by the courts is the source of much consternation. They lament, How can something that is so obvious be viewed so differently by the courts? There are two possible explanations: The first is that judges are incompetent; the second is that the content of property rights in land is not at all clear, so successive courts must sift through conflicting claims and, Solomon-like, determine precisely where the controlling property interest lies. As one cannot easily regard judges as incompetent, the second explanation is more likely.

As one thinks about private property in land—particularly in the American experience—the subject must be approached rather pragmatically. One must ask, What is the American idea of land that allows one to understand different outcomes for the sanctity of private property over the past century? The answer, quite simply, is that the empirical content of private property—that is, the essence of private property—is *discovered* as the courts struggle with conflicting claims. Although some people believe that property rights are clear—and that courts play the important role of merely sanctifying that clarity—the pattern is, in fact, the other way around. Property rights are unclear and in dispute; this is precisely why disputants end up in court. Both parties claim to have a right, and of course they cannot both be correct in their conflicting claims.

The problem is not to ratify existing property rights, but to discover and clarify the precise property right to which each party is entitled in the future. It is impossible to read the history of private property—from the Greek city-states, through feudal Europe, and on to the American frontier—and reach a different conclusion regarding the empirical content of private property. This conclusion—that the content and extent of private property is discovered as the logical outcome of conflict resolution—carries with it four correlated ideas. These associated ideas act as the causal engines behind the inevitable and continuous process of discovering rights. These themes help to explain the evolution of private land in the American experience. They are (1) the nexus between land, labor, and liberty; (2) the centrality of collective consent; (3) the march of time and the inevitable transitions the passage of time implies; and (4) the essential triad of property conflicts.

LAND, LABOR, AND LIBERTY

Since the Enlightenment, few ideas about land have been as durable as those concerning land as a guarantor of individual liberty. By the mid-fifteenth century, feudalism had vanished from the English countryside. The great landlords had begun to take an interest in land as an economic asset. But this new role for large-estate owners required some justification that went beyond mere meddling in the affairs of state. Almost two hundred years would pass before the English philosopher John Locke appeared to legitimize possessive individualism over land. Whereas prior interests in land among the comfortable classes had been for the purpose of influence in matters of state, Locke managed to link land to a more charming idea: liberty. To Locke land became the essential instrument through which liberty was attained. One acquired land by laboring on it, by mixing one's labor with the land.

The relieved acceptance of Lockean ideas among the English gentry coincided with the age of exploration and conquest in the new world, to the everlasting detriment of native peoples who were "in the way" of the European ideas of manifest destiny. Locke believed that humans, especially Europeans, were endowed with a special obligation to take possession of God's commons. By being endowed with these natural rights, then, the act of conquest and "improvement" converted the commons into the conqueror's individual (private) property. Although the natives might have been roaming about on God's commons, they were not considered serious landlords. After all, they had not planted any hedges or built any fences. Obviously (or so it seemed at the time), the Indians did not regard themselves as "landowners."

Locke's followers found comfort in this line of argument. Latter-day Lockeans find this idea absolutely mesmerizing. The French anarchist Pierre Joseph Proudhon was only half right: Private property is not necessarily theft, but a lot of theft has ended up as private property; furthermore, that theft had a Lockean sanction in the name of "natural rights." The beloved U.S. president Thomas Jefferson gave this notion a facade of respectability. After all, the Indians were not mixing much labor with the land. The Homestead Act of 1862 institutionalized Lockean thought. The European "settlers" mixed a lot of labor with someone else's land, and when the original occupants of that land protested the acquisition, the settlers had a rationale for systematic annihilation. The Lockean myth served them very well indeed, but that does not make Locke right on logical, philosophical, or moral grounds.[6]

Over the years Locke's labor theory of property has withstood attack and disbelief, probably because of its appeal to the American values of individualism, reverence for hard work, ambivalence about government intervention, and the lack of a good alternative theory of property acquisition. Locke offered an alternative to prevailing Christian doctrine that land should be held by the righteous, and to Aristotelian consequentialism that land should be held by those who use it properly. But Locke's labor theory of property justifies less than it condemns. First, by asserting that property rights exist prior to the existence of a civil society (a state), the theory fosters the confusion between possession and ownership. Individuals can possess land and other physical objects, but only a state (or a comparable authority system) can define that possession as constituting ownership. Ironically, the Lockean theory of how one acquires land—which, once acquired, will ensure liberty for the landholder—denies the social idea of ownership. For how can a possessor of land ask the state to ratify that pre-state possession—indeed, to declare it "ownership" and thus to protect it against other claimants—when the beneficiary of that legal transformation denies the legitimacy of the state as the source of rights in land? Locke's theory encourages aggrieved landowners to ask the state to protect their property rights (often by compensation with tax revenues), while at the same time denying that the state was at all pertinent to the granting of those property rights.

Second, Locke failed to address the scope of the rights acquired by mixing labor with land.[7] Throughout history, slaves devoted an enormous amount of labor to improving land, but they did not acquire a property interest in that land. If all humans are born with natural rights, then why did not slaves or Native Americans acquire land by mixing their labor with the land? An equally important question, How much land does a group acquire because of laboring on it? Just the immediate parcel, or all of that which they intend to improve through the application of their labor? Third, Locke saw private property as the great protector against a predatory state. This appeal persists as the favorite defense of private property by those who have it or hope to get it. Those without private property remain to be convinced.

Property rights in land cannot stand as a defense of liberty for the simple reason that not everyone possesses—or can hope to acquire—landed property. Does liberty extend only to those who hold land? Liberty is too important a concept to rest on something that not everyone has or is able to acquire. Those opposed to or leery of government intervention imagine that their freedom, their liberty, is assured by their possessions, including land. But the history of the world's revolutions would suggest otherwise. Revolutions have arisen precisely because of the skewed distribution of the property interests in land and other assets. Simply put, individual liberty cannot logically be grounded in property rights in land.

Locke sought to find a justification for private property, the better to defend the social and economic position of those who already possessed a great deal of land. Locke's search for a social and political justification for the private control of land, the major economic asset in early modern England at the time, points to a fundamental problem with the private control of land: namely, the potentially contentious nature of that control. Those things that are not seen as natural and obvious will always require some justification; were they obvious, their justification would be superfluous. In fact, almost all social arrangements—except, perhaps, the family—require an explanation. But why must there be a justification for private ownership? The answer is not obvious, and this brings the discussion to the problem of collective consent.

COLLECTIVE CONSENT

Any collection of individuals requires certain things of each member of the group. The inevitability of scarcity—whether of food, of materials, or of mere space—creates the potential for conflict. But this potential produces an equally pressing demand for dependence and collaboration. Out of the interplay of scarcity and dependence arises the problem—and the promise—of order. Order and predictability give collective enterprises such as nation-states (or clans or villages) the foundation for interaction on a daily basis. Out of this interaction, provisioning takes place and the group's long-run security is assured.

This social provisioning is the fundamental problem facing the nation-state. It has certainly been so in the history of the United States. For example, in Wisconsin the northern part of the state is still called "the cut over region"; and the "pinery." Wisconsin timber has built Chicago twice, originally and then after the great fire in 1871. As the United States was settled by successive waves of immigrants, provisioning was the primary idea of the land's social purpose. But provisioning went beyond land. Western water law is a novel construction necessitated by the special circumstances in this new and mostly arid region. Mining and timber laws also had to be crafted to suit the needs of provisioning.

Of course, as the land filled up, it offered a certain liberty for most of those who endeavored to "tame the West." Native groups already living on the land during this migration may be excused a certain lack of enthusiasm for this great "attainment of liberty." The settlers arrived and conquered the West—or more correctly, they conquered the people who were already living in the West. The land these migrants took under their control was central to their provisioning and the provisioning of others in the young nation. The gift of land—at this time it was indeed a gift from the federal government—was predicated on the perceived social benefits that would arise by seeing to it that the West was properly filled with non-Spanish immigrants.

Much of the literature that romanticizes the West focuses on the hardy pioneers and the taming of the frontier. Lost in the patriotic celebration of this great individual drama is the larger national interest in the gift of land to those with the spunk, or the lack of otherwise good opportunities, to undertake the hardship in coming West. This typifies the difference between the private interest in land and the social interest in it. During this settlement period, these two interests were in perfect harmony. This is not always so, however. Whether in harmony or in conflict, we must not overlook the reality that individuals hold assets—whether land or other assets—only at the implicit consent of all society members: thus, the centrality of consent. On the subject of consent with respect to the holding of private property, the great English historian R. H. Tawney wrote:

> Property was to be an aid to creative work, not an alternative to it. . . .
> The law of the village bound the peasant to use his land, not as he himself might find most profitable, but to grow the corn the village needed.
> . . . Property reposed in short, not merely upon convenience, or the appetite for gain, but on a moral principle. It was protected not only for the sake of those who owned, but for the sake of those who worked and of those for whom their work provided. It was protected, because, without security for property, wealth could not be produced or the business of society carried on.[8]

Herein lies the basis for understanding the evolving content of land rights in any social setting. Land rights are granted by the polity because of the larger social benefits that arise therefrom. It serves everyone that a few individuals own and contribute to the social provisioning that secures a better life for the rest of the people. But that grant of ownership, that consent, must always be predicated upon the larger social good. Things such as land are protected not because they are "property"; rather, those protected things become—by that conscious social action—"property." One must be ever alert not to confuse cause and effect.

Certain political lamentation has arisen lately among politicians and landowners because the period of great philosophical debates about individualism happened to coincide with the formative years in the new world. These debates informed the founding of a nation. No wonder many Americans find full-blown acquisitiveness and possessive individualism so agreeable. This leads to a situation in which individuals claim that any redefinition of their land-based actions requires that they be compensated from the tax receipts of the public purse. Others are equally adamant that this not be allowed. This conflict, which was rather shrill after 1994's midterm congressional elections, seems to have cooled down somewhat since then.

What is it about land that excites such emotions? In the West, land still symbolizes some quaint idea of freedom and the frontier. The idea of land—and property rights—is a static and durable idea to many Americans. Some merely wish to be left alone on the land. Others hope to get rich from it. Land in the American experience is a refuge, a lottery ticket, and an embodiment of something quite unique. But the idea of land cannot be static, nor can land be considered apart from the underlying problem of how a collective body deals with time and the transitions necessitated thereby.

TIME AND TRANSITIONS

Time confounds expectations and defeats certitude. Things that are true today will be found out tomorrow to be half-truths or falsehoods. The lingering emotional appeal of property rights in land is that Americans imagine that although other things may change, property rights have not, will not, and indeed cannot change. This is not true, of course. Most Americans live in neighborhoods that are stabilized by zoning laws (this represents change). Landowners once imagined that they controlled everything to the earth's core and to the heavens above. If that had been true, air travel would either be impossible or very expensive. This presumptive ownership changed as a result of conflicts that were eventually resolved in the nation's courts; the courts were forced to determine just how far the property interests of a landowner ran. As previously noted, that which ultimately gains protection can be called a property right.

Individuals today hold a much diminished ownership interest in their land than they once did—or imagined they did. And the pace of that diminution is probably directly related to the pace at which America's population is growing. It is easy to forget how very young the United States is, particularly the western part of the country. The American West has been "settled" for less than one hundred years. Arizona and New Mexico were admitted to the United States simultaneously eighty-eight years ago. Oregon statehood occurred in 1859, but full settlement did not come to pass until much later.

To be sure, the economic history of private land is a very long story. For some perspective on land in America, especially in the American West, consider the following: It took the first five kings of England (William, William II, Henry, Stephen, and Henry II) approximately 120 years (1066–1189) to suppress the Anglo-Saxon barons and convert the land from its autonomous control by the barons into a feudal gift from the crown. Most of England's marvelous castles were built during this period, which tells us something about the state of war and peace on that small land. But no sooner had feudalism been imposed in England than it was on the decline. Indeed, within another generation (by 1215), the barons forced William the Conqueror's great-grandson John to sign the Magna Carta. Yet another transition was under way—one that replaced feudalism with the increasingly centralized state. The feudal structure was much too devolved and decentralized to require the sort of protest embodied in the Magna Carta. The brief burst of English feudal revitalization under William and his sons soon gave way to the rise of a landed class intent on governance. The Magna Carta is testimony to that fact. This major realignment of land rights—toward feudalism and then back again—took less than 150 years. By those standards, not much has happened in America, and yet there has been much change in the content of ownership.

Property rights are the socially recognized rules of control over the use of, and income from, particular assets and circumstances. Because social circumstances change, property rights must also change. Societies are more stable if property rights are not constantly in a state of flux and transition, but societies cannot survive in the face of rigid and unchanging institutions. The challenge is to offer stability in institutional arrangements (including property rights) but to avoid rigidity: flexibility without chaos. Dynamic economic systems require a recognition of which rights structures must be preserved, and which ones must bend to the necessities of a changing world. Transitions in the ownership interest of land arise from changes in the socioeconomic circumstances within which land is used. Conflicting claims are made with respect to land control and land use. These claims call into question the existing presumptions concerning ownership. What is to be done when these circumstances arise? The law as written ("black letter" law) and the law as practiced (case law) are manifestations of prior actions, conflicts, and expressions of individual and public purposes and prior efforts to define and shape the future by drawing on the past.

Current conflicts are the engine in this intertemporal redefinition of who Americans are and who they shall become. The law reflects yesterday's influence and interests, and through its application the law seeks to bind the future. The law is a compilation of reflected interests from the past. Indeed, one might think of the law as a mirror on the past that provides images of the future. Those who believe that property rights should never change embrace a naive view of social dynamics and a rather sweepingly innocent perspective of human history. The final question, therefore, concerns how and why property rights change. This brings the discussion to the three central participants in institutional change.

THE ESSENTIAL TRIAD

The fundamental issue surrounding land-use conflicts is the idea that those who own private property—and those who speak on their behalf—insist that by virtue of this ownership, they have absolute rights. But, as Tawney wrote, the notion of absolute rights is impossible in a civil society:

> The State has no absolute rights; they are limited by its commission. The individual has no absolute rights; they are relative to the function which he performs in the community of which he is a member, because, unless they are so limited, the consequences must be something in the nature of private war. All rights . . . are conditional and derivative, because all power should be conditional and derivative. They are derived

from the end or purpose of the society in which they exist. They are conditional on being used to contribute to the attainment of that end, not to thwart it.[9]

The impossibility of absolute rights to which Tawney alludes is predicated on the reality of rights. To have a right is to have the ability and the capacity to require some authority system to act on one's behalf; that is, to act so as to protect one's particular interest against the interest of others. A right is a manifestation of power on the part of the right holder. For example, those who claim they have a right to smoke in public buildings are asserting that they can enlist the authorities to enforce that act over the protests of those who are outraged at such an act. If the would-be smokers cannot get the authorities to stand behind their claims, they are bluffing. More important, they are using "rights talk" in the hope of influencing the outcome in a way favorable to their interests. In keeping with the earlier theme of time and transitions, it was not so very long ago that these people would have indeed had a right to smoke in public buildings, and those opposed would have had to suffer in silence. The nature and content of rights thus change in profound ways in response to new tastes and social norms.

Therefore, a right is the capacity to call on the collective power to stand behind one's claim to an action or benefit stream. It is important to note that rights only have meaning when there is some authority system that agrees to defend a right holder's interest in a particular outcome. A right holder has the "capacity to compel" (to require) the state to act in a certain way. The effective protection from this authority is nothing other than a correlated duty or obligation for the general public. A right is a triadic relationship that encompasses the object or circumstances of interest, the individual or group related to that interest, and all others who have a duty to respect the right. For example, earlier in the twentieth century, smokers' rights were given force by the nonsmokers' duty to suffer in silence. Public authorities would have defended smokers' rights to smoke, and for nonsmokers that defense would have comprised a duty. Today, however, authorities stand ready to defend nonsmokers' right to clean air, and it is the smokers' duty to smoke outside.

The essential triad emphasizes that rights are not relationships between an individual and an object or an action. Nor are property rights correctly understood as a conflict between the interests of an owner against an oppressive government. Rather, property rights consist of relationships between two individuals (or groups) with respect to land. One of the interests will likely be the owner. The government intervenes as a necessary participant only because the disputants force its involvement. By entering the dispute, the government—in the form of the courts—must decide which set of competing claims shall be protected with a right. The landowner most likely insists that by virtue of ownership, his or her interests prevail. But the outcome of recent land-use disputes in the courts suggests otherwise. As previously indicated, property is not protected because it is property. Rather, that which wins protection becomes, because of that protection, property. In stark terms, what one owns depends on what the others say one owns—not what one says one owns. This brings the discussion back to the centrality of consent and to the German philosopher Immanuel Kant's idea of intelligible possession as distinct from empirical possession. Intelligible possession requires the application of pure reason, while empirical possession entails only physical control. The essence of a civil society, therefore, is reason leading to intelligible possession.

As the authority system, the state gives and takes away rights by its willingness—or its unwillingness—to agree to protect one's claims to something. Property is the stream of benefits, and rights to property offer security over that benefit stream.[10] For example, when one purchases a piece of land, its price is a reflection of the present discounted value of its future benefit stream. The nature and magnitude of that benefit stream depends on how one chooses to use the asset and the bundle of rights that the collective says one holds over that asset. Although land is often called "property," the real property is the benefit stream that one then owns, that one knows will be protected with the authority of a governing structure. If the property will not be protected, one's willingness to pay for it shall be reduced to reflect this less secure status.

But rights, and changes in rights, are always contentious. For example, one might ask why it is politically and socially acceptable to prevent the cultivation of marijuana, or to operate a house of prostitution on American real estate, while a law to protect the habitat for endangered flora and fauna, or a law to protect buildings of unique historical significance, is seen as a fundamental invasion of our "rights"? Why is it now recognized that soil erosion, pesticide applications, and a range of other activities can be regulated, yet regulating habitat is still so very contentious? The answer is that the government and the general public are still working their way through a continual redefinition of the empirical content of property rights in land. Unless one can make the case that land is a factor of production distinct from other factors of production—capital, labor, and management—there is no logical basis for compensating landowners but not owners of other assets when economic and social conditions change. The market value of all factors of production is buffeted by new, and often unforeseen, circumstances. Many Americans watch the stock market each day to monitor their investments. Many consult other indicators of their economic positions. Accordingly, the owners of all factors of production—not just land—often experience "windfalls and wipeouts."

The essential triad suggests that the content of ownership is a social creation that requires the consent of nonowners, who—when conflicts arise—stand alongside landowners as both make their best case to the sole force in society that can arbitrate such disputes. Through the court system, government chooses one interest over the other. To do nothing is to reward the party well served by the status quo ante. To choose the interest of the other party is to expose government to the accusation that it does not "protect" property rights. But the problem of choice is not one of protecting—or failing to protect—property rights. Rather, the problem is to discover the more socially compelling property claim.

CONCLUSION

Through the property rights in land, land in the United States has historically been advanced as the protector of individual liberty—a task that is logically impossible. Furthermore, much land, particularly that devoted to housing, has historically played the role of a savings account for old age. Finally, land has often been seen as part of a grand lottery in which one might strike it rich if a developer finds one's little corner of America especially compelling—or if a freeway passes nearby. Land in the American idea is still viewed as part of the frontier, and property rights in land are imagined to be both clear and unchanging. But the frontier is gone and Americans must now confront the challenge of understanding property rights in land in innovative ways. Rights can never be absolute;

property and property rights must continue to change as new circumstances arise. Social coherence demands that these redefinitions not appear arbitrary and capricious; this is why the courts are so careful with procedural matters. But change is inevitable, and therein lies the strength and vibrancy of the American economy and American politics. To suppose that property rights can be absolute—and static—is a sure guarantee of eventual revolution, and that is the last thing the "property rights" groups could want.

NOTES

1. *Babbitt v Sweet Home Chapter of Communities for a Great Oregon*, 515 U.S. 687 (1995).

2. Daniel W. Bromley, "Regulatory Takings: Coherent Concept or Logical Contradiction?" *Vermont Law Review* 17 (1993): 647–82.

3. Though not without a bitter dissent by the three conservative U.S. Supreme Court justices William Rehnquist, Antonin Scalia, and Clarence Thomas.

4. Prominent here are the four cases *Just v Marinette County*, 201 NW 2d 761 (WI 1972); *Keystone Bituminous Coal Ass'n v DeBenedictus*, 480 US 470 (1987); *Miller et al. v Schoene*, 276 US 272 (1928); and *Penn Central Transportation Co. v New York City*, 438 US 104 (1978).

5. Prominent here are the three cases *Pennsylvania Coal Co. v Mahon*, 260 US 393 (1922); *Lucas v South Carolina Coastal Council*, 505 U.S. 1003 (1992); and *Nollan v California Coastal Commission*, 483 U.S. 825 (1987).

6. John Christman, *The Myth of Property: Toward an Egalitarian Theory of Ownership* (Oxford: Oxford University Press, 1994).

7. Lawrence C. Becker, *Property Rights: Philosophical Foundations* (London: Routledge and Kegan Paul, 1977).

8. R. H. Tawney, "Property and Creative Work," in *Property: Mainstream and Critical Positions,* ed. C. B. MacPherson (Toronto: University of Toronto Press, 1981), 139.

9. R. H. Tawney, *The Acquisitive Society* (New York: Harcourt, Brace, and World, 1948), 50–51.

10. Daniel W. Bromley, *Environment and Economy: Property Rights and Public Policy* (Oxford: Blackwell, 1991).

Property Rights, Freedom, and Evolving Social Order

BRUCE YANDLE

W
hat is law? What are private rights, and how do they evolve? What do these ideas have to do with freedom? These questions lie at the heart of any discussion about property rights. Developing answers to these questions requires a two-pronged focus: On the one hand, one must examine the fundamental philosophical debates, and on the other hand, one must look at the practical actions taken by ordinary citizens throughout history. Law deals with abstractions and intellectual thought, and property rights evolve through concrete experiences. How these allow for the release and expression of the human spirit joins the philosophical to the practical. Therefore, a state of social harmony can be approached only when human experience is based on a shared understanding of law that somehow meets the expectations of freedom.[1] When the definition of law conflicts with human experience, there is disharmony and controversy.

Across the nation people are debating the meaning of the law of property. The debate, which some writers call a constitutional dialogue that has never really ended, can be framed in a number of ways.[2] It is about informal order-generating mechanisms versus formal order-generating mechanisms, natural law versus positive law, centralized control versus decentralized action, spontaneous order versus hierarchical control, custom and tradition versus statutes and regulation. The debate is about social processes that yield unpredictable but voluntarily derived outcomes versus the attempts by "men of systems" to shape those processes for other purposes.[3] It is about an evolutionary process through which ideas collide and become either more or less accepted.

This chapter examines the philosophical issues that surround these questions of property rights, freedom, and law. It explores this evolutionary process and the collision of ideas. In this sense the chapter is about *memetics*, the study of how ideas and beliefs spread in a society.[4] In this new science, competing ideas are called *memes*. Just as competition among genes explains part of the evolutionary pattern that forms biological life, competition among memes determines outcomes for social life. This discussion considers a private property meme that competes with a public property meme, a formal government meme that competes with a society meme.[5] By using the generalized terminology of memes, one can avoid some of the emotional content that often accompanies such discussions of property rights, freedom, and order. The chapter begins with a personal story about a community in rural Georgia, where my wife and I spend our holidays and summers. Notions of property rights, freedom, and law, as well as useful examples of conflict and controversy, emerge from this story. The discussion illustrates competing bodies of law and conflicting memes. Next, the chapter considers the evolutionary struggle that ensues during the formation of property rights. Finally, the chapter examines the current struggle between competing property rights memes and offers evidence from empirical studies that illuminates the nature of the struggle in the western United States.

BLUEBIRD BOXES AND LAW COMMON TO THE PEOPLE

A few bluebird boxes stand on land that my wife, Dot, and I own in rural Round Oak, Georgia. Cultivated plants commonly called butterfly shrubs attract the fragile butterflies to the old house's porches. Hummingbird feeders attached to the porches sway in the summer breeze. These small but important assets are located on our property. The place has been in our family for almost one hundred years; it is not for sale. Our right to have bluebird boxes benefits from the security of law that is common to the community; this provides a set of "negative rights." It is the same kind of law that Justinian's scribes recorded for the Roman Empire in 534; it is "discovered law." Among these negative rights in the community is the right not to be disturbed or harmed without our permission. In turn, our neighbors enjoy the right not to be bothered by us. These rights define zones of freedom and autonomy that allow for self-discovery, creativity, and the generation of innovative thoughts and products.

The rules of informal law limit these zones of freedom, however. If when exercising my freedom to cultivate land, runoff from my land pollutes the drinking water of my neighbor's cattle, my neighbor has a potential cause of action against me. If his use of herbicides damages my apple trees, I have a potential cause of action against him. These zones of freedom are thus defined by negative rights. These ancient common law rights are based on rules that emerged from natural law; this law of the land, therefore, has existed since "time out of mind." If our property is damaged or we are threatened for having butterfly shrubs and bird feeders, we can call the sheriff and gain protection. We have never had to do that; our neighbors watch our place, and we theirs. Our small community, which is unincorporated, enforces these rights. Extended lines of kinship and long-standing patterns of landownership are dominant characteristics of the area. There is no local government, but laws are followed and maintained and sanctioned by the sheriff, who carries a gun. The property rights held in Round Oak, which is located in Jones County, provide a private sphere of action, a zone that cannot be invaded by outsiders without our or the neighbors' permission.

Not too far from our house, a neighbor plants, cultivates, and harvests trees. He unconsciously relies on the security of these property rights when making fifteen-year plans for improving the soil, selecting seedlings, planting, and harvesting. When harvested, the trees make their way to a Georgia Pacific mill that produces merchant lumber and plywood. Chips from the process are carried by train to a mill that converts the chips to energy and paper. The paper mill, located on private property in the next county, discharges waste into the Ocmulgee River. When I was in high school, some forty-five years ago, a good friend was employed at the mill. He and other employees continually monitored the chemistry of the mill's discharge and the receiving waters of the Ocmulgee River. There were no water-quality statutes that required this, however; rather, landowners downstream held the common law right not to have deteriorated water pass their land. In the 1950s such private property memes were dominant. Indeed, so dominant that some special interest groups began to agitate for federal legislation to secure a stronger voice in determining water-quality rules. And in the 1970s meaningful meme competition over control of environmental rights emerged.

Today the railroad that carries the chips is located on private property. The train tracks are just across the state highway from our house. The highway and its right-of-way are public property. Each year, without my permission, highway workers trim some of our crepe myrtle because the tree infringes on the right-of-way. In doing so, the highway department is serving a larger public interest, a meme that competes with the local private property meme. We understand this and do not object to the practice, but they can only go so far and they understand that. In this way we limit the zone of meme competition. The railroad was built 120 years ago; the railroad company's deed to the right-of-way has infrequently been contested. My neighbor the tree farmer, the paper mill, the railroad company, and I enjoy private spheres of action that cannot be invaded by other private parties without our permission. These rules of law are common to the people; they are a vital part of the informal order. Such informal order refers to an evolved social order based on rules of just conduct and common sense that are fundamental to a free society. Participants in the informal order follow unwritten rules, often doing so unconsciously. As economics Nobel laureate F. A. Hayek has observed:

> Man is as much a rule-following animal as a purpose-seeking one. And he is successful not because he knows why he ought to observe the rules which he does observe, or is even capable of stating all these rules in words, but because his thinking and acting are governed by rules which by a process of selection have evolved in the society in which he lives, and which are thus the product of the experience of generations.[6]

This informal order serves a vital purpose; otherwise, it would cease to exist. In the deepest sense of the word, it is economic. But the existence of this order can be eclipsed and erased by formal actions that rely on statutes, regulations, and politics. The informal order that sanctions property rules and leaves an unspecified but constrained zone of freedom is based on the unanimous consent of right holders; it relies on a rule of law. The formal order—which depends on statutes and regulations and frequently defines rights and corresponding duties—relies on a rule of majoritarian politics. The ground is thus set for conflict when the two order-generating systems collide.

Historian and former Librarian of Congress Daniel J. Boorstin has examined some dimensions of this conflict in his review of American law.[7] He describes two competing systems of law: one termed "immanent" (based on an indwelling necessity, defined as values or norms), and the other called "instrumental" (based on legislative law). Both systems are order generators. Without directly saying, Boorstin is speaking of memes, or the competing ideas about order. Like Hayek, he is fond of informal law because it reflects the power of commonly held values. However, he is troubled by the struggle that arises when a homogeneous group, which finds order informally, confronts a heterogeneous group, which relies on formal rules. Boorstin illustrates the notion of indwelling law and the conflicts that can arise between different groups by discussing colonial Pennsylvania and the early controlling Quaker community that relied on William Penn's "Frame of the Government of Pennsylvania."[8] Boorstin explains how the Quakers, "who insisted on preserving the law which dwelt within them," saw their informal order eroded by a legislature controlled by non-Quakers. Once the nonbelievers were in power, the Quakers worked quietly to influence the larger society; they were strangers in their own state. Boorstin does not relate why the political meme was able to displace the idea of indwelling law, however.

Many years ago Jones County, Georgia, was part of the territory of the Cherokee Indian Nation. The Cherokee had a system of property rights, which were gained by conquest, that was later recognized by a treaty with the U.S. government. Until rights to this land were transferred to Jones County, and then raffled off to Revolutionary War veterans and citizen freeholders, the Cherokee enjoyed a private sphere of action. But their desires for freedom were defeated by the American body politic that successfully endeavored to obtain Cherokee land rights through a combination of harassment and fraud that was sanctioned by the state and federal governments. The final destruction of Cherokee rights and the tribe's forced movement went forward despite a Supreme Court opinion that disagreed with the Jackson administration.[9] The Court opinion was based partly on a natural-rights theory of property and voluntary consent between right holders and rights common to the people. In effect, the Court argued that the compound republic had simply taken Cherokee property rights. Before the arrival of the Cherokee—and before them, the arrival of other Native American tribes—the land was considered a commons. The arrival of sedentary people brought a system of rights and laws that conserved the commons and enabled people to accumulate resources and improve their life expectancies.

Trees, butterflies, bluebirds, paper mills, railroad tracks, and land are real entities, things that form part of our accumulated wealth. But the property rights that surround these entities are pure abstractions, social inventions that distinguish communities of human beings from other life forms. Invisible rights set boundaries that define and protect families, homes, schools, businesses, and industrial facilities. Whether defined by the state or merely sanctioned by it, property rights form the basis for all trade and commerce. Indeed, what one calls "property" is valuable because of the underlying rights that connect the things to specific human beings. For example, Dot and I speak of our country home. My neighbor talks about his trees; the railroad company speaks of its right-of-way. The Cherokee spoke of their land. The sanctity of these rights encourages conservation and long-term planning. Dot and I take pains to maintain our home; we enjoy the place, but we also expect to pass the property rights to our children. The right to exclude or transfer to others compels us to maintain assets that might otherwise erode. In this way property rights of some form provide the foundation of all social life.

PROPERTY RIGHTS: THE EVOLUTIONARY STRUGGLE

This brief description of life in Jones County could represent countless locales in the United States. Bundles of private property rights that evolved from custom, tradition, and country courthouses form the bedrock of community life and comprise a system of private law that, more often than not, silently supports the common transactions of day-to-day life in America. Resorting to litigation is the exception, not the rule; property rights lawsuits are indeed a minuscule part of the majority of private life. This system of law and property rights antedated the founding of the nation and the birth of the Constitution. This common law can be traced directly to England, to a time when a national government did not exist; indeed, even the concept of nations did not exist. Legal scholars trace what they term "law common to the people" to the dawn of history. The precise origin of private property rights is simply unknowable. In this sense, private property rights per se are not the inventions of governments, parliaments, presidents, and kings; rather, they are a social phenomenon, part of a Darwinian process that has to do with people, survival, and the accumulation of resources. But they can be and are indeed recognized, sanctioned, and formalized by government. Law and the theory of society should not be confused with politics and government.

Although rights common to the people did not emerge from governments, governments have had much to do with their development. Governments were invented to provide more security to rights than might be obtained otherwise and to transfer wealth from one group to another. When governments were invented, shaped, and reformed, some founders took pains to restrict government actions that might disturb the sanctity of their private rights; they were fearful of government's redistributional tendencies. These rights protectors attempted to reinforce the process that supported the private property meme. At the same time, others saw the machinery of government as a means to achieve another vision, one more favorable to their public property preferences. In this way, private and public property rights memes competed.

The Magna Carta itself, issued in 1215, supports the private meme: "No freeman shall be deprived of his free tenement or liberties or fee custom but by lawful judgment of his peers and by the law of the land." The phrase "law of the land" was used at the time to define common law. Four hundred years later, after struggling with a despotic ruler, the people of England through Parliament in 1635 wrote their Petition of Rights, which holds: "Englishmen are free in their property, which cannot be taken by government." It is not surprising that the free English people who formed the United States and penned the Constitution wrote what is called "the takings clause": "Nor shall private property be taken for public use without just compensation." There was really nothing novel about the statement, which some of the founders thought to be self-evident and redundant. When the Constitution was adopted, law common to the people had been operating in the older colonies for more than a century. But supporters of the private property meme wanted more assurance that the idea would be preserved explicitly in the Constitution. The inclusion of the statement in the Constitution enhanced the chances for meme survival.

Takings-clause requirements were extended to the states by the Fourteenth Amendment in 1868, which holds that "any State [shall not] deprive any person of . . . property, without due process of law." Today, protection of private property from state-government takings is buttressed by state constitutions, forty-eight of which contain takings clauses similar to that found in the federal Constitution. In addition, twenty-four state constitutions extend protection to property that is "damaged" by government action, even if it is not "taken." But ensuring the protection of private property rights is far from being a settled issue. The controversies that continue to surround the idea of private property rights suggest that they are still in jeopardy. By definition, assets are attractive to many people, including those who hold common law rights to said assets. For adherents to this meme, the boundaries that restrain government actions are merely parchment. To others, however, these boundaries define sacred rights that are "naturally" theirs. Of course, any government powerful enough to protect one's private rights is also powerful enough to redefine those rights.

Systems of property rights go hand-in-hand with land settlement. Those who first established rules for sharing a common pasture unwittingly invented law and property rights. Logic alone suggests that land-based people would have been the first to establish informal mechanisms for sharing and conserving land and then transferring land rights to others. Systems of rights based on custom, tradition, and shared norms would have been more dominant, the more rooted and close-knit the people. By comparison, formal systems of order that relied on an impersonal government would have been more costly. In contrast, communities of transient people who shared little in the way of custom, tradition, and language, would have found informal order to be costly. In those settings, formal or political law would have been more dominant. Therefore, the two memes—different ideas about law and property rights—compete across places and time.

Legal scholar Robert Ellickson investigated informal order among California farmers and developed a hypothesis about close-knit groups similar to those typically found in rural America.[10] He identified problems when the state legislature sought to impose external law on an internal order, but he also observed the benefits of state intervention as a safeguard against parochialism. Ellickson saw other forces challenge the informal order as well. As he observed, "Many current trends, such as increasing urbanization, the spread of liability insurance, and the advent of the welfare state, are continuing to weaken the informal-control system and expand the domain of [the state]."[11]

The property rights controversy and meme competition relates to constitutional boundaries that distinguish political from private actions. In this light, state and federal constitutions limit the scope of politics and provide a sanctuary for the common law rights of ordinary citizens. But in another way, the common law rights of ordinary people stand in the way of accomplishing the larger goals of the body politic as expressed through a majoritarian government. One perspective is the thesis; the other is the antithesis. The interaction of statute and common law, positive and natural law, yields a struggling synthesis that continuously defines one's world and the rights of ordinary people.

Noted legal scholar Harold J. Berman has taken a deeply pessimistic view of the developing synthesis in his formidable study of Western legal traditions.[12] He believes that Western legal traditions are rooted in traditional community regimes that embodied heavy doses of common values and social norms. For constitutional reasons a majoritarian state tends to be dominant in struggles between the informal and formal systems. Berman writes that "it is only when the different legal regimes of all these communities—local, regional, national, ethnic, professional, political, intellectual, spiritual, and others—are swallowed up in the law of the nation-state that history becomes tyrannical."[13] Berman also discusses the explosive growth of the modern administrative state that seeks to enforce rules and regulations over all facets of life. He concludes: "The law is becoming more fragmented, more subjective, geared more to expediency and less to morality, concerned more with immediate consequences and less with consistency and continuity. Thus the historical soil of the Western legal tradition is being washed away in the twentieth century, and the tradition itself is threatened with collapse."[14]

Wetlands, endangered species protection, and statute-based shields that deny common-law rights provide fruitful examples for exploring tensions between informal and formal ordering systems. Regarding endangered species, Congress has empowered regulators, by statute, to engage in activities that can and do interfere with traditional common law rights. In the case of wetlands, regulatory agencies (acting as agents of Congress but without explicit statutory authority) have defined activities that allow for the attenuation of private rights. In addition, the Clean Water Act of 1972 and a host of state legislation have taken environmental rights previously held by ordinary citizens. For example, until 1972 in Illinois citizens could bring common law suits against Wisconsin polluters who damaged Chicago's drinking water; they received redress. Those environmental rights were taken by the Clean Water Act. Today, matters involving interstate pollution are in the hands of federal regulators. With common law, owners of adjacent land could bring suit against hog farmers if odors and other unpleasantness reduced land value or interfered with property enjoyment. Today, right holders in thirty-five states cannot readily bring action against neighboring animal-feeding operations that inflict uninvited environmental costs; the polluters are shielded by statute. Private property rights have thus been converted to public rights and transferred to administrative agency. In this arena the public right meme has won the conflict against private property memes.

This conversion of private to public rights expanded significantly in the 1970s and 1980s. Consider my country home in Georgia. If the American bluebird were to become listed as an endangered species, a conversion of rights would occur immediately, and U.S. government agents could therefore dictate what we can do on our land. If wetlands are found on my neighbor's land, for example, federal authorities can mandate how and where he will plant and harvest trees. The logic of these mandates rests on the notion that politics should override the "law of the land" when important social benefits are at stake. Others view the same actions as an unfair infringement of their property rights. If previously held rights are to be transferred, the prospective owner should be willing to pay for the rights received. Otherwise, the transfer will not be valid in a common law sense.

As a result, people in Jones County, Georgia, are wary about providing habitat for the red-cockaded woodpecker, since they might lose their use of a large swath of land if the bird is discovered. One well-known conservationist learned this the hard way.[15] Ben Cone of North Carolina took steps to maintain woodpecker habitat on his forest land, but then learned that he would lose the right to harvest timber without compensation. Cone carried his case to the U.S. Court of Claims, where he settled out of court with the U.S. Department of the Interior. Timber operators in the

Pacific Northwest have been known to revise their harvest plans and in some cases clear-cut to avoid encounters with wetland regulators and endangered species. The results are that species habitat is lost, affected land values fall, and previously profitable ventures become loss leaders.

DRAWING INFERENCES ABOUT MEMES
FROM STATISTICAL STUDIES

Ideas about property rights are caught in a competitive struggle. What can be inferred about these two memes and regional patterns of outcomes? The results of two statistical studies shed some light on meme vitality in the eastern and western United States, an admittedly diverse set of communities. First, the ongoing property rights movement of the 1990s seems to be strong evidence that ordinary citizens across the nation are more than concerned about federal encroachments on private property rights.[16] But before jumping to that conclusion, data must be further probed.

In the eastern United States the property rights movement is inflamed by regulatory "takings" associated with enforcement of the Endangered Species Act and the control of wetlands inspired by the Clean Water Act. Added to these are federal designations of historic corridors, wild and scenic rivers, and other regulatory actions that have brought unwanted control of land use to private rights holders. Among western states these issues are joined by federal actions that limit access to vast holdings of federal land and revisions of long-standing grazing rights.[17] Some view the federal government as out of control, disregarding the sanctity of private property rights, and always deferring to the interests of environmentalists in an effort to shut off gainful uses of land by private citizens. Others see the federal government as their only avenue for accomplishing vital and sometimes unappreciated environmental goals to restore and preserve nature's sanctuary for future generations. But it is not so much these differences in perspectives that matter to property rights advocates as it is the means for accomplishing environmentalists' goals. If a group desires land rights, the property rights advocates say, those who want the land can obtain it by simply buying it. But such ideas are anathema to public property memes. Payment implies recognition of private rights, which means maintaining the rights status quo. Taking without payment implies victory of the public over the private rights meme.

Concern over property rights protection led in the early 1990s to failed efforts to gain federal legislation. Later, the 104th Congress added property rights protection to the "Contract with America"; no final action was taken. Disappointed by the failed effort, property rights advocates moved to the state level. By September 1996 some form of property rights legislation and related governor's executive orders were in place in twenty-five states. Five of these have statutes that set trigger points for compensation when government regulations reduce land values. By late 1996 every state west of the Mississippi (except Arizona, Oklahoma, and North Dakota) was either debating or had passed legislation.

In 1994 two of my colleagues and I analyzed the effort to introduce state property rights legislation and developed a statistical model that predicts which states would entertain such action.[18] The results of this research provided estimates of the partial effects of certain characteristics. This 1994 model indicates a higher probability of property rights protection in states with large amounts of federal land, with a larger ratio of legislators to population, and for those states that border a body of water. States with a higher rating for environmentalism were less likely to introduce legislation as were those with a higher state debt per capita. An examination of the statistical results on a state-by-state basis reveals where the model underpredicts and overpredicts outcomes. Sampling eight western states allows us to draw some inferences regarding the strength of competing property rights memes.

At the time of our research, Arizona had not introduced legislation; the model predicted a low probability for Arizona. California had introduced legislation, and the model predicted a probability of 99.8 percent for the action. Idaho had introduced legislation, and the model predicted a 100 percent probability. Kansas had also introduced legislation (99.5 percent probability). Louisiana had introduced legislation (67.1 percent probability). New Mexico had introduced legislation (91.9 percent probability). Oregon had also introduced legislation (99.7 percent probability). Finally, Texas had introduced legislation, but the probability of the action was only 55.6 percent. Notice that our model did not contain a variable that accounted for the strength of memes. Consider Louisiana and Texas again: The model predicted a low level of probability for a property rights law, but facts state otherwise. From this we can infer a relatively strong private property rights meme in those two states.

In an ongoing study of the environmental movement, researchers at Clemson University's Center for Policy and Legal Studies examined the determinants of memberships in four major environmental organizations.[19] The organizations were the Sierra Club, the Nature Conservancy, the National Audubon Society, and the Natural Resources Defense Fund. Using 1990, 1991, 1992, and 1993 membership data for fifty states, a regression model was constructed that included independent variables for explaining the variation in memberships. The variables were per capita income, income growth, population density, the percent of population in the 18 to 34 age group, the League of Conservation Voters (LCV) rating for the state's congressional delegation, the number of hazardous waste sites per square mile, and the percent of land owned by the federal government. The model, which used logged variables, was estimated first for states east of the Mississippi River. A separate model was then run for states west of the Mississippi River, excluding Alaska and Hawaii.

Robust statistical results were obtained for the eastern and western models. But significant and distinct differences were observed, which suggests something about competing memes. For example, income, population density, and the LCV rating were highly significant in the eastern states model but not in the western states. The signs on income and LCV were positive. The sign on population density was negative. The amount of federal land is highly significant and positive in predicting memberships for western states but significant and negative for eastern states. Other differences related to the age variable, which was significant and negative in the East but not significant in the West.

These results suggest that environmentalism and meme competition are a distinctly different phenomenon in the West. My research assistant, Brian Kropp, offered the following explanation: Consumers can gain three types of value from environmental assets—use value, existence value, and option value.[20] For example, at Yellowstone National Park some consumers will actually visit, hike, and camp in the park; they will obtain use value. Others seldom if ever take the opportunity to visit, but they gain utility from knowing that the park is there; they gain satisfaction from existence and the possible option to visit.

In western states consumers can more readily visit and enjoy nature's splendor, thus explaining the significance of the amount of federal land in the western estimates. Easterners, however, express their interest by joining environmental organizations when income and their LCV preferences are high enough. Environmentalists in the East support federal legislation that protects their "green" interests; they are "buying" an option. The amount of federal land carries a negative sign in the eastern estimate. In other words, access to the state enables eastern supporters of public property memes to obtain rights in the West, while western supporters of public property memes seem to care very little about supplanting private rights in the East. The data reinforce the idea that tensions result when communities that have an underlying informal order based on a land ethic have political encounters with those that rely on an urban formal ordering system.

FINAL THOUGHTS

Efforts by competing groups to redefine property rules involve competing ideas of property rights, order, and freedom. In a majoritarian republic, for example, both groups can call on the body politic for assistance in their cause. By using the metaphor of meme competition, this chapter has examined the historical and current dimensions of an ancient struggle that seems ever-present in human settlements. All parties in the struggle recognize the necessity of having property rules, but there is sharp disagreement regarding the laws that define private spheres of action. For one group, freedom involves actions that can take place as long as costs are not imposed on those who occupy similar private spheres of action. This group calls on government to sanction negative rights that have evolved in community settings. For the other group, freedom involves the right to redefine or eliminate evolved private spheres of action. This group appeals to the body politic for expansion of positive rights that will encompass all communities.

The relative strength of these two memes—belief in private versus public approaches to property rights management—is partly determined by degrees of social homogeneity, the degree to which a population is committed to the land, and the relative dominance of kinship patterns and the use of norms, customs, and traditions for defining property rights. The private property meme that relates to land rights is strongest among people who have historically relied on the land for income and satisfaction. They understand the long-run importance of laws that give stability to land use. By contrast, the public property meme is most powerful in urban settings that are typically managed through formal law, statutes, and regulations. Although some dimensions of private property rights are valued highly in densely populated settings, private rights that relate to natural resources and open land are not.

Paradoxically, success for the public property meme in eroding the legitimacy of private property rights carries with it a contagion for further expansion of government's redistributive powers. With that expansion, links between recognized costs and benefits are replaced by bureaucratic efforts to build synthetic substitutes for market forces. Political power rises; the negative rights of ordinary citizens decline. Ultimately, however, all people seek secure spheres of action for family and possessions. If these spheres disappear, the nation risks becoming a commons fraught with high risk for the tragedies that are inherent in that system of natural resource management.

NOTES

1. See Bruce Yandle, "Organic Constitutions and Common Law," *Constitutional Political Economy* 2 (1991): 225–41.

2. In *We the People* (Cambridge: Harvard University Press, 1991), Bruce A. Ackerman argues that constitutional changes can and have occurred in the United States even without explicit replacement of, or amendment to, the formal constitutional document. In Ackerman's view political forces, augmented by judicial collaboration, can change the Constitution even if the words of the document remain unaltered.

3. "Men of systems" refers to Adam Smith's discussion of politicians who seek to alter social processes. See Smith, *The Theory of Moral Sentiments* (1759; reprint, Indianapolis: Liberty Fund Press, 1979), 233–34.

4. For more on memetics, see Aaron Lynch, *Thought Contagion: How Belief Spreads through Society* (New York: Basic Books, 1996). Lynch's exposition is motivated by Richard Dawkins's original exposition in *The Selfish Gene* (Oxford: Oxford University Press, 1989).

5. Writers on legal theory draw a clear distinction between nation-states and societies. I too draw on that distinction here. See Otto Gierke, *Natural Law and Theory of Society: 1500 to 1800* (1934; reprint, Boston: Beacon Press, 1960).

6. F. A. Hayek, *Law, Legislation, and Liberty: A New Statement of the Liberal Principles of Justice and Political Economy*, vol. 1 (Chicago: University of Chicago Press, 1973), 11.

7. Daniel J. Boorstin, *The Decline of Radicalism: Reflections on America Today* (New York: Vintage, 1970), 71–96. (I express appreciation to Frank Varty for calling this to my attention.)

8. Boorstin, *Decline of Radicalism*, 76–79.

9. See *Samuel A. Worcester, Plaintiff in Error v The State of Georgia*, 31 US 515 (1832) and *The Cherokee Nation v The State of Georgia*, 30 US 1 (1831). For background and discussion, see David Williams, *The Georgia Gold Rush: Twenty-Niners, Cherokees, and Gold Fever* (Columbia: University of South Carolina Press, 1993), 37–46.

10. Robert Ellickson, *Order without Law: How Neighbors Dispute* (Cambridge: Harvard University Press, 1991), 250.

11. Ibid., 284.

12. Harold J. Berman, *Law and Revolution* (Cambridge: Harvard University Press, 1983).

13. Ibid., 17.

14. Ibid., 39.

15. This refers to Ben Cone of North Carolina. For further discussion, see Lee Ann Welch, "Property Rights Conflicts under the Endangered Species Act," in *Land Rights: The 1990's Property Rights Rebellion*, ed. Bruce Yandle (Lanham, Md.: Rowman & Littlefield, 1995), 151–97.

16. For more, see Yandle, ed., *Land Rights*.

17. See Roger Clegg, ed., *Farmers, Ranchers, and Environmental Law* (Washington, D.C.: National Legal Center for the Public Interest, 1995). Also see William Perry Pendley, *War on the West: Government Tyranny on America's Great Frontier* (Washington, D.C.: Regnery Publishing, 1995).

18. See Donald J. Boudreaux, Jody Lipford, and Bruce Yandle, "Regulatory Takings and Constitutional Repair: The 1990's Property Rights Rebellion," *Constitutional Political Economy* 6 (1995): 171–90.

19. See Brian Kropp, "Environmental Interest Groups: What Makes Them Tick?" Clemson University Center for Policy and Legal Studies, Clemson, S.C., November 1995.

20. Ibid.

New Property Rights Debates

The Dialectics of Naming, Blaming, and Claiming

SARAH PRALLE AND MICHAEL W. McCANN

"In no other country in the world is the love of property keener or more alert than in the United States," observed the French writer Alexis de Tocqueville more than a century and a half ago. "Everyone," he added, "having some possession to defend, recognizes the right to property in principle."[1] Indeed, he contended that it was this ubiquitous commitment to property that most distinguished the emerging "democratic" order from the older aristocratic society whose passing he lamented. In other words, the ideal of property represented a sort of defining metaphor at the heart of the American political tradition. From the start, the idea of property has been intimately related to expressed aspirations for the cognate ideals of individual liberty, limited government, republican virtue, and distributive justice that have animated American public life.

This common commitment to the principle of property, however, has rarely secured consensus on any particular construction of the concept itself. It is hardly an exaggeration to claim that virtually every period of substantial political debate and struggle in the United States since colonial days has been shaped by and expressive of rival conceptions of property. To be sure, such antagonisms have turned in large part on different material interests at stake. The diverse social positions of various key actors in the larger socioeconomic order clearly have been important in each debate. But political struggles have also involved deep differences in understandings about the very meaning of property, the complex structures of rules and entitlements that particular conceptions of property entail, and the very ways of life for "virtuous" citizens that those commitments to property have expressed. In short, the language of property in the American legal and political tradition has constituted a pervasively "contested terrain." A brief review of the country's history illustrates the point.[2]

CONSTITUTIONAL PROPERTY RIGHTS
IN HISTORICAL PERSPECTIVE

This abridged constitutional chronicle begins with the founding figures at the constitutional convention. Virtually all of the participants agreed with James Madison that "the first object of government . . . [is] the protection of the different and unequal faculties of acquiring property."[3] But this consensus on the commitment to property was matched by keen disagreement about what property required for its maintenance and the forms of social life that it secured. Many visions on the subject of property were excluded from the Philadelphia convention; among those who were permitted voice, differences of opinion were numerous and substantial. Madison represented the pragmatic middle position: balancing property rights and political rights secured by a strong, expansionist federal government. To the right were the unabashedly elitist advocates of antimajoritarian class dominance, such as Gouverneur Morris. To the left were the more democratic elements, led by such figures as James Wilson, who closely linked property ownership to the possibilities of self-governing republican communities. These different representatives thus articulated not only different principles of government organization to protect and advance property, but also quite novel visions of what a property-based society might look like, become, and mean in practice.[4]

Most of the nation's subsequent history involved struggles over, and changes in, the basic legal structures, entitlements, and meanings of those rights to property secured by the Constitution. In particular, the early nineteenth century witnessed increasing conflicts as small-scale agrarian interests were overridden by the interests, position, and ideals of dynamic corporate, industrial, and speculative property advocates. As the great legal historian J. Willard Hurst summarized, "The bulk of nineteenth century cases which develop vested rights doctrine" were committed to "dynamic rather than static property, property in motion or at risk rather than property secure and at rest."[5] Cultural struggles over these different conceptions of property dominated politics in the first half of the century, as individuals and emerging corporate groups sought to wrest control from the residual aristocratic elements of civil society and the state. These conflicts dovetailed with and were absorbed into the divisive constitutional battle between North and South, which essentially were two different cultures grounded in very different sociolegal conceptions of property: "free" (or alienated) and slave. The North's eventual victory represented the triumph of one proprietarian tradition over another, as well as a reaffirmation of property ideals in general. In defending free soil and free labor, Abraham Lincoln proclaimed, "Property is the fruit of labor; property is desirable; is a positive good in the world," thus providing his blessing to the war's certain outcome before his death.[6]

The ideals of property took on new meanings as they structured the high-stakes, often bloody, battles over the next half-century, dividing big business interests from agrarian populists and urban labor, each of which developed their own visions about property's promises and legal requirements in American society. The federal courts rushed into this battle with the greatest display of judicial activism in the nation's history. On the one hand, a majority of Supreme Court justices further elevated the symbolic significance of property to near canonical status. Brandishing two lethal swords of constitutional doctrine—the "dual federalism" of commerce clause authority and the "substantive due process" constructions of the Fourteenth Amendment—the Court slashed away at scores of state and federal regulatory statutes infringing on the discretionary power of both corporate and individual property owners. These legal protections clearly favored one vision of property, but the struggles of farmers, workers, and other interested parties continued to keep alive different visions of propertied ways of life and the virtues they would nurture in free citizens.[7]

The New Deal eventually provided yet a new legal bargain, enforced by the federal government, among these contending interests. This guiding vision validated the triumph of corporate interests and designs while granting at least minimal, and important, formal avenues of representation to workers, small property interests, and various middle-class reformers. This deal was, after some recalcitrance, blessed by the highest court in the land. In the 1938 decision of *U.S. v. Carolene Products Co.*, the Court articulated the evolving constitutional logic of the New Deal legacy. On the one hand, Justice Harlan Fiske Stone announced the emerging consensus that there shall be a "presumption of constitutionality" for government regulation of private property to secure the common good. Judicial review of government action interfering with property need only be subjected to a low standard of minimal "rationality." On the other hand, "there shall be narrower scope for the operation of the presumption of constitutionality," where regulations affect specific personal liberties outlined in the Constitution, the rights of minorities, and the functioning of basic democratic processes.[8]

The new constitutional "double standard" and its social vision was well exemplified in the emerging doctrine of "takings." Mandated by the Constitution's Fifth Amendment, as well as by most state constitutions, the provision itself has been usually interpreted as a specific elaboration of more general due-process protections. The text reads: "No person shall be deprived of life, liberty or property; nor shall private property be taken for public use, without just compensation." The provision's very words suggest two basic issues at stake. The first issue concerns the purposes of state appropriation. The specification of "public use" traditionally had been read as a restrictive criterion, thus limiting state eminent-domain and regulatory actions to those clearly providing public goods or services. In the post–New Deal era, however, this restriction has been read in "narrow" ways: "The concept of public welfare is broad and inclusive," the High Court ruled in 1954.[9] The second issue, following from the first, concerns provision of a "reasonable return" as compensation to owners whose property is taken in whole or in part. In short, government has been given relatively free rein to take, regulate, and coordinate property as long as payment is provided for physical takings and extreme costs imposed on private owners.

Of course, this new consensus hardly ended conflict and debate regarding the appropriate meaning and protections for property in the American polity. Corporations, small business interests, and conservative advocates have continued to battle against state regulations, alleging a variety of defenses regarding both particularistic private freedoms and competing visions of the public good. In return, representatives of labor, racial and ethnic minorities, women, and consumers (among others) have pushed for more government controls over the freedom and power of propertied interests. These groups have advanced various competing notions, at times elevating public goods over property, while at other times reconstructing the very meaning of property to justify greater collective state control.

Among the most interesting of these efforts at legal mobilization were liberal-progressive claims about entitlements to "new" types of property. Law professor Charles Reich played a critical role in developing the conceptual claim. Traditionally, he argued, "the institution we call property guards the troubled boundary between individual man and the state."[10] However, traditional distinctions between "private" and "public," between "property" and "state," have always been problematic; they have been virtually eroded in the modern corporate era. It now is clear, Reich contended, that the state itself is the primary legal source of much goods distribution in modern society, including for the wealthy and corporate interests (through tax breaks, subsidies, testing services) as well as for the less powerful in society. He specifically applied this argument about needed procedural entitlements of property rights to protecting the freedoms and autonomy of poor persons who are dependent on state welfare benefits. Other progressive thinkers, such as C. B. MacPherson and Frank Michelman, applied this idea to a range of other revenues, relations, and goods in modern society.[11]

More than a few such advocates boldly extended the "new property" logic to include various types of "public goods." In particular, environmental legal reformers insisted on the need to "stop short and ask ourselves how we want to redefine the rights of property," to provide protection for natural resources. Legal advocate Joseph Sax contributed immensely to this argument. Invoking an ancient "public trust" theory of "common property resources," he argued in the 1960s that the courts should "treat environmental resources as property to be maintained and protected for the benefit of its owners"—the public at large.[12] He demonstrated the potential value of applying traditional principles of private nuisance law to judicial determinations of public "takings" issues. The archetypal polarity between public authority and private property thus could be redefined as a dispute among several competing but equal property rights claims, including claims for collective resources such as ambient air, water, and land. In short, the public "right to a decent environment . . . should be phrased in a way to put them on a plane with traditional property rights."[13]

This liberal "new property" logic failed to win many converts among judges in federal or state courts. In 1970, however, the Supreme Court recognized legislatively defined welfare benefits as a form of property deserving procedural protections in *Goldberg v. Kelly*, and it flirted with various other procedural rights related to new property claims.[14] But for the most part, the new egalitarian legal logic left little imprint on formal law. In fact, its greatest effect may have been to catalyze conservative counter-mobilization around reinvigorating property rights discourse in general, and opening new routes for reassertion of traditional private property rights claims against state intervention in particular. Over the past decade scholars and legal advocates have advanced various claims for revitalizing traditional proprietarian conceptions of substantive due process and fortifying private takings claims of compensation for government regulatory burdens.[15] Moreover, in the 1980s big and small business alike, developers, and private owners began to mount a backlash against liberal-progressive advocates, especially environmentalists. As in earlier periods, these recent struggles have reflected not only differences in material interest among groups, but also opposing conceptions of property and its relation to the public good that signify yet larger social visions of free and virtuous ways of life. Yet, like the progressive-liberal visions of new property, these more recent conservative claims have had only a modest impact on constitutional legal doctrine, and significant transformations in the near future are unlikely. Overall, despite the undeniable conservative trimming of civil liberties and expansion of property-based protections in recent years, the original New Deal double-standard logic remains largely intact.

BEYOND THE COURTS

The continuing efforts of contending political groups to mobilize traditional property rights doctrines for new causes is interesting in itself; these efforts reveal much about the conservatism of the country's legal traditions and institutions. But it is a mistake to focus on courts as the only, or even the primary, arena of legal mobilization and political contestation over property rights in the contemporary period.[16] Rather, the most lively expressions of "naming, blaming, and claiming" around property rights in land-use disputes today is taking place in legislative arenas, initiative and referenda processes, administrative forums, and the mass media.[17] More than ever, these confrontations are not just about narrow rules and specific entitlements. Instead, they involve contending allegations regarding who rights claimants are, the ways of life that they represent, and the virtues (or vices) that they bring to public life. The following discussion interrogates some aspects of recent clashes between environmental groups and their opponents.

On November 7, 1995, voters in Washington state rejected one of the most radical property rights proposals that has emerged under the banner known as the property rights movement. The measure would have compensated property owners for *any* reductions in land value that result from environmental and other land-use regulations. Although this initiative was more extreme than others of its kind—adopting a broad definition of "property" (among other things)—it was not unique in its general thrust. In the past decade the issue of property rights has secured a place on the American political agenda, due largely to the efforts of a loose coalition of industries, public interest law firms, right-wing think tanks, and individual citizens dedicated to changing how the government regulates public and private land.

The new property rights movement has resurrected the discourse of property and the Fifth Amendment "takings" clause, arguing in the courts for a broad interpretation of what constitutes a "taking" of property and thus is deserving of compensation. Although legal scholars have duly debated the resurgence of takings claims and the Supreme Court's lukewarm reception of them, the public debate around the movement has not been restricted to legal or technical discourse about the merits of land-use regulations. Indeed, today's debates include sometimes vociferous exchanges between advocates and opponents about each other's respective motives, legitimacy, and character. These contests involve efforts by both environmentalists and property rights activists to persuade the public at large and the policy makers in particular that they are genuine and public-minded, while their opponents are self-interested and malevolent. At its most extreme, property rights activists and environmentalists characterize each other as the "enemy" needing to be destroyed. Such strategies are common in politics. As suggested by the political scientist Murray J. Edelman, "They help to give the political spectacle its power to arouse passions, fears, and hopes."[18] An enemy provides a clear target for group action and helps groups build internal cohesion, recruit and empower members, and build commitment to a cause.[19] In addition, this interactive process of character construction and character assassination reinforces certain cultural perspectives, whether imagined or real.

In some respects, these naming, blaming, and claiming contests are driven by the fact that appeals to property rights, although powerful, are not self-legitimating. Property rights advocates have had to defend their claims against those who embrace a different concept of what responsibilities are inherent in property ownership. Environmentalists have attacked the perspective implicit in the property rights argument, questioning the argument's individualistic orientation. For their part, environmentalists have encountered a rather formidable opponent. Their appeals to the "common good" and "community" as a way of combating property rights claims are tenuous, particularly in an age in which there has been "an abandonment of the concept of the public interest."[20] In America's pluralistic society, policy outcomes are seen as the end result of competition among interest groups, making it difficult for any one group to convincingly claim that it speaks for the common good; that is, the politically savvy public suspects that all players advocate some special interest. In such a climate the different groups avidly compete for credibility, making appeals to the "common good" in hopes that the public can be persuaded that such a thing indeed exists.

The remainder of this discussion examines the dialectics of naming, blaming, and claiming between property rights advocates and environmentalists, suggesting that these processes take place on different planes. Specifically, claims are made about the grassroots nature of the movements, the participants' character, and their motivations for getting involved. The discussion illustrates how these dynamics have encouraged groups on both sides to see their struggle as one of good over evil, of public-minded citizens against selfish special interests, and of outcasts against the mainstream.

The Property Rights Debates

Within the property rights debates, there is a rhetorical struggle between environmentalists and property rights advocates concerning who is genuinely organized at the grassroots. The designation "grassroots" carries with it a positive construction, implying a democratic movement representing the average citizen's interests; that is, the "grassroots" designation contributes to what social movement scholars call legitimacy of numbers, whereby a political group achieves legitimacy by demonstrating that "a committed and mobilized citizenry supports political change."[21] If a group is not organized at the grassroots, it is easier to accuse it of working for "special interests," a particularly unpopular label in today's political climate.

Recognizing this, property rights leaders portray themselves as managing a movement of thousands of citizens around the country, all of whom object to government regulation of private property and public lands. For example, Nancie G. Marzulla, president of Defenders of Property Rights, has stated that the property rights movement is a rare event in the nation's history, "where countless ordinary people . . . have organized at the grassroots level to make their voices heard by legislative bodies nationwide."[22] Environmentalists have questioned the movement's grassroots claims. By emphasizing the connections between self-described grassroots property rights groups and their corporate sponsors, environmental groups hope to tarnish the movement's image. A recent statement by a California chapter of Earth First! is typical in this regard: "The Mountain States Legal Foundation [a non-profit property rights foundation] is nothing more than a mouthpiece for the (un)wise (ab)use movement. *It is anything but real grassroots.* Any organization that gets the vast majority of its funding from corporations with an economic interest in raping Western landscape . . . obviously *is not a people movement.*"[23]

The environmentalists' strategy is to portray property rights activists as corporate mouthpieces, while painting themselves as genuine citizen-activists. Any grassroots activity by their opponents, environmentalists claim, has been extorted through the actions of employers in the resource-extraction industries. There is some evidence that supports these accusations. Logging companies, for example, have actively sought the involvement of distressed workers in the timber industry to protest against environmental regulations. Timber companies have gone so far as to give workers the day off with pay and provide transportation to protest rallies as a way of encouraging local involvement.[24] Such protests provide a necessary antidote to the image of an elite, corporate-sponsored movement. Indeed, Ron Arnold, a leader in the anti-environmental movement, is reported to have told Canadian timber giant Macmillan Bloedel, "Give them [citizen groups] the money. You stop defending yourselves, let them do it, and you get the hell out of the way. Because citizens' groups have credibility and industries don't."[25]

The environmental movement is also vulnerable to charges of elitism, a fact that has not gone unnoticed by property rights proponents. Much of the grassroots environmental activism of the 1970s has been gradually replaced by formal organizations headquartered in Washington, D.C., that have little contact with their grassroots constituency beyond routine mail and phone solicitations.[26] Charges of elitism have come from within the environmental movement as well, most forcefully from environmental justice activists who criticize the mainstream movement for the notable absence of minorities in leadership positions and for the scant attention paid to environmental concerns in inner cities. These internal disputes lend some credibility to the claims of the property rights activists, fueling the interchange of accusations and counteraccusations.

The political discussion over property is not unlike other heated political debates in America, where claimants label their opponents as extreme, irrational, and outside the mainstream. Environmentalists, eager to make allies with the average, property-owning citizen, argue that the demands of the property rights movement are extreme, and that the movement's leaders are right-wing fanatics. For example, Carl Pope, the executive director of the Sierra Club, has said that "it is not accidental that the property rights movement overlaps so heavily with the members of the militia and other advocates of establishing public order on the basis of an armed populace, with justice flowing to the fastest draw." Others focus more generally on "greedy" corporations and "renegade" property owners who have threatened federal land-use officials with violence.

This negative construction of property rights activists has not been wholly accepted by the media. Nevertheless, one journalist who clearly sides with environmentalists concedes: "Most of these rebellious landowners are good, God-fearing Americans who remind us of our self-reliant, pioneer ancestors. It's not hard to have a measure of sympathy for them when they tell their tales of hardship inflicted by overly strict enforcement of government regulations. It gives them standing in this debate that seems more genuine that that of city dwellers."[27] Of course, the self-described association between property rights proponents and self-reliant, rugged individualists does not comport well with the construction of these same people as victims who need what amounts to government subsidies to survive economically. But the reference to our pioneer ancestors is a powerful one. In conjuring images of the past, activists can locate themselves in the country's mythical history, imagining their fight as a continuation of what has come before them.

These reassuring images come at a time when many of the traditional values associated with these symbols are being severely challenged. Ranching, farming, and mining of the West is increasingly the job of large corporations, not cowboys and pioneers. For example, in Catron County, New Mexico, a hotbed of wise-use and property rights activism, ranching is no longer economically feasible for many of its citizens. Indeed, a significant portion of the highest-paid workers in the county (20 to 30 percent) are government employees who work for the same agencies that are allegedly the source of the ranchers' woes.[28]

As the economic base of the West changes, the social fabric of communities may begin to unravel, if it is not already doing so. New residents are moving into rural communities, some of whom do not share the "cowboy culture" of the old-timers. The property rights argument thus becomes a means of articulating values and praising behaviors that are increasingly difficult to live by or locate. In other words, it is a debate over the validity of two different ways of life, each of which has an imagined quality to it. In Catron County, for example, property rights activists reference a "cowboy culture" that is an "endangered way of life requiring special protection."[29] In response, environmentalists insist that the most important cultures in the West are the indigenous cultures, the Native American tribes whose lifeways were virtually abolished by the intrusion of cowboys and their attendant ideology. For many environmentalists Native American culture is associated with environmental sustainability and ecological wisdom. When environmentalists argue that this is the more authentic western culture, they are pointing to both an idealized past and future—one in which ecological concerns will outweigh commercial ones.

A simplistic reading of property rights battles, both current and historic, suggests that property claims tend to pit particularistic, private interests against efforts to restrict these rights in the name of advancing some version of the common good. But underneath the obvious "private rights versus public interest" debate, claimants offer competing versions and interpretations of the common good. This makes it possible, rhetorically, for both sides to claim that they are acting altruistically and that their opponents are acting out of self-interest. In the debate over a property rights initiative in Washington state, for example, the environmental coalition used the rhetoric of the common good to argue against Referendum 48, a regulatory takings bill. As stated in a fact sheet of the "No on 48 Campaign," Referendum 48 put "special interests over public interests." It is an example of "special interest legislation that is not in the public interest" being bankrolled by "vested special interests . . . because they all stand to make millions of dollars."[30] The supporters of this property rights legislation, according to opponents, were motivated by greed, seeing dollar signs where they themselves saw clean air and water, protected salmon habitat, and livable communities.

But property rights groups have argued that it is the environmentalists who act out of self-interest. According to one property rights activist in southern California, slow-growth advocates are people "who had gotten into a lifeboat and then wanted to pull up the ladder so that no one else could get in."[31] Much of the property rights literature refers to a selfishness on the part of urban environmentalists, who allegedly want to lock up federal lands and prevent growth to preserve their own natural playgrounds. Property rights advocates thus insist that they are working for the common good, while identifying slow-growth advocates and environmentalists as elitists motivated by narrow and selfish interests. This argument reflects a faith in the market, in the notion that aggregated individual interests will produce the public interest. Property rights advocates see industry and its employees as part of the "producing class" who do "real work" by producing things and investing in the economic development of the community and the nation.[32]

The property rights movement also tries to preempt or counter accusations that they are self-interested by expanding the scope of the movement's goals. In these expanded constructions of the movement's agenda, the advocacy of property rights becomes, in Marzulla's words, a "fight for freedom and individual rights," the "line drawn in the sand between tyranny and liberty," the "civil rights issue of the 1990s."[33] If basic American values are at stake—indeed, if the integrity of the Constitution is at stake—it is harder to argue that property rights advocates are simply out for their self-interest.

"Deserving" and "Undeserving" Beneficiaries

A final set of claims in the property rights debate revolves around who benefits from property rights initiatives and who loses. These debates go to the heart of public policy, for they address society's distribution of benefits and burdens. Moreover, they include explicit and implicit messages about whom society considers "deserving" and "undeserving." These contests are important in that "undeserving" individuals and groups are less likely to earn sympathy from the public and policy makers, while "deserving" groups elicit a more positive response.[34] A positioning of various property rights activists and potential policy beneficiaries along an "undeserving-deserving" continuum illustrates their relative social construction in relationship to each other (table 1). These groups are potential beneficiaries of "takings" legislation, which would compensate private property owners whose property value is diminished through government regulation.

As one might suspect, the property rights movement has focused on the more deserving members along this continuum. The horror stories that property rights advocates tell about excessive government regulation usually involve individual property owners who are unable to develop their land because of, in the words of U.S. Representative W. J. "Billy" Tauzin of Louisiana, "some sort of bluenosed lizard that the Fish and Wildlife Service deemed threatened or endangered."[35] Clearly, homeowners are a sympathetic group of potential policy beneficiaries of property rights laws: To own a home is still the American dream, and the right to exclusive control over one's property is still a powerful myth. "Moms and Pops" whose retirement nest egg is bound up in land that cannot be developed are a subgroup of particularly sympathetic homeowners.

In an article by two directors of a conservative anti-environmental think tank, various stories—of two retirees, of assorted small-property owners, of a church that was unable to build on a wetland, and of a small farmer—are related to demonstrate the need for regulatory reform.[36] Stories about farmers conjure images of small family farms; these images then "connect urban America to an arguably more virtuous agrarian past, the

TABLE 1. Hypothesized Distribution of Propery Rights Activists
and Beneficiaries along a Deserving/Undeserving Continuum

(+) Positive/Deserving		(−) Negative/Undeserving
◄──►		
Homeowners	Real-estate developers (small)	Polluting/destructive
Small farmers	Small businesses affected by	industries
Unemployed workers	environmental regulations	Large corporations

SOURCE: Compiled by the authors.

symbolic loss of which would disturb more than a few citizens."[37] Property rights activists argue that their agenda will help these farmers, ensuring the survival of important agrarian values such as independence, hard work, and even democracy itself. In short, property rights advocates give attention to the "average" property owner who might benefit from the easing of environmental regulations. In a rather direct attempt to clarify who will benefit from property rights legislation, U.S. Representative John T. Doolittle of California has stated: "It is so imperative that we understand that . . . we are not talking about standing up for large landowners. . . . We are talking about the little guy, everyone in this country who owns a piece of property, has worked hard to get that, and would like not to see it wiped out."[38]

Large corporations, particularly those that are already heavily subsidized, are considered the less deserving beneficiaries of property rights laws and as such are rarely mentioned in the property rights literature. When corporations are mentioned, they tend to be more "sympathetic" corporations, as when U.S. Representative Richard W. Pombo of California told the story of a hospital in southern California, the construction of which was delayed because of environmental laws.[39] The plight of one mining company is mentioned in a pro–property rights article, but the story is told from the perspective of mining employees, not the company itself. Some workers allegedly joined forces with the mining company (which was at the time being sued for violating environmental laws) because they feared losing their jobs if the company was forced to conduct an environmental impact statement.[40]

The task facing property rights proponents—to convince the public and policy makers that they are out for the "little guy"—is a formidable one, given that almost three-quarters of all privately held land in the United States is owned by less than five percent of the population. Some property rights groups, perhaps recognizing this problem, have chosen to publicly distance themselves from large landowning corporations who are trying to ride the property rights bandwagon. The most publicized split has been between groups who represent individual private property owners and those who represent individuals and industries who hold government leases on public lands. For example, Peggy Reigle, founder of the Fairness to Landowners Committee, turned down a wise-use Activist of the Year award in 1992, explaining that "it was to the benefit of the Wise-Use Movement to adopt us . . . to get emotion for public lands issues to be the same as emotion for private property ownership, and the two are not the same."[41] Reigle and others recognize that their constituents carry a more positive public image than, for instance, mining companies who continue to receive large subsidies from the U.S. government for mining on public lands. The mobilization of antitax groups along with environmentalists against state takings initiatives suggests that public denunciations for this sort are important to the larger success of the property rights movement.

In their public dialogue, environmentalists focus on the undeserving members of the property rights movement. For example, Doug Harbrecht of the National Wildlife Federation has argued that the primary beneficiaries of takings legislation will be large landowners rather than the "average Janes and Joes."[42] U.S. Representative Nancy Pelosi of California, in arguing against a proposed property rights bill, said that the bill would "create an entitlement program for polluters, a billion-dollar sweepstakes for land speculators."[43] Opponents of takings legislation not only deny that small landowners would be the primary beneficiaries of these laws, but they also argue that takings law would actually hurt the average American: "Today . . . special interest groups are promoting a radical new understanding of private property rights that would adversely affect 65 million homeowners in this country. . . . Zoning and other land use regulations preserve the beauty and stability of a neighborhood, supporting the rights of every property rights owner in the community."[44]

In this statement, "homeowners"—who property rights advocates claim are victims of government regulations—are recast as the potential victims of property rights laws. Positively constructed groups thus become a symbolic battleground on which property rights advocates and environmentalists argue. These battles are important insofar as they have the potential to preclude a real debate about who and what interests are most likely to benefit from the property rights agenda. The myth of the small independent farmer, for example, may mobilize support for property rights initiatives, but it hides the fact that agricultural production in America is heavily subsidized by the government and increasingly the business of large corporations. Given the amount of land such corporations control, big payoffs to agribusiness would no doubt be in order were property rights laws to go into effect.

Some of this information is clearly filtering into the debate through the efforts of property rights opponents, but environmentalists have also relied on appeals to mythical, ambiguous symbols that may do more to obscure than to illuminate the issues at hand. Environmentalists have persisted in making a connection between environmentalism, community, and the common good, sometimes without recognizing that appeals to community invite people to identify it in insular and narrow terms. That is, what ranchers perceive as community is very different from the environmentalists' version. These more indigenous understandings of community have been used in places like Catron County as a means of exclusion and mobilization against environmentalists. As such, arguing that "the community" will be hurt by property rights laws is misleading, given the varying ways in which the term is understood. The obvious lack of specificity suggests that both sides in the debate can appropriate the term, leading to a political debate in which both sides are talking past one another.

PROPERTY RIGHTS AND THE POLITICS OF BLAME

Today's property rights debates continue an important historical trend in America, one in which property, both rhetorically and materially, is the battleground on which different economic, social, and cultural conflicts take place. The appeal to property rights has created and reinforced particular legal and social orders in America, while providing those who challenge them fertile opportunity to do so. Such challenges illustrate the fact that there is little consensus about the very meaning of property and the responsibilities inherent in property ownership. More important, perhaps, is that property discourse has been and continues to be a way of talking about the virtues of competing ways of life. The resilience of property rights discourse, despite property's diminished constitutional status, is better understood when examined in this light.

An important component of the dialogue today between property rights advocates and their opponents is the naming, blaming, and claiming contests, which at times seem to dominate public debates. In these contests the legitimacy, character, and motives of the participants themselves are the subject of debate. This rhetoric becomes part of the overall message that environmentalists and property rights activists are advancing. Both sides construct and promote disturbing images—of the gun-toting property rights fanatic or the elite, out-of-touch urban environmentalist, for example—which serve as symbolic resources in the fight over property rights. Symbolic resources are increasingly recognized as important tools used by activists in highly contested policy debates.[45] These resources exist alongside material resources such as votes and campaign contributions that are typically mobilized by interest groups in American politics. Judging from the extent of these image wars, both environmentalists and property rights proponents find such symbolic resources useful for mobilizing supporters, discrediting their opponents, and advancing their cause. The strategic importance of these contests has not prevented some observers from critiquing them, however. Jan Beyea of the National Audubon Society, for example, has accused the environmental movement of practicing the "politics of blame." He warns that "environmentalists need to be very careful to watch their own psychological state. Many of my friends . . . get such a psychological reward from being in the battle, the good guys against the bad guys, that they lose sight of what they are trying to do."[46]

More recent incantations of these sentiments can be found in calls for "civility" in political discourse. It is not uncommon these days to hear politicians, political pundits, and even the pope lamenting the demise of civil discourse in American politics. People worry about an era in which political discussions about important policy issues quickly degenerate into debates about the character of politicians and political groups. Name-calling, it is suggested, has replaced informed and intelligent political discussions. The result is a less informed but more acrimonious and cynical citizenry. Of course, it is questionable whether there ever was a golden age of public discourse in America, when contestants in political conflicts gracefully debated the merits and demerits of policy proposals without commenting on their opponents' character. Rather than worry about the death of civil discourse, it is a concern that such contests deflect attention from the root causes of economic and social problems. By focusing on an alleged enemy as the source of a problem, the historical, political, and economic causes may be obscured. Attention is given to malevolent actors in the here-and-now rather than the more deeply rooted and difficult structural sources of conflict.[47] Such blame-shifting is evident in the property rights movement, which tends to characterize environmentalists as the "bogeyman," responsible for the woes of ranchers, loggers, farmers, and homeowners alike. Although the activities and successes of the environmental movement over the past twenty-five years have, no doubt, forced some changes in the practices of resource-extraction industries, they have not been alone in doing so. Management's decisions regarding the mechanization of logging mills and the practice of raw log exporting, for example, are at least partly to blame for job losses in the timber industry. These other explanations for shrinking opportunities in the industry are overshadowed to the extent that the spotlight is on environmentalists' activities.

This analysis suggests that naming, blaming, and claiming contests are a significant way in which political actors define themselves, justify their involvement in an issue, and argue about competing ways of life. As such, these contests are not likely to disappear. Indeed, vilification strategies may even increase activism and commitment by political actors and may well be the result of an impassioned (rather than cynical) politics. As one writer recently said, "civic, not civil, discourse is what matters, and civic discourse mandates the assigning of blame."[48] The naming and blaming between environmentalists and property rights activists may not signify the end of reasoned political discussion but the presence of deep conflicts in society, conflicts that are being played out by committed activists in relatively open debates.

NOTES

1. Alexis de Tocqueville, *Democracy in America* (Garden City, N.Y.: Anchor Books, 1969), 639, 238.

2. On the idea of contested terrain in American political culture, see Daniel T. Rodgers, *Contested Truths: Keywords in American Politics since Independence* (New York: Basic Books, 1987). Much of the discussion in this section is based on an earlier paper by Michael W. McCann, "Resurrection and Reform: Perspectives on Property in American Constitutional Tradition," *Politics and Society* 12 (1984): 143–76.

3. James Madison, "Federalist #10," in *The Federalist Papers*, introduction by Clinton L. Rossiter (New York: New American Library, 1961), 79.

4. My characterizations and the general argument here draw on Jennifer Nedelsky, *Private Property and the Limits of American Constitutionalism: The Madisonian Framework and Its Legacy* (Chicago: University of Chicago Press, 1990).

5. J. Willard Hurst, *Law and the Conditions of Freedom in the Nineteenth-Century U.S.* (Madison: University of Wisconsin Press, 1956), 24.

6. Th. H. Williams, ed., *Abraham Lincoln: Selected Speeches, Messages, and Letters* (New York: Holt, Rinehart, and Winston, 1957), 260; Eric Foner, *Free Soil, Free Labor, Free Men: The Ideology of the Republican Party before the Civil War* (Oxford: Oxford University Press, 1970).

7. See Alan F. Westin, "The Supreme Court, the Populist Movement, and the Campaign of 1896," *Journal of Politics* 15 (1953): 3–41.

8. See footnote 4 of *U.S. v Carolene Products Co.*, 304 US 144 (1938). For further discussion, see Richard Funston, "The Double Standard of Constitutional Protection in the Era of the Welfare State," *Political Science Quarterly* 90 (1975): 261–92.

9. See McCann, "Resurrection and Reform," 147–50.

10. Charles Reich, "The New Property," *Yale Law Journal* 73 (1964): 733.

11. C. B. MacPherson, "Human Rights as Property Rights," *Dissent* (winter 1977): 76; Frank Michelman, "Property as a Constitutional Right," *Washington and Lee Law Review* 38 (1982): 1101.

12. Joseph Sax, *Defending the Environment* (New York: Vintage, 1970), 161. See also Sax, "Takings, Private Property, and Public Rights," *Yale Law Journal* 81 (1971): 50.

13. Sax, *Defending the Environment*, 151.

14. *Goldberg v Kelly*, 394 US 254 (1970).

15. Bernard H. Siegan, *Economic Liberties and the Constitution* (Chicago: University of Chicago Press, 1980); Richard A. Epstein, *Takings: Private Property and the Power of Eminent Domain* (Cambridge: Harvard University Press, 1985).

16. For a broad approach to the politics of "legal mobilization," see Stuart Scheingold, *The Politics of Rights: Lawyers, Public Policy, and Political Change* (New Haven, Conn.: Yale University Press, 1974); Michael W. McCann, *Rights at Work: Pay Equity Reform and the Politics of Legal Mobilization* (Chicago: University of Chicago Press, 1994).

17. The phrase "naming, blaming, and claiming" comes from sociolegal research on disputing practices. See William Felstiner, Richard Abel, and Austin Sarat, "The Emergence and Transformation of Disputes: Naming, Blaming, and Claiming," *Law and Society Review* 15 (1980): 631–55.

18. Murray J. Edelman, *Constructing the Political Spectacle* (Chicago: University of Chicago Press, 1988), 66.

19. For a discussion of these dynamics in the abortion debates, see Marsha Vanderford, "Vilification and Social Movements: A Case Study of Pro-Life and Pro-Choice Rhetoric," *Quarterly Journal of Speech* 75 (1989): 166–82.

20. Kai N. Lee, *Compass and Gyroscope: Integrating Science and Politics for the Environment* (Washington, D.C.: Island Press, 1993), 96.

21. Bert Useem and Mayer N. Zald, "From Pressure Group to Social Movement: Efforts to Promote Use of Nuclear Power," in *Social Movements in an Organizational Society: Collected Essays*, ed. Mayer N. Zald and John D. McCarthy (New Brunswick, N.J.: Transaction Books, 1987), 280.

22. Nancie G. Marzulla, "The Property Rights Movement: How It Began and Where It Is Headed," in *Land Rights: The 1990's Property Rights Rebellion*, ed. Bruce Yandle (Lanham, Md.: Rowman and Littlefield, 1995), 3.

23. Tom Jones, letter to the editor, *Los Angeles Times*, December 5, 1995, p. B8. Emphasis added.

24. Tarso Ramos, "Wise Use in the West: The Case of the Northwest Timber Industry," in *Let the People Judge: Wise Use and the Private Property Rights Movement*, ed. John D. Echeverria and Raymond Booth Eby (Washington, D.C.: Island Press, 1995), 86.

25. Quoted in David Helvarg, "The War on Greens," *The Nation*, November 28, 1994, p. 648.

26. See Michael W. McCann, *Taking Reform Seriously: Perspectives on Public Interest Liberalism* (Ithaca, N.Y.: Cornell University Press, 1986); and Robert Gottlieb, *Forcing the Spring: The Transformation of the American Environmental Movement* (Washington, D.C.: Island Press, 1993).

27. David Horsey, "Greens on the Run: GOP Wave Threatening Environmental Regulations," *Seattle Post-Intelligencer*, November 5, 1995, p. E1.

28. Mark Dowie, "With Liberty and Firepower for All," *Outside,* November 1995.

29. Ibid., 65.

30. No on 48 Campaign, "Reject Referendum 48," fact sheet, October 1995.

31. Quoted in Richard Madsen, "Contentless Consensus: The Political Discourse of a Segmented Society," in *America at Century's End,* ed. Alan Wolfe (Berkeley: University of California Press), 449.

32. Ibid., 446.

33. Marzulla, "Property Rights Movement," 3.

34. Anne Schneider and Helen Ingram, "Social Construction of Target Populations: Implications for Politics and Policy," *American Political Science Review* 87 (1993): 334–47.

35. *Congressional Record,* 104th Cong., 1st sess. 1995, 141, no. 40, Daily ed.: H2592.

36. Asan V. Corda and Mark D. La Rochelle, "The New Populism: The Rise of the Property Rights Movement," *Common Sense* 1 (1994): 79–98.

37. Christopher Bosso, "The Contextual Bases of Problem Definition," in *The Politics of Problem Definition: Shaping the Policy Agenda,* ed. David A. Rochefort and Roger W. Cobb (Lawrence: University of Kansas Press, 1994), 187. Emphasis in original.

38. *Congressional Record,* 104th Cong., 1st sess. 1995, 141, no. 40, Daily ed.: H2592.

39. *Congressional Record,* 104th Cong., 1st sess. 1995, 141, no. 40, Daily ed.: H2691.

40. Margaret Kritz, "Land Mine," *National Journal* 25 (1993): 2531.

41. Quoted in Kate O'Callaghan, "Whose Agenda for America?" *Audubon* (September–October 1992): 90.

42. Doug Harbrecht, "A Question of Property Rights and Wrongs," *National Wildlife* 32 (1994): 4–12.

43. *Congressional Record,* 104th Cong., 1st sess. 1995, 141, no. 40, Daily ed.: H2605.

44. National Audubon Society, "The Takings Issue: Undermining True Private Property Protections," in *National Audubon Society's 1995 Congressional Guide* (online edition), November 1995, p. 7.

45. See, for example, Steven Davis, "The Role of Communication and Symbolism in Interest Group Competition: The Case of the Siskiyou National Forest, 1983–1992," *Political Communication* 12 (1995): 27–42.

46. Quoted in Theodore Roszak, "Green Guilt and Ecological Overload," *New York Times*, June 9, 1992, p. A27.

47. See Edelman, *Constructing the Political Spectacle*.

48. Tony Kushner, "Matthew's Passion," reprinted in *Harper's Magazine*, January 1999, p. 26.

PART II
URBAN AND RURAL
VANTAGE POINTS
ON PROPERTY

Land for Cities, Scenery for City People

Managing Urbanization in the American Grain

CARL ABBOTT

Cities and their residents make multiple claims on their places and regions. At one end of the conceptual spectrum there is the most basic claim of all: Underpinning all discussions of urban planning, development policy, and growth management is the expectation that cities have the simple right to exist, that the residents of concentrated settlements are justified in converting natural landscapes or rural land to workshops and dwelling places. We realize how axiomatic this claim is only when the contrary message demands attention, whether expressed in the actions of the monomaniacal Khmer Rouge or in the writings of the bucolic utopians who regard urbanization as an original sin. At a far remove are the complex ways in which cities (or their promoters and spokespersons) craft an urban identity from characteristics of a surrounding rural region. Such conceptual appropriation is certainly the rule rather than the exception in western North America. Portlanders use telephoto magic to incorporate distant Mount Hood into nearly every promotional image. Denver claims to be the Mile High Capital of the Rocky Mountain empire. Phoenix lies in the Valley of the Sun (at least since advertising firms coined the slogan in the 1930s). Fort Worth is "where the West begins," and Fort Worthers protest when east-tilted Dallas erects a herd of oversized bronze longhorns to proclaim its own image of "westernness."

For a discussion of "land in the West," however, some of the most interesting claims lie in the middle ground between the foundational and the rhetorical. This chapter briefly inventories and then categorizes the different demands that cities as civic entities make on their sites and regions. It then discusses the ways in which various land-control regimes respond to these public claims. The first set of claims revolves around the presumed right to utilize—to urbanize—a particular place or landscape. These claims underlie the creation of towns, cities, and their larger metropolitan areas as distinct configurations of buildings, roads, pipes, and wires. A second set of claims involves the presumed right to use resources at a distance. This cluster justifies the enlistment or conscription of a surrounding hinterland in the fulfillment of metropolitan needs.

CLAIMS THAT CITIES MAKE

Cities are economic machines that make civilization possible. Their purpose is to increase the efficiency of production by facilitating the exchange and processing of goods and ideas. In so doing, cities reduce the costs of necessities and luxuries. Cities more than pay for themselves by making it easier for human beings to gain protection from the cold, shelter from the rain, and respite from hunger. Were we to abjure cities and the comforts of civilized society, we would be huddled with Lear on the windswept heath, crying into the storm. This is the trade-off that legitimates urban claims on their landscapes and their environs. Twentieth-century Americans seldom perform the explicit calculus, but most accept that the economic benefits of cities outweigh the virtues of the fields or forests that these cities replaced. Knowing that time will soon enough have its way, few of us are rushing to cast down the walls, rip up the pavements, and invite the fireweed and thistles to repossess our towns and cities. Only on the margins do communities explicitly weigh the relative virtues of a few more subdivisions against a few more berry fields or orange groves.

The first cluster of claims can be summarized as the right to build. On the frontiers of North America, the founders of Euro-American cities asserted title and occupied portions of the landscape for the express purpose of town making. As outposts grew into cities, they took land out of its natural state or out of primary production to serve the urban purposes of processing, exchanging, and negotiating, and to house the city dwellers who performed these functions. North Americans expect a successful city to be physically expansive. Its commerce should swell in volume and reach. Its factories should serve expanding markets and spin off new products. Its universities should create new research enterprises and attract new students. These growing activities require new factories, wharves, rail yards, office towers, classroom buildings, highways, parking lots, and houses.

In this context of growth, city makers assume the right not simply to exist but to grow horizontally by converting rural and resource land to urban uses. The "urbanized area" is the census category that measures the extent of such lands. Unlike the better-known "metropolitan area" (an economic concept), the urbanized area is the land that is actually settled at urban densities—the aggregate urban footprint, if you will. In the Northwest's four states (Idaho, Montana, Oregon, and Washington), for example, urbanized areas in 1990 ranged from 20 square miles for Great Falls, Montana, to 604 square miles for Seattle. Combined, these urbanized areas held 5,122,000 people—that is, 54 percent of the total regional population on 0.5 percent of the regional land.

Also implicit in the urbanization process is the assumed right not just to build but also to reshape the landscape to human convenience and need, exercising the same dominion that farmers have always wielded over agricultural lands. City makers raise up the valleys and lay low the mountains, make the crooked straight and the rough places smooth. They drain marshes, fill ravines with rubble, and hide creeks in culverts. They trim down hills, as in the famous example of Seattle's long battle with its unpromising site. Seattle land developer R. H. Thomson expressed this manipulating impulse when he wrote scornfully of the anti-levelers: "Some people seemed to think that because there were hills in Seattle originally, some of them ought to be left there, no difference how injurious a heavy grade over a hill may be to the property behind that hill."[1]

The second cluster of claims annexes hinterlands to cities. Urbanites assume the right to use resources and control land at a distance through purchase, legislative allocation, and regulation. Implicit in this claim to have urban interests and needs considered in rural resource decisions is an extended assumption about social and economic dominance. Like France or Britain during the age of imperialism, major metropolitan areas cast long shadows and stake out vast spheres of influence. Most obviously, city people use outlying lands and resources to stoke and serve the urban metabolism.[2] Metropolitan areas take in energy and feedstocks, fuel their operations and growth, and cast off waste products. Cities reach into the countryside for building materials, natural gas, coal, and electricity. Water flows through kitchen faucets, fire hydrants, and factory valves because feats of engineering are matched with creative institutional arrangements. Municipalities purchase private water rights, legislatures allocate water supplies, and a variety of public entities direct the purchase or regulation of watersheds.[3] In return, cities cast particulates and chemicals into the sky, drain lawn fertilizer and street residues into streams, and ship garbage to landfills.

Beyond the maintenance needs of the urban metabolism, city residents also mold rural resource communities and districts in their own image around the goal of recreation. In the early twentieth century, municipalities such as Denver and Portland purchased outlying park lands, business interests agitated for the creation of national parks, and affluent households rode railroad lines to summer colonies. The automobile age that followed World War II democratized outdoor recreation and turned lake shores, ocean fronts, deserts, and mountain valleys into vast second-home districts—the "coastal condomania" and "sagebrush subdivisions" that Oregon governor Tom McCall inveighed against more than a quarter-century ago. Increasingly in the 1990s, a slot machine tsunami is washing over the rural West in the further interests of entertainment for urban populations.[4]

By extension, city-based interests restructure the social fabric of resource and recreation communities through investment, control of trade, and environmental regulation. The results have been especially visible in the western states, where much of the debate over environmental issues has been a civil war in which the long reach of the urban West has triggered battles over resource policy.[5] Metropolitan outreach as an economic process involves capital investment, control of transportation systems, and recreational use. As a political process, it involves the mobilization of legislative and regulatory power. Ultimately, both sets of claims carry the same implication: that the urbanization or urban incorporation of rural territories is regular and right. On the metropolitan fringe the claims result in the suburbanization of exurban places. Beyond the fringe the claim of dominant interest has most commonly meant the conversion of resource-producing districts into "weekendlands" for city folks—and the reshaping of these areas in the image of the expansive city.

TABLE 1. The Claims Cities Make

Land for cities: Incorporation on the fringe
The right to build
The right to expand
The right to alter the landscape
Scenery for city people: Incorporation at a distance
The right to purchase
The right to legal allocations
The right to regulate

It is important to repeat that these are civic claims, legitimated because they serve community needs. The agents who act on these claims are sometimes private individuals such as home builders, shopping mall developers, and second-home purchasers. But these agents can also be public entities, including city governments, nonprofit environmental organizations, regional service agencies, state legislatures, and even the U.S. Congress. Historians have long recognized that nineteenth-century Americans saw only a fuzzy line between the promotion of individual interest and community future. "To induce immigrants to come here and settle the vacant lands," wrote an early Chicagoan, "to control and center here the trade and travel of the West . . . to induce capitalists to make investments here in works of public and private improvement, are, all of them, objects worthy of the best exertions of her citizens."[6] This line remains just as indistinct in the late twentieth century.

From their immediate sites cities claim the right to build, to adapt the landscape, and to expand laterally into previously nonurban land. From their surrounding regions they claim the control of vital resources to serve physical, economic, and social needs, acquiring everything from water for city factories to scenery for city people (table 1). In the American polity, public claims on the use of land commonly operate within a political and regulatory system that recognizes the primacy (or perhaps the inevitability) of urban needs and uses. However, a number of states and communities, including several in the West, are currently formulating and experimenting with approaches that try to balance the needs and claims of both city and country. Most important is the growth-boundary alternative to the indefinite expansion of metropolitan areas and the greenline approach to the incorporation and control of hinterlands. This chapter explores both the traditional and the alternative planning regimes for urban growth. Examining the standard, now familiar claims on site and region as well as the alternative approaches results in a typology of ways to think about managing the growing reach of metropolitan communities within the framework of American urban and regional planning (table 2).

THE EXURBAN FUTURE:
PLANNED SPRAWL OR URBAN CONTAINMENT?

How should Americans deal with metropolitan land hunger? Given the powerful and legitimate claims of expansive cities for more land, how do Americans plan and manage the land conversion process? "Planned sprawl" is by far the most common approach to the interaction of city and country on the suburban frontier. Reflecting long-standing national values about the primacy of productive activities, planned sprawl is based on the deep-seated policy assumption that land conversion on the urban fringe is normal and desirable. Americans have historically assumed that farmers can justly shoulder aside hunters; they have assumed that capital can properly be applied to turn dry desert sands into pastures of plenty. So too they have acted as if all "urbanizable" land is up for grabs. The phrase "highest and best use" holds specific connotations in land-use law, but it also carries the linguistic implication that the most intensive use as valued by the private land market is the socially preferred use.

In the realms of regional planning and land-use regulation, central cities, their suburbs, and rural communities that lie in the metropolitan pathway use land-use controls and economic development policy to encourage the conversion of "buildable" land. On first glance, the land regulation system might seem designed to limit growth. In fact, it was developed in the 1910s and 1920s to rationalize investment decisions. In historical context, land-use planning is a sturdy survivor of the Progressive Era impulses to streamline economic change and to conserve resources in the name of long-term growth.[7] As a consequence, regulations such as zoning and direct sprawl often identify areas exempt from development, such as parks, wetlands, or aquifer recharge zones. The goal, however, is to put together the most efficient development package in the interests of overall growth. Planners have therefore found themselves boosters of development. In large cities they have worked as allies and agents of the economic growth coalitions. Especially during the 1980s and 1990s, with the increasing emphasis on public-private partnerships, a major theme of planning has been entrepreneurial deal making. Indeed, one study has characterized development planning as "the only game in town."[8]

Just as striking is the role of fringe communities in abetting metropolitan expansion. In the neoregionalist writing of the 1990s, there is sometimes a romantic belief that rural communities and small towns are engaged in desperate and underequipped cultural defense against the panzer divisions of the growing metropolis. Theoretical essays and case studies are filled with much talk about social and cultural resistance. In fact, however, most outlying communities are cooperative agents of their own transformation. Small-town politics is the province of growth machines that mirror those of big cities. Property owners, local merchants, community banks, local newspaper publishers, city managers, and many others see benefits from growth, and they plan accordingly. They zone land for commercial and industrial use and organize economic development districts to entice tenants. They welcome big box retailers, fast-food chains, and large residential developers; so, by the way, do workers in communities where resource industry jobs are drying up. A recent study of towns on Chicago's exurban fringe confirms the strong tendency to zone and rezone to attract both residential and commercial growth.[9]

Another example is North Plains, Oregon, on the edge of the Portland metro area. City officials in this town of twelve hundred are planning for up to eight thousand new residents on more than a square mile of adjacent land. The city has to accept growth or wither, one city council member has said: "The fact of the matter is all this land around us could be annexed and developed by Hillsboro. Then you've got all these people running around talking about hanging on to farmland. I believe that if a farmer was offered the right amount of money by a developer, he'll sell in a minute."[10] As these sentiments suggest, planned sprawl thrives in a fragmented political system. Cutthroat competition makes each metropolitan area eager for the most accommodating growth package. Towns on the metropolitan fringe engage in the same competition, often driven by the desire to capture increased property taxes or retail sales taxes. Planned sprawl democratizes the American dream of a real-estate killing. Metro-politan expansion into exurban and rural fringes has seldom involved the plunder and rape of unwilling communities. Much more often, it has pro-ceeded as a passionate consensual embrace. "We welcome Wal-Mart," say signs along Highway 30 leading into St. Helens, Oregon, where many res-idents hope for Wal-Mart jobs. Because of the mutually beneficial rela-tionship, there is basic truth to the adage that politicians, developers, and many other citizens are in bed together.

In sharp contrast to planned sprawl, urban containment strategies adopt some of the same tools of land-use regulation but use them to a dif-ferent end. Containment utilizes open-space reserves ("greenbelts"), ur-banization boundaries ("urban growth boundaries" or UGBs), and designation of satellite cities to limit development to predetermined areas. If planned sprawl uses "yes, when" zoning, containment uses "yes, no" zoning. Advocates of urban containment typically rely on the cen-tury-long intellectual heritage of British planner and social reformer Ebenezer Howard's proposals for "garden cities"—freestanding satellite cities separated from the metropolis and from each other by zones of agri-cultural land. European versions of this containment strategy have often established rural greenbelts that are intended to mark the limits of metro-politan expansion, although growth pressures have often required the ad-dition of satellite "new towns" beyond the greenbelt.[11]

American versions of this concept define a flexible growth boundary around urban areas that is intended to move outward gradually and care-fully. For example, Oregon's statewide land-use planning system, adopted in 1974, requires towns and cities to designate UGBs within which future urban uses will be located. Such uses include residential subdivisions, re-tail stores, offices, and manufacturing facilities. The state guidelines man-date that new housing on high-quality resource lands outside UGBs be tied directly to the production of farm or forest products, and that new commercial development be intended to serve rural populations and communities. In contrast, development at urban intensities outside a UGB requires the special finding that no urban land is available to accom-modate the proposed use. Washington state legislation from 1990–91 similarly requires municipalities in both populous and fast-growing coun-ties to define and enforce UGBs adequate to hold twenty years of expected development. New Jersey's 1992 statewide comprehensive plan requires

TABLE 2. Planning Regimes for Urban Growth

	Planning Approaches	
	Traditional	*Alternative*
Growth on metropolitan containment periphery	Planned sprawl	Urban
Control of distant resources	Economic development planning	Greenline partnerships

municipalities to draw "community development boundaries" around cities and towns that define the maximum area that will ultimately be developed. San Jose, California, in April 1996 adopted its own growth cordon and a number of other California cities have since joined it.[12]

Urban containment presumably meets the needs of both city and country. It benefits urban property holders by turning urban land into an inelastic commodity and raising its value. It serves the interests of rural resource producers by offering institutional protections against disruptive urban intrusions and leapfrogging development. In more philosophical terms, containment tries to privilege the rural social ecology by limiting the spread of urban activities *and* to persuade urbanites that compact cities are socially and culturally more vibrant than sprawling ones.[13] In the Oregon rhetoric justifying statewide land-use planning and UGBs, the rural benefit always comes first: Trying to protect an agricultural way of life is primary; developing compact cities is a byproduct. In the bottom-line culture of the United States, however, urban containment has needed economic as well as social justification. Since the Real Estate Research Corporation's famous 1974 report *The Costs of Sprawl*, opponents of urban sprawl have mobilized economic justifications for their argument that the centered metropolis should also be compact. A series of studies have shown that the concentration of urbanized land within radial corridors and nodes preserves green spaces and farm lands, reduces energy consumption and automobile mileage, and keeps infrastructure affordable.[14]

Containment works best when there is consensus that the off-limits land has special value. This might be economic value for resource production as reflected in high per-acre valuation. It might be social and cultural value as reflected in a widely shared sense of place that singles out particular landscapes and districts. Residents of Oregon's Willamette Valley, for example, live with daily reminders that high-quality farm land and urbanizable land are limited commodities. Metropolitan Portland is already nudging against the natural barriers of the Coast Range and the Cascade foothills. Motorists along I-5 in the mid-Valley can see forested mountains both to the west and to the east. This sense of the Valley as a finite region helped to make a statewide land-use planning program acceptable in the 1970s. A similar sense of limits has helped in the adoption of growth management approaches in small eastern states with valued rural environments and in the passage of Washington's growth management program. The applicable metaphor here is one of chaste friendship. In 1898 Howard asserted that garden cities would bring the marriage of city and country, but the UGB approach treats city and country more like roommates with separate bedrooms, for urban containment requires mutual forbearance.[15] Rural and exurban landowners have to accept limits on land profits, while city dwellers have to live with a bit of un-American crowding.

ACTION AT A DISTANCE:
BOARDING-HOUSE REACH AND GREENLINE PARTNERSHIPS

Looking beyond the daily social and economic system of the metropolitan area, how do Americans deal with the wider urban claims on regional resources? The boarding-house reach of city people has pushed metropolitan commuting zones seventy-five to one hundred miles from large city centers and recreation zones twice that distance. With this reach, how can city dwellers manage the desire to use rural resources, rural scenery, and rural places themselves?[16] The standard management framework for this urban reach has been "economic development planning." Like suburban land conversion, economic development planning and promotion is a public-private partnership linking local governments, regional and state development agencies, federal bureaus, and chambers of commerce. The goal is outside investment in the interests of local job creation. The techniques are land assembly, public infrastructure investment, place market-ing, and tax incentives.

Such planning in rural areas has a long heritage. More than a century ago, middle western towns responded to declines in their agricultural base with early versions of smokestack chasing. Western cities rolled out the red carpet for railroad tycoons; they wined, dined, bought shares of wa-tered stock, and gave away public property in the search for investment.[17] At the end of the twentieth century, rural economic development dis-tricts and small town elites from coast to coast continue to recruit tenants for new industrial parks.[18] The invasion of the "summer people" (or the "winter people" in the western mountains) is part of the same economic development process. Worn-out resource towns convert to tourism as city people search out scenery.

The tendency within each locale has been to create miniatures of planned sprawl with all land ripe for sale and development. Second-home smallpox scars the face of mountainsides. RVs encircle the lake shores, sport-utility vehicles crawl up logging roads to trailhead parking lots, and vehicles of all descriptions crowd new fast-food and motel strips. At its worst, the consequence is "Aspenization"—the headlong transformation of local economic and social systems that has occurred in many western recreational hot spots, pricing workers out of housing and pushing local businesses out of the pathways of corporate bulldozers.[19] The appropriate metaphor is a bit uncertain here. Because much economic development work is little more than offering up locational advantages and physical at-tractions to the highest bidders, there is an element of prostitution. Less pejoratively, one might think in terms of an old-fashioned arranged mar-riage in which developable resources and sites are the dowry, the invited corporations and investors the eligible spouse.

In contrast to the economic development approach, "partnership" strategies are both problematic and promising. Drawing on the European idea of "greenline parks," they try to create mechanisms for managing the peaceful and creative coexistence of urban and rural uses (and lifestyles) within the same broadly defined region. They are particularly relevant for areas beyond the suburban frontier, where urban areas expect to find a va-riety of resources that range from water to scenery. "Greenline partner-ships" are an idea borrowed from Europe and the United Kingdom. The term comes from the idea of drawing a "green" line on a map to define a district of high scenic or cultural value and devising special land-management regulations to sustain its character over time. "Greenlining" is intended for working or living landscapes, not wilderness. It envisions the conservation of valued regions through special regulations rather than massive land acquisition. Greenline controls can preserve natural resources, social institutions, and historic landscapes while allowing local residents to continue their previous livelihoods from land-based industries. For example, in the United Kingdom the national parks are specially regulated landscapes rather than public reserves in the American style.[20]

As partnerships, greenline approaches give rural and urban claims roughly equal standing. California's innovative coastal zone management program of the late 1960s was an early effort to balance development and landscape preservation.[21] Other examples in the United States include New York's Adirondack Park, the New Jersey Pinelands, and the Columbia River Gorge National Scenic Area in the Pacific Northwest.[22] The gorge area program is a clear demonstration of both the possibilities and the potential problems. The Columbia Gorge is a historic resource-producing region that is home to roughly sixty thousand people in parts of Oregon and Washington. The gorge is not a pristine environment. Over nearly two centuries, American traders and settlers have drastically altered its natural environment. They have impounded the river, carved its shores for roads and railroads, cut over its bluffs, and decimated its salmon runs. Nevertheless, the gorge remains a visually stunning landscape.

Creation of the Columbia River Gorge National Scenic Area by federal legislation in 1986 reflected the power of Portlanders to shape a regional agenda around the goal of scenic protection. Indeed, the legislation climaxed a steady expansion of Portland's use of the gorge as a recreation zone. The Scenic Area Act, however, added the second goal of economic development to the first goal of resource preservation. In effect, the task of the specified management agencies, the USDA Forest Service and the bi-state Columbia River Gorge Commission, is to preserve and create jobs for country people while managing scenery for city people. Senator Mark Hatfield reflected this understanding of the Scenic Area when he told a gorge audience that the legislation "was never intended to dry up those communities in the gorge or to be a blow to the future of those communities."[23]

Such a greenline partnership is a multiple balancing act, however. As an effort to plan for environmentally sensitive economic development, this kind of partnership faces the challenge of reconciling sometimes competing activities within a limited space. Protection of natural areas competes with resource production; both may conflict with new industries such as tourism. Closely related is the need to mediate between differing and sometimes clashing community cultures and worldviews that belong to an "old West" of loggers and ranchers and a "new West" of bureaucrats and Internet entrepreneurs. The intent of the Scenic Area and similar programs such as the Pinelands National Reserve–Pinelands Commission is to plan and manage the piecemeal changes that cumulatively overwhelm resource regions. Substantive goals try to balance the forces of change against the claims of existing social and economic systems. Implementation requires ranchers, loggers, and farmers to learn the customs of committee work and bureaucracies. It likewise expects sophisticated interest groups to accept rural communities as partners and agents of change. Ultimately, the greenline approach and the debates it engenders are about the possibilities of sharing the power to make land development decisions—a sort of ideal marriage of equals in which each partner respects the strengths and character of the other.

CONCLUSION

Americans plan and expand their cities within a powerful set of assumptions about the character of land as a commodity. Inside many Americans is a land speculator clamoring to make a killing. Homeowners in rundown neighborhoods are often happy to sell to gentrifiers; many farmers look forward to unloading burdensome acreage on city slickers. Bill and Hillary Clinton have gotten in hot water for their efforts to profit from land development deals, but they simply followed in the footsteps of George Washington's Potomac River improvement schemes. If the traditional approaches to the planning of urban growth are "Washingtonian," the alternatives outlined in this chapter are efforts to introduce additional goals that offset or moderate the land development impulse. Urban planner Scott Campbell recently defined planning as an effort to balance three goals: economic growth, environmental protection, and social equity. In these terms, urban containment systems try to add the environmental benefits of compact cities to the evaluation of land development. Greenline approaches add both environmental protection and social equity as potentially coequal goals.[24]

Whatever their abstract merits, what is the political feasibility of alternative approaches to identifying land for cities and scenery for city people? Urban containment has been most popular in parts of the Northeast and the West. These may be areas where residents place special value on the rural and natural environs of large cities, or (as in the West) where residents share a sense that they live in the last, best place. One Washington state official has said, "A lot of people in this part of the world are from somewhere else. They really treasure the environment they've found here. They don't want to repeat the mistakes other places have made."[25] Greenline partnerships as large-scale planning efforts share the metropolitan roots of urban containment. They are efforts to rationalize and control rather than stop the process of metropolitan incorporation. They have tended to occur when the political influence of cities such as New York or Portland has been enlisted on behalf of extraurban preservation. To date, both strategies have depended on state-level action for successful implementation. Single municipalities that try their own containment programs find their efforts undermined by the growth competition of neighboring communities. Greenline programs have required state action to circumvent the old economic development planning schemes of local growth coalitions. Those interested in alternatives to land development as usual should most fruitfully invest their energy in building state planning alliances.

Finally, the testing and refinement of similar planning experiments depends on the development of a civic dialogue that engages multiple interests and communities in ongoing discussion. Resembling some of the ideas of the social theorist Jurgen Habermas, successful efforts to balance the claims of growth, environment, and equity require continual civic conversation in which policies and programs are tested and refined. Experts learn from citizens and citizens from experts in a constant refining of ideas; in this way the public realm takes on a life and value of its own. Ideally, gradually increasing consensus becomes a valuable and positive product in itself. A compact city or a greenlined region may start as a compromise among conflicting interests, but these partnerships may evolve into an understanding of shared needs and goals in which private claims and the common good are brought into new balance.[26]

NOTES

1. R. H. Thomson quoted in Roger Sale, *Seattle: Past to Present* (Seattle: University of Washington Press, 1976), 74.

2. Abel Wolman, "The Metabolism of Cities," *Scientific American* (March 1965): 179–90.

3. There is a vast literature on the urban reach for water supplies. Studies of cities in rainy regions tend to emphasize technical and institutional innovation in positive terms, such as Nelson Blake, *Water for the Cities: A History of Urban Water Supply Problems* (Syracuse, N.Y.: Syracuse University Press, 1958); Rick Harmon, "The Bull Run Watershed: Portland's Enduring Jewel," *Oregon Historical Quarterly* 96 (1995): 242–70. Studies of the search for water by cities in the arid West tend to treat the importation of supplies as dubious at best, as thievery at worst. For example, see William L. Kahrl, *Water and Power: The Conflict over Los Angeles' Water Supply in the Owens Valley* (Berkeley: University of California Press, 1982); John Walton, *Western Times and Water Wars: State, Culture, and Rebellion in California* (Berkeley: University of California Press, 1991); Mark Reisner, *Cadillac Desert: The American West and Its Disappearing Water* (New York: Penguin Books, 1987).

4. The descriptions of recreation zones are based on census data on the location of "homes held for occasional use." Richard White, *Land Use, Environment, and Social Change: The Shaping of Island County, Washington* (Seattle: University of Washington Press, 1980), describes the growing recreational use of one part of the rural Northwest.

5. The urban dimension of western environmental politics is discussed in Samuel Hays, *Beauty, Health, and Permanence: Environmental Politics in the United States, 1955–1985* (New York: Cambridge University Press, 1987); Kathleen Ferguson, "Toward a Geography of Environmentalism in the United States," M.A. thesis, California State University, Hayward, 1985; Thomas A. Wikle, "Geographical Patterns of Membership in U.S. Environmental Organizations," *Professional Geographer* 47 (February 1995): 41–48; and Frank J. Popper, *The Politics of Land-Use Reform* (Madison: University of Wisconsin Press, 1981).

6. J. W. Norris, *Norris's Business Directory and Statistics of the City of Chicago in 1896* (Chicago, 1896), 4.

7. On the Progressive Era impulse, see the classic study by Sam Hays, *Conservation and the Gospel of Efficiency* (Cambridge: Harvard University Press, 1959). On the Progressive origins of the city planning profession, see Richard Fogelsong, *Planning the Capitalist City* (Princeton, N.J.: Princeton University Press, 1986); Mansel Blackford, *The Lost Dream: Businessmen and City Planning on the Pacific Coast, 1890–1920* (Columbus: Ohio State University Press, 1993); William Wilson, *The City Beautiful Movement* (Baltimore, Md.: Johns Hopkins University Press, 1989); Blaine Brownell, *The Urban Ethos in the South, 1920–1930* (Baton Rouge: Louisiana State University Press, 1975); Judd Kahn, *Imperial San Francisco: Politics and Planning in an American City, 1897–1906* (Lincoln: University of Nebraska Press, 1979).

8. Christopher Silver, *Twentieth-Century Richmond: Planning, Politics, and Race* (Knoxville: University of Tennessee Press, 1984); Lisa Peattie, Stephen Cornell, and Martin Rein, "Development Planning as the Only Game in Town," *Journal of Planning Education and Research* 5 (fall 1985): 17–25.

9. A classic study of the capture of planning efforts by local economic and political interests is Philip Selznick, *TVA and the Grassroots* (Berkeley: University of California Press, 1949).

10. Alex Pulaski, "Growing Pains Spread," *The Oregonian*, November 13, 1996, p. D1.

11. On Ebenezer Howard and his influence, see Robert Fishman, *Urban Utopias in the Twentieth Century* (New York: Basic Books, 1977); Peter Hall, *Cities of Tomorrow* (London: Blackwell, 1986); Stanley Buder, *Visionaries and Planners: The Garden City Movement and the Modern Community* (New York: Oxford University Press, 1990).

12. Vermont (1988) and Maine (1988) created statewide planning goals for localities that include the clear separation of urban areas and countryside. See Scott A. Bollens, "State Growth Management: Intergovernmental Frameworks and Policy Objectives," *Journal of the American Planning Association* 58 (1992): 454–66; John DeGrove, *The New Frontier for Land Policy: Planning and Growth Management in the States* (Cambridge, Mass.: Lincoln Institute of Land Policy, 1992); Dennis Gale, "Eight State-Sponsored Growth Management Programs," *Journal of the American Planning Association* 58 (1992): 425–39; Jay M. Stein, ed., *Growth Management: The Planning Challenge of the 1990s* (Beverly Hills, Calif.: Sage Publications, 1993).

13. For a recent argument in favor of urban containment for the sake of rural communities, see Thomas Daniels and Mark Lapping, "The Two Rural Americas Need More, Not Less Planning," *Journal of the American Planning Association* 62 (1996): 285–88.

14. Real Estate Research Corporation, *The Costs of Sprawl: Environmental and Economic Costs of Alternative Residential Development Patterns at the Urban Fringe* (Washington, D.C.: Government Printing Office, 1974); James E. Frank, *The Costs of Alternative Development* (Washington, D.C.: Urban Land Institute, 1989); Michael Bernick and Robert Cervero, *Transit Villages in the Twenty-First Century* (New York: McGraw-Hill, 1997).

15. Ebenezer Howard, *Tomorrow: A Peaceful Path to Real Reform* (London: S. Sonnenschein, 1898).

16. For a general discussion of metropolitan reach in the American West, see Carl Abbott, *The Metropolitan Frontier: Cities in the Modern American West* (Tucson: University of Arizona Press, 1993), 149–72.

17. Lewis Atherton, *Main Street on the Middle Border* (Bloomington: Indiana University Press, 1954). The 1892 banquet hosted by Everett, Washington, for James J. Hill, as the tycoon planned the western terminus for his Great Northern Railroad, was one of dozens of comparable cases. Norman H. Clark, *Mill Town: A Social History of Everett, Washington* (Seattle: University of Washington Press, 1970).

18. Meredith Ramsey, *Community, Culture, and Economic Development: The Social Roots of Local Action* (Albany: SUNY Press, 1996).

19. "Aspenization" as a "devil's bargain" is analyzed by Hal Rothman in *Devil's Bargains: Tourism in the Twentieth-Century American West* (Lawrence: University Press of Kansas, 1998). Thomas Michael Power, *Lost Landscapes and Failed Economies: The Search for a Value of Place* (Washington, D.C.: Island Press, 1996), argues to the contrary that tourism can be a positive economic transition.

20. The greenline idea is discussed in Marjorie Corbett, ed., *Greenline Parks: Land Conservation Trends for the Eighties and Beyond* (Washington, D.C.: National Parks and Conservation Association, 1983); Charles E. Little, *Green-Line Parks: An Approach to Preserving Recreational Landscapes in Urban Areas* (Washington, D.C.: Library of Congress, Congressional Research Service, 1975); and Stephen C. Harper, Laura L. Falk, and Edward W. Rankin, *The Northern Forest Lands Study of New England and New York* (Rutland, Vt.: U.S. Forest Service, 1990).

21. Melvin B. Mogulof, *Saving the Coast: California's Experiment in Intergovernmental Land-Use Control* (Lexington, Mass.: Lexington Books, 1975).

22. On the Adirondacks, see Richard Liroff and G. Gordon Davis, *Protecting Open Space: Land Use Control in the Adirondack Park* (Cambridge, Mass.: Ballinger, 1981); Michael K. Heiman, *The Quiet Evolution: Power, Planning, and Profits in New York State* (New York: Praeger, 1986); Holly Nelson and Alan J. Hahn, *State Policy and Local Influence in the Adirondacks* (Ithaca, N.Y.: Cornell University Center for Environmental Research, 1980); Alan J. Hahn and Cynthia D. Dyballa, "State Environmental Planning and Local Influence," *Journal of the American Planning Association* (1981): 324–35; Richard Booth, "New York's Adirondack Park Agency," in *Managing Land-Use Conflicts: Case Studies in Special Area Management*, ed. David J. Brower and Daniel S. Carol (Durham, N.C.: Duke University Press, 1987).

On the Pinelands, see Robert J. Mason, *Contested Lands: Conflict and Compromise in New Jersey's Pine Barrens* (Philadelphia, Pa.: Temple University Press, 1992); Jonathan Berger and John W. Sinton, *Water, Earth, and Fire: Land Use and Environmental Planning in the New Jersey Pine Barrens* (Baltimore, Md.: Johns Hopkins University Press, 1985); Beryl Robichaud Collins and Emily W. B. Russell, eds., *Protecting the New Jersey Pinelands* (New Brunswick, N.J.: Rutgers University Press, 1988); Richard M. Hluchan, "Overview of Pinelands Preservation Plan," *New Jersey Lawyer* (August 1983): 21–25; Kevin J. Rielley, Wendy U. Larsen, and Clifford L. Weaver, "Partnership in the Pinelands," in *Land Reform, American Style*, ed. Charles C. Geisler and Frank J. Popper (Totowa, N.J.: Rowman and Allanheld, 1984); Richard F. Babcock and Charles L. Sieman, *The Zoning Game Revisited* (Cambridge, Mass.: Lincoln Institute of Land Policy, 1985); Daniel S. Carol, "New Jersey Pinelands Commission," in *Managing Land-Use Conflicts*, ed. Brower and Carol; R. J. Lilieholm and J. Romm, "Pinelands National Reserve: An Intergovernmental Approach to Nature Preservation," *Environmental Management* 16 (1993): 335–43.

Basic to understanding the political background and arguments about Columbia River Gorge protection is Bowen Blair Jr., "The Columbia River Gorge National Scenic Area: The Act, Its Genesis, and Legislative History," *Environmental Law* 17 (1986–87): 863–969. For its origins and implementation, see Carl Abbott, Sy Adler, and Margery Post Abbott, *Planning a New West: The Columbia River Gorge National Scenic Area* (Corvallis: Oregon State University Press, 1997).

23. "Hatfield Makes Stops in Gorge," *Gorge Weekly*, June 9, 1995.

24. Scott Campbell, "Green Cities, Growing Cities, Just Cities? Urban Planning and the Contradictions of Sustainable Development," *Journal of the American Planning Association* 62 (1996): 296–312.

25. Quotation in Tom Hylton, *Save Our Land, Save Our Towns* (Harrisburg, Pa.: R B Books, 1995), 101. Contrast this sense of a limited supply of farmland with the very different sense of unbounded land surrounding a city such as Indianapolis or Des Moines.

26. Jurgen Habermas, *The Theory of Communicative Action* (Boston: Beacon Press, 1984); John Forester, *Planning in the Face of Power* (Berkeley: University of California Press, 1989); Judith Innes, "Planning Theory's Emerging Paradigm: Communicative Action and Interactive Practice," *Journal of Planning Education and Research* 14 (1995): 128–35, and "Planning through Consensus Building: A New View of the Comprehensive Planning Ideal," *Journal of the American Planning Association* 62 (1996): 460–72.

From Open Range to Closed Range
on the Public Lands

WILLIAM D. ROWLEY

L ivestock grazing on public or common lands spans the history of the nation's westward expansion. European Americans introduced large grazing animals to the "new world"—horses, cows, sheep, pigs, and goats.[1] The animals demanded extensive grazing grounds that took them to coastal savannas, to the forests and mountains, to the rolling prairies, and finally to the plains and mountains of the American West. In each instance these animals altered the land's ecology.[2] Grazing lands often became private, but in the West they typically remained public. The mixture of private and public grazing lands gave rise to a host of problems and quarrels that continue to wrack the western range.

In the years after the Civil War the demise of the great bison herds in the grasslands of the West and the confinement of Indian tribes to reservations opened vast lands to the invasion of what General Phil Sheridan described as the era of the "speckled cattle." From 1867 to 1887 a veritable cattle kingdom reigned from the eastern plains states to the Rocky Mountains. It was built on the northern movement of Texas longhorns and the introduction of finer breeds from the East.[3] Long trail drives moved cattle north from Texas and Indian Territory (what is now Oklahoma) to the railheads in Kansas, Nebraska, and even Wyoming. Lush northern ranges encouraged stock operators to establish base ranches claimed from the public domain under the various U.S. land laws. By the 1870s ranch holdings reached as far north as the Dakotas and Montana and even to parts of the northern Great Basin in Nevada. From these islands of private land or base ranches, cattle grazed over thousands of acres that comprised the surrounding sea of public range. Sometimes there was no base ranch, and owners put their animals directly onto the public range. This distinction between ranch and range is important. Stock operators used the public domain as a gigantic grazing commons.

Western stock owners could not afford to own outright the thousands of acres of marginal western grazing land needed to support the numbers of stock necessary for an economically viable operation. One scholar noted in the early twentieth century: "The land laws made it nearly impossible for one owner to acquire legally the thousands of acres that were needed to support a large herd." In addition, without the control of a water source, there could be no cattle ranch, "and control of the water rendered the unwatered hinterland of the region useless so far as other cattlemen were concerned."[4] But U.S. land law favored the acquisition of only small acreage by western standards (160 to 640 acres). When the governmental scientist and famed Colorado River explorer John Wesley Powell looked at the western plains and mountains in the late 1870s, he recommended in his *Report on the Arid Lands of the United States* that Congress grant landed estates in this region of at least 2,560 acres. This allowed a rancher-farmer grazing lands, irrigated acreage, surface water sources from streams, and woodlands for fencing and fuel.[5] Congress never moved to grant land in these recommended large parcels, however. It rejected fostering landed baronial holdings in the West.

Because the land laws favored only smaller holdings, stock interests sought leasing arrangements over large acreage on the public domain to secure their usage over time. Again, Congress declined. Many people, members of Congress included, argued that long-term leasing threatened to freeze much of the West into a permanent grazing economy, to bar the growth of diversified stock and crop farming, and to discourage the influx of population into the region. Even local boosters in the western communities surrounded by an open-range grazing economy supported the congressional view. The future, they insisted, should be shaped by population growth on farms and in communities, not by the maintenance of the pastoral stage of development. Aspiring stock owners, including sheep owners, looked with suspicion at a system of long-term quasi land tenure for cattle outfits that possessed the power to bar newcomers. Railroad companies, desiring population growth along their routes, objected to a permanent labeling of the lands for grazing purposes only. They hoped for a future that included not only carrying cattle, but for the lucrative trade of carrying crops out of the region and returning manufactured goods to a growing local population.

DESPOLIATION OF THE PUBLIC RANGE

All of these voices denounced any system of leasing on the public domain that constricted the area's future and, most important, limited new enterprises seeking opportunities. These voices from the West were strong and reinforced Congress's commitment to a Jeffersonian land policy, one that projected a vision of the West as a land of small farmers who were sturdy citizens of the republic.[6] Congress's refusal to shape land laws to benefit stock interests prompted open range outfits to unlawfully fence the public domain. Stock operators defiantly asserted their need to have permanent resource-use rights over designated sectors of the range. In response, Congress demanded the removal of "illegal enclosures" from the public domain.[7]

Meanwhile, drought and winter attacked herds on overstocked and depleted ranges. During the summers and winters of 1885 through 1888 the southern plains suffered. The winter of 1886–87 ravaged the northern plains, and the White Winter of 1889–90 struck the herds of the northern Great Basin.[8] These weather-related disasters revealed overgrazing and a disorganized industry that could not restrain itself from depleting the grazing commons. The absence of an overarching authority to impose range regulations and provide long-term security for individual grazing areas endangered all classes of stock operators. One shrewd historian acknowledged the difficulty faced by the graziers, but wisely noted that "the chief sufferer, and the one destined to exact the greatest measure of revenge, was the range itself."[9]

Not only did cattle graziers compete for the range resources among themselves; sheep added another dimension to the competitive picture. As early as 1876, the president of the Colorado Cattle Growers' Association said that sheep and cattle interests had nothing in common save "grazing on the same grass." He dismissed as "simply nonsense" the idea that the range could not be overstocked and that the resource was unlimited.[10] After the destructive winters for cattle in the late 1880s, sheep made impressive advances into the western ranges. As competitive grazers, sheep had many advantages over cattle. They used browse as well as grasses and could survive on eating snow as a water source. Sheepherders directed their flocks to areas not easily found by freely roaming cattle. Sheep provided revenue both from their meat and from the sale of wool, which often enjoyed tariff protection from foreign imports. In some areas of the public range the race to the mountain pastures in the spring became an ecological disaster. "That which was free for all to use, came to be regarded as free for all to despoil."[11] An 1885 report to Congress regarded the struggles for the free and open range among large and small cattle people, the sheep interests, and settlers with detachment. It said that the often violent confrontations were "but the natural and unavoidable result of the interaction of productive forces in the development of the resources of the country." This optimistic view of the laissez-faire range situation concluded that out of such struggle came "the advancement of the commercial and industrial interests of a great people."[12]

With the prevailing policies discouraging large acquisitions of the public domain and preventing lease options, chaotic conditions predominated on many western ranges by the 1890s. Congress toyed with the remedy of irrigation for the western arid lands to encourage the small farmer settlement many had envisioned for western lands. Congress once again called on Powell to deliver a report on the West's arid lands and to survey the lands for irrigation sites. His work ended abruptly in 1890 after a fight with Congress. Western senators and congressmen objected to Powell's strategy of withdrawing so much land from entry while a careful irrigation survey went forward that might take years to complete.[13]

Irrigation, of course, required water in storage reservoirs in the arid West. Advocates of forest protection seized the opportunity to point out that forest protection was essential to the protection of watersheds for these reservoirs. One source dismissed both the agricultural and grazing potential of forest lands and saw them only as "great moisture reserves." The irrigation cause became an additional reason to advocate the creation of government forest reservations on public lands. Bernhard E. Fernow, Gifford Pinchot's predecessor as head of the Bureau of Forestry in the Department of Agriculture, saw government forest reservations as a major step in moving resource policies from laissez-faire ones (full of waste and destructive competition) to *faire marche* policies (providing guidance and direction for the protection of social and natural resources). The reservations would seek to protect forest resources from plunder and water supplies for irrigation.[14] Powell, who was no friend of the forests, believed that trees consumed water, denying it to reservoirs and streams. Although Fernow and others criticized Powell for this "pseudo science," it is widely noted by Powell's admirers that he stood for carefully planned irrigation and local community management of water and other resources.[15]

By 1891 Congress approved the General Revision Act, which repealed many land laws but, most important, it authorized the president to proclaim forest reservations on public lands. Over the next fifteen years Presidents Benjamin Harrison, Grover Cleveland, William McKinley, and Theodore Roosevelt withdrew millions of acres to create a gigantic public forest reserve system. Although the public range question was obscured by the new interest in forested lands, it must be emphasized that the establishment of forest reservations on the public domain offered the first step toward implementing a system of governmental grazing regulation on public lands.

Six years later, Congress finally spelled out the management goals of the reserves in the Forest Organic (Management) Act of 1897. Two purposes of the forests emerged paramount in the act: (1) to secure "favorable conditions of water flows," and (2) "to furnish a continuous supply of timber for use and necessities of the citizens of the United States." There was no mention of grazing other than a vague reference to the power of government to regulate the "use and occupancy" of the forests. An earlier report from the National Academy of Sciences criticized the unrestricted grazing that was occurring on the newly created forest reserves. The report addressed a question of persistent dispute on public grazing lands. Sheep pasturage as well as other grazing had occurred for so many years that stock operators "have come to believe that they have acquired vested rights in the public forests." To allow continued grazing, said the report, "commits an injustice to persons engaged in this industry in other parts of the country, who are obliged to own or hire their pastures." The act's failure to explicitly mention grazing underlined the developing controversy over its continuation on public forest lands.[16]

The U.S. Department of the Interior began to develop a structure for grazing administration under the new act. Debates raged over whether to admit sheep to forest ranges, but in the end the department determined that sheep could be admitted to selected forests and that grazing was a legitimate resource use on the lands. Like the uses of all forest resources, access to forage was to be granted on the basis of privilege. Administrators and early "forest guards" began a permit system with preference going first to nearby landowners, then to longtime users who owned land, and last to itinerants ("tramp herders"). The process outlined a system of privileged permits for admitting graziers to forest ranges. As initiated by the General Land Office (GLO), the program emphasized that admission to the reserves was a government-granted privilege to stock operators. It also said that the secretary of the interior, under whose department the forests were then managed (until transfer to the U.S. Forest Service in the Department of Agriculture in 1906), "may make such rules and regulations and establish such service as will insure the object of such reservations, namely to regulate their *occupancy and use* and to preserve the forest hereon from destruction." This was a wide mandate to an administrative agency, and the GLO had little experience in management and certainly in the way of effective, dynamic leadership in Washington, D.C., or in the forests to carry out the mandate.[17]

The terms, privilege, allotment, and admission reinforced the government's contention that stock operators did not possess proprietary rights to graze on the reserves. Forest administrators spoke of a "restrictive right" as opposed to what the stock interests sometimes wished to consider a "prescriptive right." The GLO began the designation of "maximum numbers" of stock to be grazed in a forest as it attempted to establish "safe limits" for individual forests. The Forest Service later adopted the criteria of "carrying capacity" according to objective scientifically prescribed methods of determination that would eventually form the foundations of the emerging discipline of range science. Although the GLO in the Interior Department pioneered a range policy, the office appeared unable to sustain the bold administrative action needed to give credibility to its policies of range control and management. That boldness awaited more charismatic leadership.

FOREST SERVICE, GRAZING SERVICE, AND THE
BUREAU OF LAND MANAGEMENT

Events conspired to bring forth leadership and inspiration. The assassination of President William McKinley in September 1901 placed Vice President Theodore Roosevelt in the White House. Roosevelt's interest in western problems and conservation was already widely known. It was no accident that forestry advocate Pinchot, now head of the Bureau of Forestry in the Department of Agriculture, visited the president shortly after Roosevelt's arrival in Washington, D.C. Pinchot urged the president to support a dynamic program of national forestry, and true to his promise, Roosevelt prominently mentioned such a program in his first annual message to Congress. Throughout Roosevelt's presidency, Pinchot remained a confidant and advisor on what Roosevelt came to call "my policy" (that is, conservation). Roosevelt believed that "the fundamental idea of forestry is the perpetuation of forests by use," and he pointed out the usefulness of the forest reserves to mining, grazing, irrigation, and other western interests. Pinchot asserted in his autobiography that Roosevelt's interest at once transformed such resource issues as forestry, irrigation, and reclamation "into national issues with continental consequence, and started them toward that high degree of public acceptance they achieved before T. R. left the White House."[18]

Pinchot himself offered leadership of charismatic proportions. In the process he recognized the problems revolving around the grazing question, which he considered "far and away the bitterest issue of the time."[19] Pinchot's initiatives brought the forest reserves out of the Department of the Interior and into the Department of Agriculture, where he assumed the position of chief forester for a new U.S. Forest Service. Congress approved of this move in the Transfer Act of February 1905, which placed the reserves to the Department of Agriculture and required the Forest Service to charge for resource sale and use. When the reserves were transferred, the secretary of agriculture sent his famous transfer letter to Pinchot, a letter written by Pinchot himself. It outlined the utilitarian philosophy that would guide the Forest Service administration and the management of resources on federal public lands. The lands were for use, but they could only be used under supervision of land managers and the rules laid out in the Forest Service's significantly named *Use Book* for the now designated "National Forests."[20] Pinchot enlisted the services of Arizona stock rancher Albert F. Potter to direct the Grazing Section of the early Forest Service. Potter's assistant, also from Arizona, Will C. Barnes, asserted that "the grazing men of the Forest Service were the shock troops who won the West for forestry."[21]

In 1906 the Forest Service initiated a program of grazing fees for the consumption of public forage in the forests. The drive for efficiency (a trait of modern bureaucracy) may well have been one of the reasons that the Service chose to impose fees so quickly after taking charge of the reserves. An appropriations act of March 3, 1905, included the authority for forest officers to make arrests for violations of regulations, the power to enforce state or territorial laws to prevent forest fires, and the command to enforce local fish and game laws. The assumption of these new powers, especially the authority to levy a grazing fee, made some in the range business feel that the iron hand of government bureaucracy was coming down hard on them. Others welcomed it as a necessity.[22]

The Forest Service faced a public-relations challenge over the fees. Stock raisers early on insisted that fees and other regulations could not be imposed by administrative fiat—that only Congress could levy taxes. At the American Forest Congress of January 1905, the secretary of the National Livestock Association spoke of the "peculiar disposition" of the western stockman that made him resent attempts to bind him to ironclad rules and regulations. The secretary said that stockmen felt they had acquired some moral rights to the ranges "which even the Government should respect."[23] Protests abounded. Many western voices charged that the fee was a tax. One Colorado newspaper read: "There seems to be no adequate reason for imposing a per capita tax or other charge on cattle allowed to graze within the limits of a reserve. Let the sale of timber cover the expense of maintaining the forest, but let grazing privileges be as free as they are on the treeless plains." A stock journal, *Ranch and Range*, referred to the fees as "taxation without representation."[24]

Colorado became a center for these bitter protests. In early 1906 Pinchot rushed to the state to meet with disgruntled stock interests. He expertly mollified many in what had become a serious attack on government forest control. Two issues were at stake. The first questioned whether the Department of Agriculture had the right to impose fees under the general administrative order to "regulate the occupancy and use of lands" under the 1897 act. The second question was also crucial but less publicized: To prevent trespass, especially by cattle, must the Forest Service fence its lands against drifting herds like other property owners according to Colorado open-range laws?

Major grazing cases came to federal courts from Colorado and California. Shortly after the Forest Service announced charges for grazing privileges, stock owner Fred Light, who lived near the Holy Cross National Forest, refused to pay fees. He contended that fees could not be collected on cattle straying into unfenced forests. The government brought suit to compel compliance with the fees and to free the forest from requirements to fence lands. Light argued that he and his wife had pioneered the country. They built a home, raised a family, and developed a herd of five hundred cattle that depended on the forests. The Lights chose their ranch site in a place that gave them access to public-land mountain ranges at a time when no one else had claimed them. Everything they had achieved, they held, they owed to the use of these pastures. Now the government claimed these lands and, although the government allowed grazing to continue, the Forest Service proposed to tax Light's cattle.

Light did not object that the fees were too high; rather, he contended that if the Forest Service possessed the right to set a fee of ten cents per head on his cattle, it could eventually impose a confiscatory $5-per-head charge. In addition, if the Service had a right to set the time of year that Light's cattle could come into and leave the forest as well as the number permitted, it could entirely prohibit his cattle grazing at some future time. If the Service had the right to prohibit Light's use of the range either through direct denial or high grazing fees, it could deny his livelihood and destroy his ranch, home, and enterprise. In January 1909 the federal circuit court in Colorado ruled in favor of the government on both the fee and the fencing issue. The *New York Times* called it a decision "of the utmost importance in the West."[25]

In California a test case arose over the power of Congress to delegate its legislative power to an administrative officer. In November 1907 the grand jury in the district court for the southern district of California indicted stock owners Pierre Grimaud and J. P. Carajous for pasturing sheep on the Sierra Forest Reserve without obtaining a permit. Lawyers for the accused maintained that their actions were not an offense against the

United States. Most important, they said "that the acts of Congress making it an offense to violate rules and regulations made and promulgated by the Secretary of Agriculture are unconstitutional, because they are an attempt by Congress to delegate its legislative power to an administrative officer." The district court accepted this view and dismissed the indictment, ruling against the government. Federal lawyers appealed the case to the U.S. Supreme Court. In May 1911 the Court ruled in favor of the government in both the Light and Grimaud cases, declaring: "From the various acts relating to the establishment and management of forest reservations it appears that they were intended to 'improve and protect the forest and secure favorable conditions of water flows.'" Any use of the reservations for pasturage therefore must be subject to the rules and regulations established by the secretary of agriculture. On some reservations, range use would be accepted, on others not at all: "What might be harmless in one forest might be harmful in another." In all cases such use was to be a matter of administrative detail. It would be impossible for Congress to regulate each forest on an individual basis. To meet the various local conditions, "Congress was merely conferring administrative functions upon an agent, and not delegating to him legislative power." The secretary had the "power to fill up the details" by the establishment of administrative rules and regulations. The Court concluded its decision by justifying its authority to rule on the matter, stating: "The offense is not against the Secretary, but as the indictment properly concluded, contrary to the laws of the United States and the peace and dignity thereof."[26]

With the fee system upheld, critical questions relating to how and who should set the fees arose. The Court alluded to these questions when it ruled that fees were for the purposes of limiting grazing and paying administration cost. Should these, however, be the sole bases upon which fees were fixed? Within a few years many administrators and members of Congress asked that fees be based on the cost of forage and established at the rate of the cost to rent similar private lands. But stock interests saw dangers in this and desired fees set only on the basis of administrative cost or, at the most, tied to the price of stock on the hoof. Clearly, fee controversies did not end with these early court decisions. The fee issue persisted through the end of the twentieth century and will probably be at the center of the range debate in the twenty-first century. Attempts to impose fees at market value have been repeatedly frustrated as Secretary of the Interior Bruce Babbit discovered in his attempt to do so in 1993–94.[27]

While the Forest Service continued to grapple with the fee question in the 1920s, at least two hundred million acres of additional public range lands remained outside of its regulations in the West.[28] Congress tried to address the problem with the Stockmen's Homestead Act of 1916, granting 640 acres of public domain to ranchers. The effort fell far short of the mark. Stock operators needed thousands of acres of land for viable western ranching. Congress refused to abandon the homestead idea, as indicated by the title of the act as well as its limited largesse.[29] Overgrazing and disputes about range rights continued to belie the tranquil, romantic image of homes on the range. Not surprisingly, in the 1920s the lands became an issue of debate locally, in Congress, and in the president's cabinet.

Announcing his intent to halt government centralization and the growth of the federal bureaucracy, President Herbert Hoover in 1929 offered the states possession of the public range lands. The administration wanted the states to take possession of public lands other than those under special designations (for example, the Forest Service). Western states expressed little enthusiasm for the proposal. It was an empty gift; no accompanying grant of mineral rights came with the proposal.[30] Hoover's defeat in the election of 1932 amidst a worsening national depression gave the next president, Franklin Roosevelt, an opportunity to address the open-range problem in his New Deal administration. In 1934 Representative E. T. Taylor from Colorado, eyeing that year's dust bowl storms, proposed what was to be known as the Taylor Grazing Act. The legislation provided for the establishment of a structure for range regulation largely under local rancher control and later overseen by a Grazing Service operating in the Department of Interior. With the Taylor Grazing Act, Congress rejected the extension of the Forest Service and the USDA Grazing Administration over these lands. The chagrin that the USDA and the Forest Service felt over this defeat was apparent in a report that they completed in 1936 on western grazing lands entitled *The Western Range*.[31] It contrasted the relative health of forest ranges with the outside lands, which had neither the benefit of grazing regulations nor the application of range science then under development in Forest Service range research efforts and in cooperating land-grant universities.

The Taylor Act authorized the formation of grazing districts by local ranchers under grazing advisory boards that exercised the power to issue, deny, and admit new graziers to the range under a permit or allotment procedure. Secretary of the Interior Harold Ickes established a Grazing Division to guide the procedure and carry out the rules of the rancher-controlled grazing boards. Although this was government intervention, many ranchers believed it adhered to the practice of "home rule on the range." [32] The legislation ignored previous proposals for permanent grazing leases, but it offered something almost as good: ten-year grazing permits with acceptably low grazing fees. Employees in the new Grazing Division, which became the Grazing Service in 1939, were largely hired from the local level to avert the hiring of exclusively college-trained men (which the Forest Service preferred and the locals did not). The Grazing Service eventually conflicted with powerful western senators, such as Pat McCarran from Nevada, over the old issue of grazing fees and the contention that it needed a larger budget for administration. Costs of range administration had been underestimated from the beginning. The conflict destroyed the Grazing Service and even its parent bureaucracy, the venerable General Land Office, by 1945. From these ruins grew the Bureau of Land Management (BLM) in 1946. The BLM compliantly remained largely under the control of local ranching interests and the representatives from western range states. The lessons of the recent history and the demise of the Grazing Service were clear to all who undertook grazing regulation in the new BLM.

Still, the BLM and the Forest Service used the grazing permit as the instrument of grazing control. The Forest Service, in contrast to the BLM's weakened position, exercised greater regulatory authority. It already had many years of experience with the permit system developing criteria for issuing permits and even for reducing the numbers that may be grazed under a permit. The effective flexing of bureaucratic muscle over the years was one reason that the stock interests did not wish to see the extension of Forest Service authority over the remaining public range. From the beginning, the Forest Service insisted that a grazing permit was a government-granted privilege to the users of public lands. Sometimes the permit was also called a "preference," to indicate that some stock operators could have the permits and others could not. The permit conferred power to the agency, and the threat of its denial, restriction, or reduction of numbers grazed under it could be used to coerce desired grazing practices from permit holders. All of this oversight acted as a constraint on the free and open range (a most desirable constraint from the perspective of range conservationists and even ranch interests, who wanted to limit competition for the range). But within this use privilege, permit, or allotment were the seeds for private claims to forage use on the public lands, that is, grazing rights.

Although it was easy enough for the Forest Service, the Grazing Service, and later the BLM to proclaim that permits did not confer rights, the workings of the private economy conspired to suggest otherwise. Chief among this private conspiracy were the bankers who backed local ranch and stock enterprises. Banks quickly recognized, as did stock operators, that public land grazing permits added value to base ranches. Permit values boosted the amount of loans issued to finance individual operations and larger mortgage loans advanced upon the total sale price of a property, if it had attached permits. These practices created a market in the sale of permits among ranchers, although denounced by agency policy. As early as 1923, courts refused to recognize or enforce contracts that included in ranch sales the permits to graze on the national forests.[33] However wrongly conceived and reinforced by banking practices, by the 1930s agency officials privately acknowledged the practice and the value added to ranch holdings by the possession of public land grazing permits. The Forest Service came to allow the transfer of permits from one grazier to another so long as the sale of the base land was bona fide, but the Service would not guarantee that the numbers allowed under that permit would continue for the new permittee. Little wonder that the permits came to assume value that could not be easily denied. If a permit were denied, the value of the base ranch fell precipitously (and there were always the rumblings that the action could in later parlance be considered a "takings").[34] In light of the strong private property and liberal traditions in the United States, the situation gradually opened the door to private property claims on public lands.[35] Although this impression grew in the minds of the ranching community, government agencies continued to assert that grazing permits were privileges granted and in no way conferred property or even use rights.

PRIVATE PROPERTY, FREE MARKETS, AND ENVIRONMENTALISTS

Another opportunity to assert private rights on the public range grew out of the practices of range improvements. Both the grazing administrators and ranching interests saw the possibilities of range improvements. These came in the forms of water developments, fences, stock driveways, rodent control, poisonous and noxious plant control, revegetation of grasses and shrubs, corrals and loading facilities, and brush control—all of which could make for the "safe" grazing of even greater numbers of stock on ranges. But who should build, maintain, initiate, and pay for these improvements? Early on, the Forest Service saw that if it accepted the aid of graziers in building or even in maintaining these improvements, it risked the claim of a private property interest on the public range. But this stance meant that the government as landowner was key to providing all improvements—an expensive proposition. By the mid-1950s grazing agencies reacted to pressure from the industry and Congress. Some moved grudgingly and others enthusiastically toward cooperative agreements with users in funding some of the expenses of range improvement programs. These policies expressed a commitment to expanding the resource to avert the need for future reductions in grazing stock. One observer saw it as "the mid-century liberal policy . . . not to disturb entrenched interests, but to attempt amelioration by increasing the size of the resource."[36]

From a late-twentieth-century perspective, range improvement paid for by private parties or even in cooperation with the government offered an additional opportunity to claim vested rights to grazing on public lands. Cooperation with permittees in building and maintaining range improvements had long been a part of Forest Service policy. But the Service was always under the obligation to compensate stock owners for their cooperation to avoid private property claims to the range. That compensation often came in the form of determining that reductions were not necessary because improvements increased the range capacity. Still, such improvements required an investment on the part of stock operators on allotments to which they had no permanent guarantee. This was certainly true under "cost-sharing contracts" for range improvements that became a standard part of Forest Service policy in the 1960s. On the one hand, some believed that the range-resource agency should "meet the stockman half-way by guaranteeing either a reasonable permanency on the land or a reimbursement for lost investment," should the allotment be denied in the future. On the other hand, taxpayers should not be expected to subsidize range improvements for private gain by increasing the range capacity. Proposals still surfaced to give permittees a property right over their permits. One argument suggested that perpetual grazing permits be created that could be sold on a free market in an open bid system. Such permits, it was claimed, would offer greater access to grazing lands and equitable distribution of the privilege according to the market forces.[37]

Free marketers have often cheered the possibility of this development and deplored "the locking up of the public range," as economist Gary Libecap put it.[38] Since the 1970s, the holy grail of the free market has been held aloft by some economists (even "free market environmentalists") as the ideal arbitrator in the distribution of goods and services.[39] Offering the bidding for the resource to those outside of the grazing community raises the real possibility of vast change and disruption of the status quo. Although this might be a first step in the removal of the "dead hand" of public ownership, it might also mean the concentration of land use, even ownership, in the hands of gigantic corporations. Still, if the public lands are commodities and contain economic resources, should they not be distributed according to that most modern of all forces, the free-market system? This fact of the modern economy may come as a rude awakening to the grazing community that has erected a quasi legal system of privatizing range rights through market control in range permits. The grazing community could appeal to tradition to close the circle of bidding, but this certainly would not be considered modern. It would be striking an alliance with the very bureaucracies against which it has long raged over issues of fees, number to be grazed, season of graze, and the financing of range improvements. The alliance is perhaps a necessity.

Others have suggested that the era of western public lands is at an end. That the region is on the verge of breaking out into a more progressive and opportunity-laden future wherein the wisdom of private management and development or nondevelopment of resources will prevail independent of public range managers driven by science and politics.[40] They assert that experience shows that government is an incompetent manager and that science can be employed for multiple and contradictory purposes. This has been no less true for the forage resources of the public lands. Here the free market might be the hammer and anvil needed to break the iron triangle involving the agencies' looking out for their own interests by pandering to the demands of their client resource users, who in turn pressure Congress to fund agency operations. With the rise of environmentalism and the free-market movement, the BLM and Forest Service found themselves caught in a dilemma. Congress listened to environmentalists who spoke of the deterioration of the public range; it listened to free-market advocates who saw mismanagement in agencies and giveaways of public resources under the permit system that allowed low grazing fees. The agencies received criticism from all sides including the traditional resource users, who themselves became befuddled with attacks of environmental organizations, free marketeers, and vacillating policies from and in the agencies.

Grazing on public lands grew into a contentious problem after 1970. Public land agencies proclaimed they administered "lands of many uses"—in adherence to multiple-use doctrine. Still, it was no secret that the dominant grazing use prevailed over the majority of public land. Environmentalists sued and won their demand for environmental impact statements for grazing plans, particularly from all BLM grazing districts under the provisions of the National Environmental Protection Act of 1969. New legislation from Congress further complicated the situation in the 1970s. In 1974 it passed the Forest and Rangeland Renewable Resources Planning Act, in 1976 the Federal Land Policy and Management Act (FLPMA), and in 1978 the Forest and Rangeland Renewable Resources Research Act. These acts sought range improvements, greater research, and new fee studies, and the FLPMA declared the permanency of federal ownership.

New fee studies raised the possibilities of increased costs for grazing, possibly to market level. In the face of falling beef prices and rising costs for public land ranchers, a new fee structure threatened disaster. The FLPMA's declaration of perpetual ownership seemed to lock the public ranges into a pattern of increased fees, reduced cattle numbers under permit, and the dictates of powerful government grazing regulators influenced by both environmentalists and advocates of market prices for rental of grazing privileges. It was a far different era from the immediate post–World War II period, when a compliant BLM stood largely at the beck and call of the western ranching interests. Frustration and anger produced the ill-fated Sagebrush Rebellion in western legislatures demanding the cession of public lands to the states.[41] This is a story unto itself, but suffice it to say that the movement failed. It failed because the states began realizing the high cost of administering the lands, the fear of imminent privatization blocking urban recreational access, and the "good neighbor" policy of President Ronald Reagan's newly elected administration that promised greater cooperation with western resource users.[42]

The Reagan administration brought a reprieve to western grazing interests in the 1980s, while environmental organizations stood aghast at the high-handed methods of Reagan's secretary of the interior, James Watt. The alarm sparked an enormous increase in the memberships of the Sierra Club, the Nature Conservancy, and the Wilderness Society, to name only a few organizations. Stock interests had long been wary of recreationists. Early on, these groups had campaigned for the expansion of deer herds, the protection of prime trout steams, and the prevention of pollution and the erosion of stream banks, but the new environmentalists demanded more. They wanted protection and even restoration of biodiversity on the ranges and a halt to range improvement projects for the sole purpose of increasing the range's capacity to hold more stock. Both demands required sharp decreases in the number of cattle permitted on the ranges. According to these new critics, the cow did not belong on western ranges. Some environmentalists declared that the ranges should be "Cattle Free by '93," to which cattle interests responded "Cattle Galore by '94." Other pro-cattle sources suggested that those who opposed cattle on the public lands harbored deep psychological problems. The issue threatened to be one of the ugliest controversies in recent debates over the public lands.[43]

The failure of the open-and-free range system originally prompted government to direct public land bureaucracies to oversee range use. The story began in controversy with the Forest Service grazing program; reached a comparative calm by the time the other public lands came under regulation with the Grazing Service and eventually the Bureau of Land Management. By the end of the twentieth century, severe complications ensnared the grazing agencies. Some bore direct relation to the economic problems of the industry and others to new forces afoot in society that looked to guard the "public equity" in the range lands. Not only must managers be responsible to earlier criteria of efficiency and conservation (that is, sustainable use), they now faced demands for nonuse of the re-sources to meet environmental, biological, and esthetic protection stan-dards. New rules, demands, and legislation all meant more regulation. The mythical and romanticized "home on the range" and the life of the "cowboy"—that symbol of American "frontier" freedom—became in-creasingly enmeshed with federal rules and government land managers. The two groups often did not get along. [44]

CONCLUSION

Historically, public land agencies brought a superficial order to the range. Close examination of the permit system, fees, and other regulations sug-gests resource users often manipulated the system for private advantage. Their successes testified to the strength of local interests in outsmarting a centralized bureaucracy. Despite the conservation movement in the Pro-gressive Era and the expansion of government in the New Deal era, west-erners often contrived the bureaucracy issue as a bugaboo to defeat Washington's moves to seriously control the use of western resources.[45] The history of the federal government's agency range regulation programs is no exception. Resource users accepted government administration of grazing so long as it reinforced a local power structure. All of this made the chal-lenges of revamping the administration's goals toward environmental pro-tection and free-market pricing of resources extremely difficult even at the end of the twentieth century—a century characterized by the centraliza-tion of policy and bureaucracy. Ironically, the existence of the "free and open" public lands in the West offered the opportunity for the creation and intervention of resource bureaucracies, some of which have made their most indelible and controversial marks in range land grazing regulation.

NOTES

1. Alfred W. Crosby, *Germs, Seeds, and Animals: Studies in Ecological History* (Armonk, N.Y.: M. E. Sharpe, 1994), 66–72.

2. Gordon G. Whitney, *From Coastal Wilderness to Fruited Plain: A History of Environmental Change in Temperate North America, 1500 to the Present* (New York:

Cambridge University Press, 1994), 164–71, 257–58; Terry G. Jordan, *North American Cattle-Ranching Frontiers: Origins, Diffusion, and Differentiation* (Albuquerque: University of New Mexico Press, 1993).

3. Walter Prescott Webb, *The Great Plains* (Boston: Grinn and Company, 1931), 205–68. The phrase "speckled cattle" is attributed to General Phil Sheridan in a speech before the Texas legislature in 1866; see LeRoy R. Hafen and Carl Coke Rister, *Western America* (New York: Prentice Hall, 1950), 545; Ernest Staples Osgood, *The Day of the Cattleman* (Minneapolis: University of Minnesota Press, 1929), 21–58.

4. Federic L. Paxson, "The Cow Country," *American Historical Review* 22 (1916): 71–72.

5. John Wesley Powell, *Report on the Arid Lands of the Arid Region of the United States*, 45th Cong., 2d sess., 1878, H. Exec. Doc. 73, pp. 21–29.

6. William D. Rowley, *U.S. Forest Service Grazing and Rangelands: A History* (College Station: Texas A&M University Press, 1985), 11–12; Paul F. Starrs, *Let the Cowboy Ride: Cattle Ranching in the American West* (Baltimore, Md.: Johns Hopkins University Press, 1998), 41; E. Louise Peffer, *The Closing of the Public Domain: Disposal and Reservation Policies, 1900–1950* (Stanford, Calif.: Stanford University Press, 1951), 26.

7. Paxson (in "Cow Country," 72, 81) speaks of the "greed of stockmen" that prompted them to fence in illegal enclosures on the public domain that "forced effective intervention by the government to break them up and to end the period of unregulated free grass."

8. James A. Young and B. Abbott Sparks, *Cattle in the Cold Desert* (Logan: Utah State University Press, 1985), 121–40.

9. Peffer, *Closing of the Public Domain*, 26.

10. As quoted in Louis Pelzer, *The Cattlemen's Frontier: A Record of the Trans-Mississippi Cattle Industry from Oxen Trains to Pooling Companies, 1850–1890* (Glendale, Calif.: Arthur H. Clark Company, 1936), 74.

11. J. J. Thornber, "The Grazing Ranges of Arizona," *Bulletin No. 65*, (Tucson) Arizona Agricultural Experiment Station (1910): 336.

12. U.S. Congress, House, *Letter from the Secretary of the Treasury Transmitting a Report from the Chief of the Bureau of Statistics [Ranch and Range Cattle Traffic]*, 48th Cong., 2d sess., 1885, H. Doc. 267, pp. 38–39.

13. See Thomas G. Alexander, *A Clash of Interests: Interior Department and the Mountain West, 1863–96* (Provo, Utah: Brigham Young University Press, 1977),

for a critical view of Powell; see also Wallace E. Stegner, *Beyond the Hundredth Meridian: John Wesley Powell and the Opening of the West* (Boston: Houghton Mifflin, 1954), for a pro-Powell perspective on this controversy.

14. "A National Forest Preserve," *The Nation*, September 6, 1883, p. 201, urged making forest reservations "only valuable as a reservoir of moisture" for rivers in the arid lands and "agriculture possible west of the 100th meridian by means of irrigation"; Bernhard E. Fernow, "The Providential Functions of Government with Special Reference to Natural Resources," *Science* 2 (1895): 257.

15. Powell, "The Non-Irrigable Lands of the Arid Region," *Century Magazine* 39 (1890): 919–20; Bernhard E. Fernow, "Pseudo-Science in Meteorology," *Science* 3 (1896): 706–8; Abbot Kinney, "Forests and Streams," *Century Magazine* 40 (1890): 637–38; see also Donald J. Pisani, *To Reclaim a Divided West: Water, Law, and Public Policy, 1850 to 1902* (Albuquerque: University of New Mexico Press, 1992), 161–63; Donald Worster, "Landscape with Hero: John Wesley Powell and the Colorado Plateau," *Southern California Quarterly* 79 (1997): 41.

16. U.S. Congress, Senate Report of the Committee Appointed by the National Academy of Sciences upon the Inauguration of a Forest Policy for the Forested Lands of the United States, 55th Cong., 1st sess., 1897, S. Doc. 105, vol. 6, p. 7.

17. Rowley, *Grazing and Rangelands*, 54 ; James Muhn and Hanson R. Stuart, *Opportunity and Challenge: The Story of the BLM* (Washington, D.C.: Government Printing Office, 1988), 29. Emphasis added.

18. Gifford Pinchot, *Breaking New Ground: An Autobiography* (New York: Harcourt, Brace, 1947), 188–90.

19. Ibid., 265.

20. Rowley, *Grazing and Rangelands*, 63–64.

21. Will C. Barnes, *Apaches and Longhorns: The Reminiscences of Will C. Barnes*, ed. Frank C. Lockwood (Los Angeles: Ward Ritchie Press, 1941), 202.

22. Karen R. Merrill, "Whose Home on the Range?" *Western Historical Quarterly* 27 (winter 1996): 433–51, notes the early acceptance by the ranch community of government range regulations (this acceptance does not prevail in later decades).

23. Fred P. Johnson, "Advantage of Cooperation between the Government and Live Stock Associations in the Regulation and Control of Grazing on Forest Reserves," in *Proceedings of the American Forest Congress* (Washington, D.C.: American Forestry Association, 1905), 229.

24. Rowley, *Grazing and Rangelands*, 64–65.

25. Paul H. Roberts, *Hoof Prints on Forest Ranges: The Early Years of National Forest Range Administration* (San Antonio, Tex.: Naylor Company, 1963), 81–82; "Forest Reserves Upheld," *New York Times*, January 6, 1909, p. 5.

26. U.S. Forest Service, Range Management Staff, *Court Cases Related to Administration of the Range Resource on Lands Administered by the Forest Service* (Washington, D.C.: Government Printing Office, 1964), 9–18.

27. "New Federal Land-Grazing Policy Doesn't Include Higher Fees," *New York Times*, February 19, 1995, p. 31.

28. "The Casement Report," *American Forests and Forest Life* 32 (December 1926): 743–44; Rowley, *Grazing and Rangelands*, 138–39.

29. Peffer, *Closing the Public Domain*, 160–63; Starrs, *Let the Cowboy Ride*, 135.

30. Peffer, *Closing the Public Domain*, 203–13; Christopher McGrory Klyza, *Who Controls Public Lands? Mining, Forestry, and Grazing Policies, 1870–1990* (Chapel Hill: University of North Carolina Press, 1996), 111.

31. U.S. Congress, *A Report on the Western Range: A Great but Neglected Natural Resource*, 74th Cong., 2d sess., 1936, S. Doc. 199, vol. 7; Debra L. Donahue, *The Western Range Revisited: Removing Livestock from Public Lands to Conserve Native Biodiversity* (Norman: University of Oklahoma Press, 1999), utilizes this title to attack livestock grazing on public lands and quotes the praise of historian Donald Worster, who terms the 1936 work "the most thorough ecological accounting we have of the first half-century of western pastoralism" (p. 45).

32. Muhn and Stuart, *Opportunity and Challenge*, 39.

33. U.S. Forest Service, *Court Cases*, 31–33.

34. Philip D. Brick and R. McGreggor Cawley, eds., *A Wolf in the Garden: The Land Rights Movement and the New Environmental Debate* (Lanham, Md.: Rowman and Littlefield, 1996), 115–34.

35. For an extremely ahistorical treatment of this position, see Wayne Hage, *Storm over Rangelands: Private Rights in Federal Lands* (Bellevue, Wash.: Free Enterprise Press, 1989); and various statements made throughout the 1990s from the organizations Wise Use and People for the West. For a closer analysis of these movements, see Richard White, "The Current Weirdness in the West," *Western Historical Quarterly* 28 (spring 1997): 5–16.

36. William Voigt Jr., *Public Grazing Lands: Use and Misuse by Industry and Government* (New Brunswick, N.J.: Rutgers University Press, 1976), 150; Clayton R. Koppes, review of Voigt's *Public Grazing Lands*, in *Journal of Forest History* 21 (October 1977): 225.

37. Rowley, *Grazing and Rangelands,* 235; L. A. Stoddart, "What Hope for Grazing on the Public Lands," *Journal of Range Management* 18 (May 1965): 111; Delworth Gardner, "A Program to Stabilize Livestock Grazing on the Public Lands," *National Wool Grower* 52 (November 1962): 14.

38. Gary Libecap, *The Locking Up of the Range: Federal Land Controls and Grazing* (San Francisco, Calif.: Pacific Institute for Public Policy, 1981).

39. Robert Kuttner, *Everything for Sale: The Virtues and Limits of Markets* (New York: Alfred A. Knopf, 1996); Thomas Michael Power, "Ideology, Wishful Thinking, and Pragmatic Reform," in *The Next West: Public Lands, Community, and Economy in the American West,* eds. John A. Boden and Donald Snow (Washington, D.C.: Island Press, 1997), 233–54.

40. Karl Hess Jr., *Visions upon the Land: Man and Nature on the Western Range* (Washington, D.C.: Island Press, 1992).

41. R. McGreggor Cawley, *Federal Land, Western Anger: The Sagebrush Rebellion and Environmental Politics* (Lawrence: University Press of Kansas, 1993); William L. Graf, *Wilderness Preservation and the Sagebrush Rebellion* (Lanham, Md.: Rowman and Littlefield, 1990).

42. C. Brant Short, *Ronald Reagan and the Public Lands: America's Conservation Debate, 1979–1984* (College Station: Texas A&M University Press, 1989).

43. Denzel and Nancy Ferguson, *Sacred Cows at the Public Trough* (Bend, Oreg.: Maverick Publications, 1983); Lynn R. Jacobs, *Waste of the West: Public Lands Ranching* (Tucson: By author, 1991); Paul Starrs, "Cattle Free by '93 and the Imperatives of Environmental Radicalism," *Ubique* 14 (1994): 1–4; Donahue, *The Western Range Revisited,* sees the controversy in terms of competing faiths: utilization vs. preservation of natural systems (p. 99).

44. Even academic writers have come to suggest that this romance be permitted to continue. See Starrs, *Let the Cowboy Ride,* as contrasted with Sharman Apt Russell, *Kill the Cowboy: A Battle of Mythologies in the New West* (Reading, Mass.: Addison Wesley, 1993), and Donahue, *The Western Range Revisited,* who uncompromisingly builds a case for the end of public land livestock grazing. The situation is filled with a bit of dramatic conflict rooted in the confrontation between antimodern impulses in American life fiercely entrenched on the range and the forces of modernization and bureaucracy reaching out to tame them. At the beginning of the twentieth century, the German sociologist Max Weber studied the rise of bureaucracies and how they supplanted charismatic leadership and innovators. There is something charismatic in the leaders of the early conservation movement (for example, Gifford Pinchot and Theodore Roosevelt). The case

could be made that these leaders institutionalized the conservation innovations that became unwieldy bureaucracies performing tasks according to the rules. All of this meant more paper work and a lifelessness that was a curse of modern society and even a threat to freedom itself. See the biography of Weber by John Patrick Diggins, *Max Weber: Politics and the Spirit of Tragedy* (New York: Basic Books, 1996).

45. Donald J. Pisani, *Water, Land, and Law in the West: The Limits of Public Policy, 1850–1920* (Lawrence: University Press of Kansas, 1996), 195–98; Lawrence A. Scaff, *Fleeing the Iron Cage: Culture, Politics, and Modernity in the Thought of Max Weber* (Berkeley: University of California Press, 1989), 228–29.

PART III
THREE CASE STUDIES
OF LAND USE

Dividing the Land

The Taylor Ranch and the Case for

Preserving the Limited Access Commons

MARÍA E. MONTOYA

S ince the late 1960s, the people of the San Luis Valley in south-central Colorado have experienced intense litigation involving private property rights and the use of a commons. The case *Espinoza v. Taylor* has pitted the local inhabitants of San Luis, Colorado, against a North Carolina lumberman for control of a seventy-seven thousand-acre tract of the Sangre de Cristo land grant. This vast area, known as the Taylor Ranch, became a source of tension and litigation when the owner, Jack Taylor, refused to allow the local Hispanos the same access to resources that their ancestors had used as a commons under previous owners. The Hispanos responded to what amounted to Taylor's closing a commons by continuing their traditional uses, which Taylor viewed as poaching and trespassing. At the height of the conflict, each side accused the other of violence and someone even took a few shots at Taylor. Because of the conflict's intensity, the Colorado state government (through the initiative of then governor Roy Romer) intervened with a rare exhibition of generosity and historical insight by proposing to purchase the land from Taylor and return some of the acreage to the original claimants—the local Hispanos in Costilla County.[1]

At the heart of the conflict is the status of the land as a commons. The Hispanos argue that since the grant's inception, this mountain tract—*la sierra*—has been used as a common area for grazing, timber cutting, and wood gathering, to name but a few uses. Moreover, the seventy-seven-thousand-acre tract sits at elevations above eight thousand feet and provides the watershed for the Culebra River Valley and its tributaries; these streams provide the water that feeds the historic *acequias* used by the Hispanos to irrigate their lands in the valley below. The locals fear that Taylor's assertion of his private property rights, as well as the Taylor family's logging activities, threaten both their use of the land as a commons and the stability of the watershed. More important, Taylor's disruption of the commons threatens the distinct nature of the San Luis community.

Since litigation began, Taylor has died and his heirs, particularly his son Zachary Taylor, would like either to make a profit or to sell the parcel: Taylor the younger has no interest in maintaining the land's historic use. At one point the state government of Colorado, through the use of lottery funds, proposed purchasing the land for a reasonable market price in order to save it from loggers and others who might overdevelop it. Perhaps more important, the Colorado state government was interested in settling the thirty-year-long legal battle between the Taylor family and the local San Luis residents. The conflict has been a seesaw of activity, with both sides winning court cases but with no final adjudication in place and no signs of a negotiated settlement in the foreseeable future between Taylor, the town of San Luis, and the Colorado state government.

For the Hispanos of Costilla County this is not merely a philosophical or legal battle. Rather, the outcome of the case, which will determine who owns and controls the tract, will directly affect the quality of their daily lives. Hispanos of the rural San Luis Valley depend on subsistence farming, and today many live near poverty level because few industries, agricultural or otherwise, exist in the vicinity to provide local wage labor. Since World War II, the valley has endured a large outmigration of its citizens, as many have left to find work in Albuquerque, Denver, Los Alamos, and Pueblo.[2] Although many emigrants retain their cultural and familial ties to the area, few economic opportunities remain to sustain them or their families on their traditional homeland. Those who stay in Costilla County and San Luis depend on wood gathering for home fuel consumption (natural gas is not available and butane is expensive), grazing for their small herds, and hunting for sustenance. When Taylor asserted his individual property rights and completely excluded the Hispanos from the land's historic uses, he also cut off a significant portion of their economy. Residents have reacted by abandoning local informal solutions and instead of dealing directly with Zachary Taylor, they have gone outside of the traditional methods of negotiating conflict and have fought back using the U.S. legal system.[3]

INTELLECTUAL FRAMEWORK

Although this story conjures up the images Hollywood typically portrays about the American West—shootouts, range wars, and quaint local color—this story is really about complex ideas regarding property and the problems between conflicting land tenure systems.[4] To understand the role of the commons in the American West, it is helpful to understand how common property systems work or do not work. Garrett Hardin's 1968 article "The Tragedy of the Commons" clearly outlined the problem created by allowing an unlimited number of people to have unlimited access to an exhaustible resource.[5] Hardin, a biologist by training who was perhaps more concerned with issues of overpopulation than land allocation, suggested that in a world of limited resources each person will act to maximize his or her own personal use of that resource. Property scholars, moreover, have suggested that each person will continue to take one more fish out of the stream or add one more cow to the pasture to benefit himself or herself. In a Hardinian model, this rational actor understands that such unrestrained use by all may destroy the resource, but given his neighbor's similar behavior, he must either continue to maximize his own gain from the commons or take the "sucker's payoff" of getting nothing while others exploit the resource to exhaustion. Either way the commons will be destroyed, so there is no incentive to constrain one's own individual exploitation.

How then does a society preserve a common-access resource in the face of humans' "natural" tendency to use that resource at a maximum level? Hardin assumed, as do many environmental historians today, that all humans act in similar and predictable ways: They tend toward capitalist exploitation.[6] Hardin was not alone in failing to take into account the important roles of culture, social custom, and religion in his analysis. In fact, both environmental activists and historians have tended to construct humans and their interactions with nature and the environment in rather flat terms.[7] A new generation of environmental historians, however, have begun to consider how different ethnic groups, genders, social

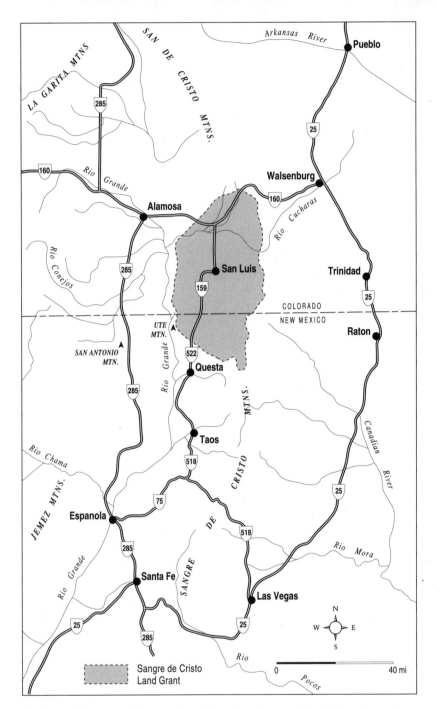

The Sangre de Cristo Land Grant, southern Colorado and northern New Mexico. Adapted from Charles L. Briggs and John R. Van Ness, eds., *Land, Water, and Culture: New Perspectives on Hispanic Land Grants* (Albuquerque: University of New Mexico Press, 1987).

and economic classes, and cultures interact with and use their "place."[8] Only through analysis of the differences between people's interactions with their landscape can the answers be found as to why society should desire and work to create thriving common-pool resources.[9]

For example, Mexican Americans in the Rio Grande watershed of southern Colorado and New Mexico have followed land-use practices that markedly differ from Euro-American land-use customs. Historians have tended to inscribe the Euro-American practices as dominant and normative in the United States.[10] But the intention here is not to conjure up romantic images of a pastoral life with shepherds tending their flocks while women work their small familial garden plots next to their adobe homes.[11] Nevertheless, Hispanos in New Mexico and Colorado have had a historical and cultural legacy of communally working the land within extended familial units.[12] Even the earliest set of legal proscriptions, the *Law of the Indies*—which governed landownership in Hispanic-influenced America—instituted and preserved communal interaction. The laws had rules about the placement and creation of plazas, the center of community life. Lawmakers believed that by first establishing the plaza, a thriving community would naturally flourish on the frontier around the common space. Furthermore, much of later Mexican land law was based on the need to preserve community and create a commons for the community's use on the frontier of the Mexican Republic's empire.[13]

Toward furthering these goals of creating communities and efficient property distribution, there were three types of land grants that a Spanish crown official, and later a Mexican governor, could grant: (1) individual, (2) empresario, and (3) community. An individual grant was limited to no more than ninety-seven thousand acres for the individual to do with as he pleased. There were no restrictions on the land; it was considered an outright gift for service rendered to the crown or the government. Individual grants were the least obviously communal type of land grants. However, although no specific mention of the community interest was made in law, there certainly was an implied one in practice. The grant's size implied that more than a single family would be involved in its use. Typically, the grantee did not subdivide the land and sell lots to many individual households. Rather, the usual practice was to become a *patrón* rather than a developer. He would create a hacienda—one type of community—to develop the land.[14] There is some discussion about whether a hacienda with patrons and peons is the kind of community a society or legal system should want to create, but nevertheless, the hacienda was a community of sorts. Haciendas built families, produced resources, and provided stable communities and outposts on an expanding frontier.

The second kind of land grant, the empresario grant, gave more land than an individual grant but carried with it a series of restrictions, including the requirement that the grantee settle citizens on the land. These grants were usually given in "frontier" locations—the most famous being the Austin colony in Texas.[15] The intent behind the empresario grant was to settle these unpopulated areas and form a permanent community that would stabilize the borders and bring the area under the control of the central government. The Mexican government gave huge parcels of land (some more than a million acres) to an empresario, who agreed to sell smaller parcels to farmers and ranchers, to establish towns, and to create a buffer on the frontier for the state. Through this system the empresarios relieved the state of the burden of creating incentives for settlement, and the state could turn over the project to enterprising businessmen who would risk their finances to possibly gain a fortune from land sales.

The third type of land grant, the community grant, was given jointly to a group who had petitioned the governor for a parcel of land so that they could form a settlement. In a community grant each individual received an allotment for a house (solar) and one or more outlots for cultivation (suertes). Settlers also had the right to use the unallotted land of the grant as a common area for the community. Uses of this land included grazing, farming, wood cutting, watering, and herb and food gathering. Individuals who held a plot in the town had open and unhindered access to the commons.[16] This idea of the government granting lands to individuals or communities directly conflicted with American ideas about individual property rights and, in particular, the homestead. American land law has tended to privilege the idea of individual over communal ownership.[17] Whether Thomas Jefferson's ideal of the virtuous yeoman farmer, the idea of the homesteader out on the Great Plains, or the 1950s American dream of owning a single-family home in the suburbs, historically Americans have been attracted to the notion of individual households owning single parcels of private property in fee, simple absolute. In the case of the Taylor Ranch, these complex concepts about property—one based on the history of Spanish-Mexican land law and the other on U.S. land law—have directly conflicted with one another.

Evident in the Taylor Ranch case and throughout the American West is a confluence of property regimes: the legacies of Native American, Hispano, and Anglo-American traditions. The issue of the commons has reemerged recently with a new wave of restoring historic property rights to Native peoples. For example, the Sioux have asked that the Black Hills be restored to them as their own property, with no encumbrances from the federal government. They also want the land restored to them as a community, not as reparations to individuals.[18] Gaming on Indian reservations has also raised this issue, as Native American communities face the task of how to divide the abundant resources that come not from the land but from tourists' pockets. Should the monies be allocated to individuals and households or kept as tribal assets? How Native Americans will manage returned lands or incoming revenues remains unclear; presumably they will be allowed to come to a self-determined consensus about rights and uses. Such concerns in the Native American community, along with the current situation of Mexican Americans in southern Colorado looking for restoration of their property rights, beg for the issue of the commons and its place in society to be revisited.

The "tragedy of the commons" literature comes out of the Anglo-American tradition in property rights, which is quick to divide between "yours" and "mine." For these authors, there is no easy way in Anglo-American law and practice for the notion of the commons to succeed. But would the commons work, even today, if one looked at a different culture? Chances are, yes. Although useful for understanding an Anglo-dominated property system, the "tragedy of the commons" scenario sheds little light on the historical nature of commons in other cultures.[19] Although the "tragedy" literature should certainly be taken into account, there may be some very unique ways of solving the conflict, looking at the historical background of the Taylor Ranch.

HISTORICAL LEGACY

The history of the Sangre de Cristo land grant finds it origins, as do many New Mexico land grants, in the administration of the Mexican provincial governor, Manuel Armijo, during the early 1840s. The governor, concerned with the hostile and encroaching movements of foreigners on his northern borders (particularly those of settlers and traders from the United States), attempted to shore up this frontier by making large land grants to close friends and to those sympathetic to his administration. By doing so, Armijo hoped that they would populate the area with loyal Mexican settlers who would secure the area against invasion. Most of these land grants were on the eastern side of the Sangre de Cristo mountains and to the north of Taos, in present-day southern Colorado and northern New Mexico.

In 1843 Stephen Luis Lee (an American-born distiller living in Taos) and Narciso Beaubien (the thirteen-year-old son of Carlos Beaubien) joined together and asked Armijo for a 1,038,195-acre grant "to encourage the agriculture of the country and place it in a flourishing condition."[20] Because of the haste with which Armijo granted them the land, grants made during his regime have had a historical reputation for being suspect, and the Sangre de Cristo grant was considered one of the most peculiar of all grants made.[21] First, Lee was an American citizen, not a Mexican. Although foreigners at this time could attain land grants if they applied along with Mexican citizens, it was not viewed by government officials and other critics as particularly wise, given the current fear of American incursions into New Mexico.[22] Second, Narciso Beaubien was only a young boy, with no stature or ability to lure citizens to the frontier to create new settlements. The grant was probably made as a gift to Narciso's father, Carlos, a prominent Canadian-turned-Mexican-citizen and the brother-in-law of Lee. Carlos, however, technically could not receive another grant under Mexican law because Armijo had already granted him half of the Beaubien-Miranda grant two years earlier. In 1848, just months after Brigadier General Stephen Watts Kearney had secured the occupation of New Mexico, an uprising in Taos against the American intruders left Governor William Bent and others, including young Narciso, dead. After his son's death, Carlos Beaubien gained full control of the Sangre de Cristo grant through inheritance and through purchase of Lee's share of the grant. Beaubien then began developing its resources and encouraging settlement on the land. The U.S. Congress in 1860 confirmed that Beaubien owned more than nine hundred thousand acres, known as the Sangre de Cristo grant.[23]

In 1862 Beaubien was elderly and in failing health. He also owed a significant amount of back taxes on the Sangre de Cristo grant, and therefore he began looking for a buyer for the entire estate. In William Gilpin, territorial governor of Colorado, Beaubien found the perfect entrepreneur to relieve him of his burden.[24] With the intention of turning around and selling the land to European investors for a profit, Gilpin purchased the grant from Beaubien's heirs in 1864 after Beaubien's death the year before. The contract made clear that the Hispano settlers living on the grant would retain rights to the commons of the grant. The provision for those living on the land grant read: "Certain settlement rights before then conceded by said Charles Beaubien to residents of the settlement of Costilla, Culebra, & Trinchera, within said tract included, shall be confirmed by said William Gilpin as made by him."[25] In 1863, before his bargaining with Gilpin, Beaubien had conveyed common areas to the towns on the Sangre de Cristo land grant.[26] Beaubien clearly intended to provide for the settlers' use of the commons for the usufructuary community rights of wood, timber, water, and pasture. In short, Gilpin knew he was purchasing the land with certain encumbrances attached to the property. He explicitly agreed to honor those obligations that Beaubien felt toward the settlers living on the grant.

THE CURRENT LEGAL SITUATION

For the next hundred years Gilpin and his successors in interest sold most of the grant to various parties.[27] In each of the conveyances from owner to owner, the rights of the local residents to use the commons were duly noted and agreed to by the new purchasers. Even Jack Taylor had been aware that the land came with a number of encumbrances, including the Hispanos' rights to continue in their usufructuary uses.[28] In fact, it was precisely because of these rights that Taylor petitioned the court to erase them. Immediately after his purchase, Taylor filed a petition in U.S. District Court to register the title of his land under the Colorado Torrens Act.[29]

The Torrens Act has a long history that originated in South Australia in 1858 under the guidance of Sir Robert Richard Torrens. Under his recording system, a landowner could petition the court to wipe away all other claims to a parcel of land. After giving proper notice to all who might have a claim to the land, conducting a hearing, and dismissing other claims, the landowner could then clear his title of rival claims, reducing it to the form of a fee, simple absolute.[30] In effect, one could now rewrite the legal history of a particular parcel of land. On the certificate of title, all other landowners (some with complex usufructuary interests in the land) were erased and the title was vested solely in the landowner who petitioned the court. This registration method and analogous ones were particularly effective in Australia, Canada, Hawaii, New Zealand, and the American West in purging parcels of complex communal rights held by a significant preexisting Native population based on their own customary property systems. In 1967 Taylor found success and the Colorado courts issued him a title under the Torrens Act that was legally free of any encumbrances.[31]

In 1981, however, some San Luis residents filed a new civil action in the Costilla County District Court to regain access and use of *la sierra,* the mountain tract of the Taylor Ranch. They made three claims for relief: (1) that the Torrens Act violated due process of law and therefore did not apply to local landowners and that when Taylor applied under the Torrens Act, he failed to properly notify the property owners who made use of the commons; (2) that their usufructuary rights were preserved under the Treaty of Guadalupe Hidalgo; and (3) that when Carlos Beaubien conveyed rights to the settlers of the Sangre de Cristo land grant in 1863, those were rights and responsibilities that ran with the land and encumbered all subsequent property owners. In the eyes of the plaintiffs, Taylor had an obligation to leave the commons open.[32]

The American Southwest has had a long history of Hispano settlers using violence to resist Anglo holders of Mexican land grants. From the nineteenth-century struggles on the Las Vegas land grant (when Las Gorras Blancas rode across the landscape cutting fences) to the late 1960s (when Reis Lopez Tijerina occupied the courthouse and shot at police officers in Tierra Amarilla), northern New Mexicans and southern Coloradoans have been fighting to preserve their property rights.[33] What differentiates the Taylor Ranch struggle is that Hispanos no longer turn to violence to make their case; instead, they now work within the U.S. legal system, with both Anglo and Hispano lawyers, to attain their rights. By claiming that their rights to due process of law have been violated, the Hispano plaintiffs have accepted the validity of U.S. law—a concession that earlier land struggle movements would not make. Their legal claims reflect a shift in position from the nineteenth-century inhabitants of Mexican land grants. No longer are the Hispanos considered foreigners suffering under the domination of a conquering government; they are now fully incorporated U.S. citizens who possess rights that have been violated.

Ironically, the claim that has worked in the Hispanos' favor has not been the more esoteric and principled arguments about the nature of communal rights under Mexican grant law or how Mexican land rights were incorporated into the U.S. system under the Treaty of Guadalupe Hidalgo. Rather, a purely procedural and legalistic objection has kept their claim alive. As previously noted, the plaintiffs claim that when Taylor applied for a clear title under the Torrens Act, he did not give proper notice to all the owners of the commons. He posted notices in the local papers but did not make any significant effort to track down owners who had long since moved away from the area, who still retained property and familial connections to the commons. The plaintiffs believe that because their rights were violated, the clear title issued under the Torrens Act should be revoked and the whole issue of who owns the commons should be reopened.

That the courts have virtually ignored the plaintiffs' claims made under the Treaty of Guadalupe Hidalgo about the nature of treaty rights and community held land grants should not come as a surprise. The relative success of the Torrens Act claim illustrates the historic reluctance of U.S. courts to introduce the Spanish-Mexican notion of complex usufructuary property rights into the U.S. property regime. Unlike the claim under treaty-based rights, in which the plaintiffs assert that they have rights as a *community*, the Torrens Act claim states that they, as individuals, were not given adequate notice to vindicate their "individual" interest in the land. But note the artificiality of the Torrens Act claim: It hardly seems to explain the real nature of the plaintiffs' grievance. The plaintiffs were not merely injured by the lack of notice, they were injured by the loss of their communal property right, an interest that the notice requirements of the Torrens Act would be inadequate to vindicate even if Taylor had honored such requirements. Properly notified individual Hispano owners, some of whom reside hundreds of miles from the San Luis Valley, may have been less likely to show up in court to vindicate their "trivial" claim to gather wood. Such usufructuary rights are considered simply too small to the individual to justify such expense, especially to those who might live far away.

This is not to say that these usufructuary rights, taken collectively, would not have considerable value. In fact, they do. But no single usufructuary claimant would have sufficient incentive to defend the rights of all, based only on his or her individual share of the commons. The Torrens Act claim is inadequate to protect the real interest of the plaintiffs—the preservation of the commons—because it is a claim designed to protect significant individual interests in the land. The Torrens Act claim simply cannot protect any notion of communal ownership in which the vested right in question belongs to a group, and no single individual is institutionally suited to protect the communal interest. Therefore, notifying individuals would have been insufficient to protect the community interest unless there had been some way to organize all of the affected community members to simultaneously challenge the 1960 Torrens action. The courts, however, have denied the Hispanos the right to act as a class and work together.[34] Rather, they must individually sue Taylor to retain their specific rights, which had once belonged to the whole community.

In short, the plaintiffs' claim against the Torrens Act is an inadequate way to recognize Spanish-Mexican communal property rights—a sort of imperfect translation of such communal rights into terms recognized by the Anglo-American system of individual property rights. But its imperfection also indicates why it is the plaintiffs' most successful claim in litigation: Such a theory of individual property rights is more familiar to the state courts than the concept of communal property created by Spanish-Mexican property law. Rather than attempt to reconstruct and enforce the law of Spanish-Mexican land grants under the terms of the Treaty of Guadalupe Hidalgo, the court naturally preferred to narrowly inquire into whether every owner received a postcard informing him or her of the pending Torrens action in 1960. Such a claim might not really reflect what the plaintiffs want: return of their communal interest. But it does reflect what the court can surely deliver: enforcement of an Anglo-American system of individual property entitlement.

The Costilla County District Court reheard the case of *Rael v. Taylor*, now *Espinoza v. Taylor*, in spring 1998 to determine the extent of these rights. The plaintiffs lost their case before Judge Gaspar Perricone, but the case is on appeal to the Colorado Court of Appeals and property rights are still contested.[35] As one can imagine, business interests and much of the legal establishment, including three Colorado Supreme Court justices, do not wish to see private property rights thrown into such turmoil. In the 1994 remand back to the district court, the dissent of Justices Vollack, Roviera, and Erickson read: "The effect of the majority opinion is to re-open a thirty-year-old decision and put into question the ownership of a considerable portion of the land in Costilla County. . . . It is the public policy of this state to make title to property more *secure* and *marketable*, not less. . . . Such a result will introduce chaos and uncertainty in the marketability of land in this state."[36] After all, it is bad for business to open up a legal argument that could throw into question the title to thousands of acres.

In the final analysis, however, clouding the title may be the only action that will persuade Taylor the younger to sell the tract for somewhere between $15 and $20 million. The Colorado state government would like to see all of this litigation disappear and would like to purchase the tract of land from Taylor with the use of state lottery money, but the two sides cannot agree on a purchase price. And although various outside interests, from the Sierra Club to Canadian lumber interests, have expressed interest in buying the land, everyone is standing back until the issue of a clear title is resolved. Even media mogul Ted Turner declined to purchase the tract. State officials—like Ken Salazar, former head of Colorado's land bureau, chair of the governor's Sangre de Cristo Land Grant Commission, and now the state's attorney general—have been sympathetic to the plight of the people of San Luis.[37] On a more cynical level, however, one could also argue that the state does not want this questioning of land titles to go any further, as there are too many old land grants in Colorado with similar histories.

ISSUES OF MANAGING COMMONS

This section discusses some theoretical considerations about how a commons might work both in this particular case and in the larger context of the American West. Lawyers, state managers, and commentators have solely focused on returning the land to the Hispanos without considering how the community might actually access and use the land. The question of who gets the land, however, is tightly woven together with how that party will use the tract. The question should therefore be: What goals do we as a society, and the people of Colorado in particular, want to accomplish, and which caretakers of the land can best meet these goals? If and when Taylor the younger relinquishes the land, either through sale or forfeit, there are at least three choices in managing this commons: (1) individual ownership, (2) government ownership, or (3) communal ownership. An examination of the historical and philosophical implications of each of these possibilities is useful.

If a certain acreage of the land were to be allotted to each confirmed recipient of the grant, a homestead-like system could be devised in which a surveyed grid would overlay all seventy-seven thousand acres. Through a lottery system each heir could choose a parcel. The major obstacle would be deciding who in fact constitutes an eligible recipient. This points to the Hispanos' original claim against Taylor's Torrens action: Taylor did not find all of the eligible property owners, as outmigration has made it extremely difficult to find the rightful claimants. A second problem would be, do all owners have an equal claim to a portion of the commons? Local residents of San Luis, Costilla County, and Colorado who live their day-to-day lives in the area probably have a stronger moral, if not legal, claim for needing the commons' resources than do those who have moved away. So those who divide the land would either have to make a bright line rule that every owner is considered equal and land would thus be allotted accordingly, or devise a complex scheme that takes into account residency, strength of claim, and perhaps even need when parceling out the tract. Furthermore, recalling the allotment process for Native Americans under the Dawes Act reminds us that division of commons into private property will probably not solve the problem of allocating resources to those who need and use them most. Private ownership in this case could accelerate the sale of the land to the lumber industry and other commercial users who have no interest in seeing the concept of the commons succeed. [38] Division of the Taylor Ranch into individual plots would ruin the San Luis community and go against the original intentions of Carlos Beaubien.

A grid simply cannot account for the rugged terrain, the aridity, and the differences within the tract of land. One of the major flaws with the "tragedy of the commons" analysis is that it assumes that the sum of the commons' parts equals the whole, but the Taylor Ranch proves otherwise. *La Sierra* is a mountain tract: Portions hold fertile valleys with water and vast acres of tall timber, while others sit above tree-level at more than twelve thousand feet. What happens to the claimant who has lived his or her entire life in San Luis working a farm, but who draws a high lottery number and can choose only from the mountain tracts? This method of individual allotment seems both unfair and inefficient, as some plots may be practically worthless economically. The Taylor Ranch works best as a commons because as a whole parcel it possesses resources that can serve and sustain the entire community in a way that allotment would surely destroy. For example, the tract provides the watershed for the *acequia* system of the valley below. Recent logging activities in the area have muddied these historic irrigation ditches and threatened the economic livelihood of the San Luis farmers.[39] Individual allotment would encourage property holders to use the land in ways that may not benefit the surrounding property and thus threaten the entire ecosystem.

Subdividing the land ignores the history of the people and the area. The people of San Luis have a historical memory of using the land in common. Forcing them to adapt to another property system seems to go against the entire proposition of returning this unique parcel of land to them in the first place. Interested bystanders, the state of Colorado, and policy makers should be willing to encourage experimentation in property holding. They should learn from past failed attempts at allotment, which tried to transform communal-based societies into communities based on individual ownership. Allotment and severalty never proved to be the rousing success that late-nineteenth-century reformers predicted, and many Native American communities lost their cohesiveness as a result of the policy.

Another solution, one that the state of Colorado has favored in the past, is that the state park system run the commons. The land would be purchased with lottery funds and then turned over to either the Department of Fish and Game or the park system for management. Opposition has come from Colorado citizens who object to this "special rights" way of dealing with the problem, and resent their lottery funds being used to make what some critics see as individual reparations to this remote Hispano community. The town of San Luis and the Taylor Ranch lie on the western side of the Sangre de Cristo mountains, isolated from the majority of the state's population. Ironically, polls show that there would be much less popular objection to making the land into a wildlife preserve (mostly elk and bear) in which few could visit and no one could "use." State officials hope to alleviate some criticism by allowing day uses such as picnicking and sport fishing, while still allowing the Hispanos their traditional uses: a multiuse commons.

Many people in San Luis have found this solution problematic, however. They know that state officials will regulate amounts of resources that can be taken, when they can be taken, and how they can be harvested. Local residents fear that state officials will not necessarily be sympathetic to their historic ways and land uses and will interfere too much. After all, there is a long history of conflict between federal and state governments and Native American groups who have sought to gather resources for religious and traditional ceremonies from federal or state lands that once belonged to them. Local Hispanos also fear that this commons, if run by the state park system and opened to camping and day uses, would merely become a tourist attraction where outsiders would come to enjoy the natural beauty of the landscape and to gawk at the quaint locals. The community has been adamant in their demand that they be allowed to decide their fate and control the land around them. The thought of merely being an extension of the Santa Fe–Taos tourist route is something they desperately want to avoid. In the end, they fear that state control, or the Leviathan solution, will be little better than Taylor's control over the land: Although they might gain limited access, they would not have complete control over the resource. The local Hispanos argue that the land belongs to the community and, as such, they would be the best caretakers.

Finally, communal ownership, although it has some significant obstacles to overcome, presents a viable alternative. The state could purchase the property with lottery funds (or condemn it through eminent domain) and return it to the owners of the land grant as a commons without any encumbrances attached. State officials would have to overcome the opposition of other state residents and embark on the difficult task of convincing late-twentieth-century citizens that they need to accept and help facilitate reparations to native peoples. But the difficult question arises: *Who* is the community? Presumably, heirs of the original owners would number in the thousands by now, and each would have varying claims to the use of the tract as a commons. To solve this problem, a system would have to be established such that those people who lived in San Luis have more rights of access and use than those living elsewhere. Perhaps a two-tier system of use could be devised whereby some would have access to take resources while others could only use them in such passive ways as camping and hiking. The important point is that the community, not the state, would decide how to use the land. Because the number of owners has grown dramatically since Carlos Beaubien first gave the commons to the people, the real problem will be preventing overuse and abuse. Some sort of regulating board made up of local residents and property holders, perhaps with the consultation of outside experts in land management, could preserve the resource while giving the largest numbers fair access.

This community should not be viewed in romantic terms as pastoral, cohesive, and entirely peaceful. The community itself has not always been able to decide on a united strategy. With Jack Taylor as the opponent, it was easy to present a united front. Now, however, there is no Jack Taylor, no clearly defined opposition. The Taylor owners want to sell: A workable sale price simply has to be negotiated and the money found. The litigation can be seen as a posturing tool used by both sides to fix the sale price. With the possibility of having the land returned to the community, conflicts have begun to arise. There are two factions. First, there are those who want to pursue only litigation; they are willing to risk everything and wait for the outcome of the legal struggle. They believe they have a legal right to the land and that they will prevail in the court system, so a compromise strategy that involves settling with the Taylor estate should not be pursued. They are the more radical (although that term is problematic) activists of the Chicano movement and its struggles; they would like to see the community preserved as a historic but working commons. Second, there are those who want to end the litigation. They are willing to let the state purchase and regulate the land with the community's input. Ideally, they would like to raise the money themselves from private funds to purchase the land. They see themselves as more modern or progressive. They are willing to discuss the possibilities of limited development in terms of timber cutting and tourist attractions, because they believe that only economically viable use of the commons can preserve the community.

What does this conflict within the community say about ethnic identity? Clearly, both factions identify with the land and want to preserve the community. One group wants to return to a pastoral, if not romantic, vision of the community and the commons, while the other wants limited development, jobs, and "progress." Who is right? Who gets to define the community? The two sides have little in common and both control a significant proportion of the community. For now, the differences are moot, as the groups put their energies into the tasks at hand. However, when the time comes to divide the lands and govern the commons, they will have to find common ground if they are to hold off outside interlopers who may not have the community's best interests in mind. Although these are difficult questions, there have been precedents for maintaining successful commons by close-knit societies. Theorists and lawyers such as Elinor Ostrom and Robert G. Ellickson have explored how tight societies can overcome Hardin's "tragedy of the commons" scenario to preserve community and alternative ways of life. They argue that when a community has enough of a common interest, individuals can overcome their desire to overuse a commons and preserve it for the greater good. For example, the *acequias* of both northern New Mexico and the San Luis Valley run under joint cooperation with little interference from the government.[40] People gather in the spring to clear the ditches and the *mayordomo*, with the backing of the community, regulates the amount and time and the usage of those living on or using the *acequia*. Presumably, this kind of model would guide the future managers of the commons.

For the citizens of San Luis and Costilla County, their sense of place, their community structure, and even their ethnic identity as Hispanos and Chicanos is specifically tied to their relationship with *la sierra* and the surrounding land. The question is whether they can come together as a cohesive community to manage the commons. And will society, apart from those who will benefit directly from the land exchange, be willing to make the necessary reparations? Although it is necessary to balance the economic costs of reopening these land grant issues, they must be balanced against the moral cost of failing to act. For years Native Americans and Mexican Americans suffered land loss at the hands of unscrupulous government officials and land dealers. It is only right that reparations now be made. The argument that land titles will be clouded and real-estate values will plummet must be rejected for the old nineteenth-century rhetoric that it is. Rather, a collaboration between government officials, business interests, and local citizens must begin to create workable solutions to these difficult economic and moral questions. The Taylor Ranch situation provides a unique opportunity and challenge to resolve some of the hundred years of chaos that land grants have created in the American Southwest.

NOTES

I wish to thank Rick Hills, Jeff Goldstein, and Michael Heller for reading earlier drafts of this chapter, and Tom Romero for his research assistance.

1. I use the term "Hispanos" because this is the term that I believe the majority of these residents use to describe themselves. Although many in the younger generation identify themselves as "Chicanos," that term clearly is a chosen political identity. The older generation tends to identify more with their Hispanic rather than their Mexican heritage. Therefore, throughout the chapter I consistently use the term "Hispano," except for those who have chosen to identify themselves as Chicano. I use the term "Mexican American" in a more general sense, when making larger observations.

2. Regarding the historic patterns on migration in the area, see Sarah Deutsch, *No Separate Refuge: Culture, Class, and Gender on an Anglo-Hispano Frontier in the American Southwest, 1840–1920* (New York: Oxford University Press, 1987). On more recent patterns of migration, see Richard Nostrand, *The Hispano Homeland* (Norman: University of Oklahoma Press, 1992).

3. Both Robert G. Ellickson and Hernando de Soto have written on the formal and informal ways that neighbors have worked out property conflicts. See Ellickson, *Order without Law: How Neighbors Settle Disputes* (Cambridge: Harvard University Press, 1991); and Hernando de Soto, *The Other Path: The Invisible Revolution in the Third World* (New York: Harper and Row, 1990).

4. This chapter originates from my larger work on Mexican land grants in the American Southwest. For a more detailed exposition about conflicting property regimes, see María E. Montoya, *Translating Property: The Maxwell Land Grant and the Conflict over Land in the American West, 1840 to 1900* (forthcoming).

5. Garrett Hardin, "The Tragedy of the Commons," *Science* 162 (1968): 1243.

6. The works of Donald Worster—particularly *Dust Bowl: The Southern Plains in the 1930s* (New York: Oxford University Press, 1979) and *Rivers of Empire: Water, Aridity, and the Growth of the American West* (New York: Pantheon, 1985)—have been most influential in bringing this perspective to environmental history.

7. William Cronon's controversial essay "The Trouble with Wilderness, or Getting Back to the Wrong Nature" in his edited collection of essays, *Uncommon Ground: Toward Reinventing Nature* (New York: W. W. Norton, 1995), clearly illustrates this point. His critique of "wilderness" and its advocates and his call for understanding nature in a larger context, which presumably would include the view of the suburban gardener and urban resident, has raised a fury among environmental activists who have objected to Cronon's deconstruction of the sacred terms "nature" and "wilderness." From their perspective there is little room for competing views of (much less uses of) nature. See, for example, the winter 1996–97 issue of *Wildearth*.

8. This literature is growing rapidly (this note may in fact be outdated upon this book's publication), but some classic examples that have influenced my own thinking include Richard White, "Are You an Environmentalist or Do You Work for a Living?" in *Uncommon Ground* and in his *Organic Machine* (New York: Hill and Wang, 1995); and Annette Kolodny, *The Lay of the Land: Metaphor as Experience and History in American Life and Letters* (Chapel Hill: University of North Carolina Press, 1975), and Kolodny, *The Land before Her: Fantasy and Experience of the American Frontiers, 1630–1860* (Chapel Hill: University of North Carolina Press, 1984). The study of Native Americans' land use and their ties to the land has enjoyed a longer historiography. See William Cronon, *Changes in the Land* (New York: Hill and Wang, 1983); Richard White, *Roots of Dependency* (Lincoln: University of Nebraska Press, 1983); and Arthur McEvoy, *The Fisherman's Problem: Ecology and the Law in California Fisheries, 1850–1980* (New York: Cambridge University Press, 1986).

9. Many of my thoughts about how different groups—including people of color and women—use and think about nature come out of the 1998 conference "And Justice for All: Racial Equality and Environmental Well-Being in the American West," which was held in Denver, Colorado, and sponsored by the Center of the American West. A collection of essays from the conference proceedings is forthcoming. Another book that influenced my thinking is Elinor Ostrom's *Governing the Commons: The Evolution of Institutions for Collective Action* (New York: Cambridge University Press, 1990).

10. For a discussion of this dominant paradigm, see Paul Wallace Gates, *The Jeffersonian Dream: Studies in the History of American Land Policy and Development* (Albuquerque: University of New Mexico Press, 1996).

11. In fact, William deBuys, *Enchantment and Exploitation: The Life and Hard Times of a New Mexico Mountain Range* (Albuquerque: University of New Mexico Press, 1985), has left little room for that notion to exist any longer.

12. For example, see Ken Orona, "River of Culture, River of Power: Identity, Modernism, and Contest in the Middle Rio Grande Valley, 1848–1947" (Ph.D. diss., Yale University, 1998).

13. For how New Mexicans established their communities, see Alvar W. Carlson, "Long-Lots on the Rio Arriba," *Annals of the Association of American Geographers* 65 (March): 48; and Carlson, "Rural Settlement Patterns in the San Luis Valley: A Comparative Study," *Colorado Magazine* 44 (1967): 110. See also Margaret Mead, *Cultural Patterns and Technical Change* (New York: New American Library, 1955), 151–77.

14. For example, Lucien B. Maxwell in New Mexico, while holding claim to two individual land grants, depended on hundreds of people who worked for him to make the enterprise successful. Although he was their boss, he formed a certain patron-client relationship with the workers. See Montoya, *Translating Property*, chapter 2.

15. The Austin colony is an interesting study in itself when discussing conflicting property regimes. Stephen Austin brought his very U.S.-centric view of property and incorporated it into the Mexican system of land grants. The result was the creation of some of the largest privately held tracts of land in the United States. As a consequence of his efforts, Texas was the only western state where the Homestead Act and the Northwest Ordinance were not imposed on the people and the landscape. Regarding the rules of empresarios, see the "Distribution of Lands to Foreigners Who Come to Colonize," Mexico's *Code of Colonization*, no. 46, January 4, 1823, as published in Matthew Reynolds, *Spanish and Mexican Land Laws* (St. Louis: Burton & Skinner Stationery Co., 1895), 171.

16. Common areas were classified according to use. For example, the *dehesa* was pasture land, the *monte* was for wood gathering, the *ejido* was located outside of town and used for recreation, and the *propio* was located in town and used for municipal funds. Victor Westphall, *Mercedes Reales: Hispanic Land Grants of the Upper Rio Grande Region* (Albuquerque: University of New Mexico Press, 1983), 9–10.

17. This is not to suggest, however, that there are not many cases of public property and community-held property. For examples in the United States and

how the U.S. legal system has dealt with these pieces of land, see Carol M. Rose, "The Comedy of the Commons: Custom, Commerce, and Inherently Public Property," in *Property and Persuasion: Essays on the History, Theory, and Rhetoric of Ownership* (Boulder, Colo.: Westview Press, 1994).

18. *The Economist*, July 23, 1994, p. 28.

19. See Robert G. Ellickson, "Property in Land," *Yale Law Journal* 102 (1993): 1319, in which he argues that it is possible for "close-knit communities" to sustain a commons.

20. Westphall, *Mercedes Reales*, 53.

21. For a detailed and interesting discussion of the time period and these grants, see Marianne L. Stoller, "Grants of Desperation, Lands of Speculation: Mexican Period Land Grants in Colorado," *Journal of the West* 19 (1980): 22. I want to thank Professor Stoller for her generosity in sharing with me her vast knowledge of Colorado land grants.

22. One particularly harsh critic of granting land to foreigners was the Taos Catholic priest, Padre Jose Antonio Martinez, who argued vigorously against Armijo granting lands to Beaubien, Bent, St. Vrain, and other Canadian and American foreigners. Martinez believed that the lands were a commons to be held by all citizens (Mexican and Indian) and could not and should not be given away to private individuals. See Montoya, *Translating Property*, chapter 2.

23. Just how and why the grant was confirmed is a curious topic unto itself. The Sangre de Cristo, Maxwell, Las Animas, and Nolan grants were all conveyed by Armijo at roughly the same time. They were later confirmed by the surveyor general of the United States, the secretary of interior, and the U.S. Congress with relatively little trouble. Because of the vast acreage and valuable locations, these areas were ripe for speculation by Anglo land-grabbers. Businessmen and politicians interested in making their fortunes off of these grants were quite influential in seeing that their boundaries were confirmed at outrageous amounts of acreage. See Howard R. Lamar, *The Far Southwest* (New Haven, Conn.: Yale University Press, 1964), 136–70; Westphall, *Mercedes Reales*, 147–92, and Victor Westphall, *Thomas B. Catron* (Tucson: University of Arizona Press, 1973), 33–38.

24. For a history of William Gilpin's life, see Howard R. Lamar, *Reader's Encyclopedia of the American West* (New Haven, Conn.: Yale University Press, 1998), 429.

25. *Rael v Taylor*, p. 3.

26. As recorded in the Costilla County book of deeds, Book 1, p. 256, as cited by the court in *Rael v Taylor*.

27. The Sangre de Cristo land grant has one of the most interesting legal histories. The sale of the large Trinchera and Costilla tracts led to some of the most influential litigation in land grant history. See *Tameling v U.S. Freehold and Immigration Company*, 93 US 644. Today, the Trinchera portion of the Sangre de Cristo land grant is owned by the heirs of Malcolm Forbes.

28. The provision read, "subject to claims of the local people by prescription or otherwise to right to pasture, wood, and lumber and so-called settlements [*sic*] right in, to and upon said land." *Rael v Taylor*, 1994 WL 161234 (Colo.), p. 3.

29. Colorado 1953 Torrens Registration Act, sections 118–01–1 to 102, 5 C.R.S. (1953), currently codified as sections 38–36–101 to -198, 16A C.R.S. (1982 and 1993 Supp.).

30. John L. McCormack, "Torrens and Recordings: Land Title and Assurance in the Computer Age," *Wm. Mitchell Law Review* 18 (winter 1992): 70–73; U.S. Department of Housing and Urban Development, *Land Title Recordation Practices: A State of the Art Study* (Washington, D.C.: U.S. Government Printing Office, 1980); and Richard W. Laugesen, "The Torrens Title System in Colorado," 39 *dicta* 40 (1962).

31. On appeal, the Tenth Circuit Court of Appeals held that the 1860 congressional confirmation of the Sangre de Cristo grant extinguished "any conflicting rights prior to the Confirmatory Act of 1860 which might have arisen or existed by reason of the original grant from Mexico." *Sanchez v Taylor*, 377 F 2d 733.

32. *Rael v Taylor*, p. 6, and the "Plaintiffs' and Interveners' Opposition to Taylor Family's Motion for Summary Judgement," April 6, 1998.

33. For examples of resistance, see Robert Rosenbaum, *Mexicano Resistance in the American Southwest: The Sacred Right of Self-Preservation* (Austin: University of Texas Press, 1981); Rudolfo Acuña, *Occupied America: A History of Chicanos* (New York: Harper and Row, 1988); and Peter Nabakov, *Tijerina and the Court House Raid* (Albuquerque: University of New Mexico Press, 1969).

34. In 1997 the trial court denied the plaintiffs their motion to file suit as a class action. This ruling is still under appeal, however. See the plaintiffs' "Opening Brief" in *Lobato v Taylor* in the Colorado Court of Appeal, case # 98CA1447.

35. Because *Espinoza v Taylor* is still in litigation, a new court decision may render this discussion outdated. Still, it is a useful discussion for the reader in considering the larger implications about commons and their place in the American West.

36. *Rael v Taylor*, p. 24. Emphasis added.

37. *Sangre de Cristo Land Grant Commission Report*, December 28, 1993.

38. See Emily Greenwald, "Allotment and Severalty: Decision-Making during the Dawes Act Era on the Nez Perce, Jicarilla Apache, and Cheyenne River Sioux Reservations," Ph.D. dissertation, Yale University, 1994. Greenwald argues that because Indians did not value land the same way that Anglos did, they often chose land that had no economic value. This caused great problems for those who envisioned the Dawes Act as a way of making Indians self-sufficient farmers. Furthermore, in some areas of the West, particularly where it was rather arid, the homestead of 160 acres was simply unworkable.

39. *La Sierra*, May 15, 1995, p. 2.

40. The local newspaper, *La Sierra*, is littered with notices of ditch meetings and warnings to those who abuse the system. See also Stanley Crawford, *Mayordomo* (Albuquerque: University of New Mexico Press, 1988).

Public Lands and Public Sentiment

A Comparative Look at National Parks

ARTHUR R. GÓMEZ

On September 18, 1996, President Bill Clinton intervened in one of the decade's most virulent conservation fights. Embraced by the vermilion majesty of the Grand Canyon, Clinton asserted the privilege of executive proclamation to declare 1.7 million acres of desert landscape in southern Utah a national monument. By this proclamation, the Grand Staircase–Escalante National Monument, with a land surface equal to twice that of the state of Rhode Island, became the largest national monument in the United States.[1] After signing the proclamation, Clinton addressed the select crowd of supporters, which included Vice President Al Gore, Secretary of the Interior Bruce Babbitt, Colorado Governor Roy Romer, and actor Robert Redford. As the sole representative of Utah, Norma Matheson (the widow of Scott Matheson, the former governor of Utah) also attended the ceremony. "Our parents and grandparents saved the Grand Canyon for us," Clinton proclaimed. "Today, we will save the Grand Escalante Canyons and the Kaiparowits Plateau of Utah for our children." The proposed national monument, located west of the Colorado River and east of Bryce Canyon National Park, will set aside for preservation purposes some of Utah's most dramatic topographic formations known variously as the Grand Staircase, the Kaiparowits Plateau, and Escalante Canyon. In the president's estimation, the new federal preserve represents "a unique combination of archeological, paleontological, geological, and biological resources, all in a relatively unspoiled state."

It was neither unprecedented nor unanticipated that Clinton exercised the executive powers ascribed to his office under the provisions of the Antiquities Act of 1906 to set aside this vast parcel of scenic and spacious desert landscape for public use. The same legislation enabled President Theodore Roosevelt in 1908 to declare—without congressional approval—the Grand Canyon a national monument in his effort to protect the popular western attraction from industrial encroachment. Although perhaps motivated more by conservation-mindedness and less by political expediency, Presidents William Howard Taft and Woodrow Wilson established Zion National Monument in Utah (1919), Herbert Hoover protected California's Death Valley (1933), Franklin Delano Roosevelt declared Arizona's Organ Pipe Cactus National Monument (1937), and Jimmy Carter created a plethora of national parks in Alaska (1978). Clinton, however, employed the historical precedent in southern Utah no doubt to avert the congressional bipartisan gridlock that has consistently plagued his administration since he assumed office.[2]

Not until January 1999, more than two years after the Grand Canyon ceremony, did it become clear to the American public that Grand Staircase–Escalante National Monument was to be the cornerstone of a more comprehensive environmental policy proposed by the Clinton administration. In his 1999 State of the Union Address, Clinton announced a $1-billion Lands Legacy Initiative designed to expand federal protection of "critical" lands across America. This bold measure, which calls for an unprecedented $900-million contribution from the Land and Water Conservation Fund (LWCF), represents the largest ever single-year investment in the preservation of America's public lands. The new program's goal is to greatly expand federal efforts to save the nation's natural treasures as well as to provide significant new resources to states and communities for the protection of local green spaces. The president's request for a 125 percent increase over fiscal year 1999 funding not only underscores the federal government's commitment to preserve irreplaceable parcels of America's natural resources, but also Clinton's resolve to forge "a new conservation vision for the twenty-first century."

Under the proposed lands program, to be administered by the Department of the Interior, the president has called on Congress to grant permanent wilderness protection to more than five million acres of land distributed among several of America's existing national parks.[3] Notably,

Arches, Bryce Canyon, Canyonlands, and Capitol Reef national parks (all located in southern Utah) are among the federal parks enumerated in the president's outline. The president's bold, new initiative thus leaves little doubt that the Clinton administration in fall 1996 viewed the establishment of the Grand Staircase–Escalante National Monument as a central feature of its overall environmental plans for the year 2000.[4] Although the new lands proposal seems to have been received with widespread applause on the national level, Clinton's executive action in Utah amplified a centuries-old conflict in the West between land-use advocates and conservation proponents. The 1996 set-aside was an especially unwelcome blow to the residents of economically depressed communities in southwestern Utah. In a virulent denunciation of the proposed monument, Congressman James V. Hansen of Utah, chair of the House Subcommittee on National Parks, charged the Clinton administration with "doing something blatantly political in appeasing Eastern environmentalists just before the presidential elections." Hansen further chided, "He is ruining both the area and its economy, seizing public lands, violating private property rights, and hurting school children."[5] The latter criticism was a reference to the loss of tax revenues to Utah's public school system that resulted from the federal set-aside.

Residents of the town of Kanab, near the Utah-Arizona border, especially protested the president's announcement because they stood to benefit from jobs that the Andalex Resources Corporation had promised to create in the area. The Dutch-owned coal mining company previously had signed agreements with the state of Utah to mine upwards of seven billion tons of high-quality, bituminous coal reserves layered deep within the recesses of the Kaiparowits Plateau. Lamenting the loss of "the largest untapped energy reserve in the country," Andalex representative Dave Shaver admitted to southern Utah's irate citizens that the Clinton administration had negotiated a land-lease swap with Andalex similar to the arrangement it had mediated between the Crown Butte New World Mine and Yellowstone National Park earlier that summer. Under this agreement, Clinton directed the secretary of the interior to trade leases with Andalex in the proposed national monument area in exchange for "more accessible and commercially marketable federal resources of equal value elsewhere in the state."[6] Although Interior Department officials made it clear that Andalex would not be forced to relinquish its mining

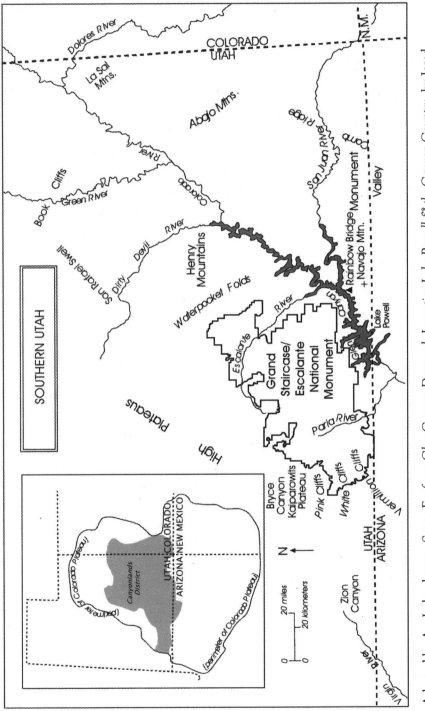

SOUTHERN UTAH

COLORADO
UTAH

Dolores River

La Sal Mtns.

Abajo Mtns.

Paria Ridge

Book Cliffs

Green River

San Juan River

Colorado River

San Rafael Swell

Dirty Devil River

Henry Mountains

Waterpocket Folds

Escalante River

Grand Staircase/ Escalante National Monument

Rainbow Bridge Monument + Navajo Mtn.

Lake Powell

Glen Canyon

Paria River

Bryce Canyon

Kaiparowits Plateau

Pink Cliffs

White Cliffs

Vermillion Cliffs

High Plateaus

Zion Canyon

Virgin River

UTAH
ARIZONA

N

0   20 miles

0   20 kilometers

Canyonlands District

UTAH COLORADO
ARIZONA NEW MEXICO

(level of Colorado Plateau)

(perimeter of Colorado Plateau)

N.M.

Adapted by Art Ireland, NPS, Santa Fe, from *Glen Canyon Dammed: Inventing Lake Powell & the Canyon Country*, by Jared Farmer. © The Arizona Board of Regents. Used by permission of the University of Arizona Press.

leases entirely, they also assured the Dutch-owned firm that the national monument designation would seriously impede any prospective mining activity.

MULTIPLE USE VERSUS PRESERVATION

In their effort to mollify critics of the newly created federal preserve, White House spokespersons argued that declaring a national monument was in many respects a compromise measure to the more restrictive wilderness area designation. Under the latter category all motorized vehicular traffic, road building, commercial resource extraction, and new mining activity are categorically prohibited. But the designation "national monument" allows limited multiple uses such as livestock grazing, hunting, and fishing. In that regard, management of the Grand Staircase–Escalante Canyon unit would continue under the Bureau of Land Management (BLM) rather than the National Park Service, thus minimizing the cost of converting state lands to national monument status. Under the terms of a rather unique partnership, grazing would continue under the auspices of the BLM, while hunting and fishing activities would become the function of state supervision. Residents of southwest Utah, however, were far from appeased. In their view federal appropriation of these state lands effectively translated to the loss of badly needed jobs.

It was no coincidence that Clinton selected the Grand Canyon as the forum to announce his proclamation. The famous chasm represents a direct physical link to the Antiquities Act of 1906. On a more symbolic level, the Grand Canyon also represents the battleground on which preservationists in general and the National Park Service in particular clashed with the mandates of a conservative Congress. Notably, Utah's Republican-led congressional delegation, consisting of Representatives Hansen and Enid Waldholtz coupled with Senators Orrin Hatch and Robert Bennett, have proven to be the most vigorous opponents of Clinton's environmental policies. Politically speaking, it appears that the Clinton administration may have determined there was little to lose in further antagonizing Utah voters with such a profound environmental statement on the eve of the presidential election.

How was it that Utah became the stage for the dramatic western "shoot-out" between state and federal leaders? First, the predominantly

Mormon state contains some of the most uniquely scenic and singularly colorful topography in the American West, indeed, in the entire United States. With the previous establishment of Zion (1919), Bryce Canyon (1928), and a multitude of other national parks over the years, the allure of Utah's canyon country holds a mysterious appeal to visitors from all over the world. Since 1990, the number of visitors who have traveled to Utah's eight national parks has totaled 25.7 million.[7] Second, the recent set-aside in no way represents the first time the executive branch has inflamed public sentiment in Utah over the issue of multiple use versus preservation. During the Kennedy administration then secretary of the interior Stewart Udall, an Arizona native and longtime devotee of recreational tourism in the West, proposed to incorporate one million acres of land near Moab in southeast Utah into a grand concept he labeled "The Golden Circle of National Parks." In spring 1961, while en route to Denver from the site of the proposed Glen Canyon Dam on the Utah-Arizona border, Udall became enthralled with the "scenic masterpiece" below him. "It was not deep and did not have the majesty of the Grand Canyon," the former secretary recalled years later in an interview, "but it had more variety."[8]

On his return to Washington, Udall recruited an entourage of political dignitaries—Senator Frank E. Moss and Congressman David S. King of Utah, Secretary of Agriculture Orville L. Freemen, and Assistant Director of the National Park Service George B. Hartzog Jr.—to join him on a rafting investigation of the canyon lands of southeast Utah. From the outset Udall challenged his colleagues to determine if they believed, as he did, that the area warranted nomination as America's newest national park. On a warm July evening, the secretary of the interior peered into a dim-lit campfire and outlined his plan for the promotion of tourism in the West. "The boundary of this remarkable region is a golden circle," Udall proclaimed, "encompassing the greatest concentration of scenic wonders to be found in the country, if not the world."[9]

The "golden circle" to which Udall referred was an imaginary line he had drawn around an area of southwestern states known as the Four Corners, linking them into a single, unified scenic region. Enclosed within that circle was a concentration of national parks unmatched anywhere in rugged beauty and cultural heritage. It was Udall's intent to set aside one million acres of Utah's prime canyon country as a national park to complete the circle already formed by Grand Canyon, Zion, Bryce, and Mesa Verde National Parks, in addition to the recently proposed Glen Canyon Dam National Recreation Area. Udall predicted that the "golden circle" would surely make the Four Corners "a region unsurpassed in tourist visitations." In the secretary's view the creation of still another park in Utah was "an investment in the economic future of the West." Interestingly, Udall (now retired and living in New Mexico) resuscitated his idea in a 1997 editorial published in the *Arizona Republic*; this time he profiled Indian reservation lands and renamed the area America's "scenic circle."[10]

Although fellow Democrats Moss and King enthusiastically embraced Udall's concept, Udall's desire to set aside one million acres of state lands as a national park rekindled long-standing animosities among contemporary western politicians. Udall's most strident detractors were Utah's senior Republican senator Wallace F. Bennett, and his GOP colleague in the state executive office, Governor George D. Clyde. More at issue than partisan rivalry was the recurring debate over multiple use versus preservation. It was common knowledge that Udall favored establishing the one-million-acre park as a scenic preserve, federally protected against mining, grazing, and all other commercial activity. This prospect was particularly unpalatable in a state that had a well-established reputation as one of the West's leading producers of consumptive energy resources.

Clyde, a political conservative and former economics professor who had helped guide Utah to industrial prominence, was the principal spokesperson for the multiple-use advocates. He criticized both the size of the proposed park and the federal government's commitment to single use. "What I object to," voiced the state executive, echoing the protests of hundreds of western politicians who avidly opposed a national conservation movement, "is locking up these areas before they have been surveyed and economically explored."[11] In a well-calculated countermove, Clyde proposed a compromise offer to the federal government. He agreed to establish a park, but with the size reduced from one million to 250,000 acres, the majority of which would remain under state, not federal, protection. Udall viewed the ploy as ridiculous and held fast to the one-million-acre proposal.

The overriding issue facing Udall—and to a lesser degree President John F. Kennedy—in 1961 was not radically different from that confronting Clinton and Babbitt today: At issue is the right of the federal government to impose its will, even in the cause of preservation, over the individual states. In retrospect, one can argue that Utah prevailed thirty-five years ago. After more than three years of acrimonious debate over Canyonlands, Udall relented and endorsed a 250,000-acre federally operated park. In a gesture that further mollified lingering concerns among the multiple-use faction, Moss amended the legislation to provide for a twenty-five-year phase-out period; time enough, Moss believed, to maximize any potential commercial uses in the park. On September 3, 1964, President Lyndon B. Johnson authorized the establishment of Canyonlands National Park.[12] Although not without certain concessions, Udall had his park, and with it the vital link to the "golden circle." In his fight to protect one million acres of Utah's premier canyon country, Udall reasoned that the millions of tourist dollars attracted into southern Utah in response to Canyonlands National Park would far surpass any potential income lost because of federal restrictions on future industrial use. Visitation statistics since the park's creation in 1964 seem to support this prediction. Although a comparatively new scenic attraction within the state, Canyonlands' 3.2 million visitations from 1985 to 1995 have contributed measurably to southeastern Utah's economy. Reflecting on that bitter struggle, Udall commented, "Teddy Roosevelt could have set the whole thing aside as a national monument in 1908 without anybody batting an eye, because nobody knew about it." Udall continued, "But in the 1960s, we had to fight our way through; there were many times when I wondered whether we would make it."[13]

THE THREAT TO CLOSE THE NATIONAL PARKS

Utah's initial reaction in the 1960s to the establishment of Canyonlands National Park was patently negative. It is no surprise, then, that the recent concerted assault by the state's congressional delegation against Clinton's long-term conservation planning for the West has been nothing short of defiance. Although not the most outspoken member of the state's delegation, Republican senator Robert Bennett now bears the standard of antifederalism and fiscal conservatism that his father, Senator Wallace Bennett, championed before him. Teamed with Senator Hatch, the most senior and highly respected member of the Utah contingent, Bennett has been candid in his opposition to the president and his administration. The most irrepressible adversary of Clinton's environmental pronouncement—and to a greater degree, to the entire national park system—was none other than the self-appointed defender of states rights in southern Utah, Congressman Hansen.

On January 4, 1995, Hansen cosponsored a bill introduced to the House by Representative Joel Hefley of Colorado and Congressman Bruce Vento of Minnesota. The bill, known as the National Park System Reform Act (House Resolution 260), proposed a comprehensive review of the national park system's then 368 units with the express purpose of identifying those that are "not worthy of the designation national park." Once passed, the law would require the director of the National Park Service to prepare within one year a plan including goals and objectives that would "carry the Park Service into the next century." The plan should specify the criteria used for the selection and retention of all of the system's urban and nonurban parks. Once elaborated, the Park Service must identify in a report to Congress "all units of the System that do not conform with the revised park criteria from the new plan."[14]

In his capacity as chair of the House Subcommittee on National Parks and the second ranking Republican on the House Committee on Resources, Hansen's personal contribution to H.R. 260 was the call to establish a National Park System Review Commission. The eleven-member, politically appointed commission would, subject to data compiled in the National Park Service director's report to Congress, recommend specific units of the park system to be designated for closure, privatization, or sale. The only exclusions, promised Hansen, would be an estimated fifty-four units, the so-called crown jewels of the system: the Grand Canyon, Yellowstone, and Yosemite National Parks. Amazingly, some of the nation's most revered historical monuments (Independence Hall, the Statue of Liberty, Mount Rushmore) and national icons (the Lincoln, Jefferson, and Washington Memorials) were not exempt from scrutiny.[15]

Critics of H.R. 260 were understandably indignant at the suggestion that an appointed commission, not the full Congress (who had for the most part been responsible for their creation), should determine the value of the nation's parks to the American public. One editorial in the *Salt Lake Tribune*, Hansen's home-state newspaper, likened the proposed parks commission to the controversial Base Realignment and Closure Commission that had been created to determine the peacetime use of military bases across the country. "National parks were created for purposes of preservation and posterity," the editorial argued, "not for the ever-shifting requirements of national defense." Presumably, the parks had an unchanging value and thus "should not be exposed to the whims of an independent commission." Acknowledging that not all units of the National Park Service met the standards of a Yellowstone or a Gettysburg battlefield, the editorial stressed that Congress still retained its authority to decommission a park, citing congressional deauthorization of the John F. Kennedy Center for the Performing Arts in 1994 as a prime example.[16]

Although some journalists supported the notion that the National Park Service undergo a strenuous self-examination, most agreed that it made little sense to set up a mechanism for park closure before all methods to increase park revenues were exhausted. "National parks are not at all like military bases," some concluded. "They need more creative ways to stay open." In effect, critics of the Hefley-Hansen panacea for the ills of the national park system shifted the blame to a parsimonious, Republican-dominated Congress. For example, the New York Times argued that in the past twenty years, Congress—not the National Park Service—had established more than eighty new parks while refusing to give the Interior Department enough money to do its job.[17] The Miami-Herald echoed support for the Times' accusations. The Republican budget resolution scheduled for debate that summer, noted the Florida daily, proposed to cut the National Park Service's annual budget request by 21 percent for fiscal year 1996. At this rate, the service would have 36 percent less money to maintain its parks by the year 2002. Meanwhile, park visitations were expected to increase from 267 million in 1995 to an estimated 300 million by the turn of the century. "The real culprit," judged the New York Times, "is Congress." Echoing the charge to the National Park Service to leave its parks "unimpaired for the enjoyment of future generations," the news media clamored, "Congress wrote the language, and Congress needs to clean up the mess it created."[18]

Not surprisingly, Hansen rebutted the media's challenge to his parks closure idea. He stood firm in his objection to the manner in which the Park Service evaluated its prospective and existing national parks. In fact,

Hansen cited numerous examples in which the public expressed skepticism toward the national park system. Foremost among the questionable parks was Steamtown National Historic Park in Pennsylvania, the subject of widespread disapproval for having no obvious historical link to the railroad industry. Others denounced Wolf Trap Farm in Virginia as more of a venue for the performing arts than a site of outstanding historical significance. Santa Monica National Recreation Area near Los Angeles, one more example, had the reputation of a city park rather than the distinction of a national preserve. Only a handful of federal units, in Hansen's estimation, aspired to the true definition of a national park; most of those, he acknowledged, appeared to be in serious financial distress.

Discussion of the woeful financial condition of the national park system was a frequent topic among the leading newspapers. According to the *New York Times*, expenditures needed to repair roads, sewer, and water facilities at the Grand Canyon alone were estimated at $350 million. A conservative estimate for the entire national park system, including perennial repairs to its twenty-two thousand historic buildings, was a staggering $4 billion. Clearly, the Park Service's 1995 budget allocation of $972 million, which barely offset the agency's operating costs, seemed minuscule when compared with the parks' horrendous maintenance backlog. Dismal financial prospects such as these, Hansen concluded, justified his plan to reduce the total number of national parks from 368 to a mere 54 premier parks. The money saved from the closure or privatization of more than 300 "less popular" parks, he persuaded, could be applied toward the operation and maintenance of the higher profile units.[19]

THE NATIONAL PARK SERVICE UNDER SIEGE

The most persuasive voice in opposition to the Hefley-Vento-Hansen rationale was that of Representative Bill Richardson of New Mexico, who resigned his House seat to accept appointments to the United Nations and the Department of Energy. An ardent conservationist, Richardson expressed dismay that the focus of H.R. 260 appeared to be more on park closure than park reform. First, he contradicted the notion that the proposed legislation would save money. "We could deauthorize all of the 30-plus units designated since 1980," Richardson said, "yet we would save less than 2 percent of the NPS's annual operation and maintenance budget." Further, he challenged Hansen's concept of the fifty-four park exemption, noting that many of the country's most treasured historical landmarks would be in jeopardy of decommissioning or closure. "What makes the Statue of Liberty any less worthy than Yellowstone or Grand Canyon National Parks?" Richardson queried. Before his departure from Congress, he prevailed upon his colleagues to strike out sections 102 and 103 of the current proposal, which dealt with management review and the Park Closure Commission. Toward this end, Richardson sought to replace the adversarial document with a new bill intended to generate increased revenue for the national park system through concession reform and entrance-fee legislation.[20]

Bent on reforming the system, not gutting it, Richardson introduced H.R. 2181 in August 1995, appropriately named the Common Sense National Park System Reform Act, as a countermeasure to what had come to be known simply as the "Hansen Bill." The legislation proposed to increase park entrance fees from the standard $3 per carload—the same admission required since 1916—to a modest $10. More substantive was the language that required park concessionaires to contribute a portion of their annual gross receipts beyond the nominal 2.8 percent into a Park Improvement Fund, the proceeds to be expended only on long-neglected repairs within the parks.[21]

H.R. 260 came up for a vote before the floor of the House on September 18, 1995. The proposal resoundingly failed passage by a vote of 231 opposed to 180 in favor. The Utah delegation predictably voted along partisan lines; Republicans Hansen and Waldholtz voted yes, while Lloyd Orton, the state's lone Democrat, dissented. For all of its defects, H.R. 260 did have some redeeming qualities. First, it articulated the need for the National Park Service to standardize the criteria by which the agency designates its new units. In an official Interior Department news release posted the following day, Babbitt acknowledged the wisdom of at least this aspect of the reform bill: "I believe that there should be good criteria for establishing new national parks." He further pledged, "I would be willing to work with Congress to ensure the quality of future additions."[22] More important, the prospect of mandatory closure of our national parks rallied the American people to their defense. The public's challenge to

Congress to seek creative methods that promised some measure of financial solvency within the national park system inspired more effective solutions toward that end. A multiyear program that began in 1996 to increase entrance fees in the parks with the explicit intent of returning 80 percent of all collections toward capital improvements and routine maintenance was clearly the bill's most positive influence.[23]

Hansen's Park Closure Commission, however, was a bad idea that galvanized public opinion against the entire piece of legislation. In presuming that only 54 of 368 units administered by the National Park Service were worthy of recognition, Hansen effectively declared open season on all urban parks, military battlefields, recreation areas, seashores, and memorials. The aftermath would have resulted in the preservation of a generic national park system with no regard for regional or ethnic distinctions—in effect, a social and political regression to pre–civil rights America. More disturbing, it appears that Hansen's insistence that park closures would produce a surplus of money to be spent on the needs of the premier parks had no foundation. Babbitt questioned how Congress, on the one hand, could seriously consider closing national parks to raise money, when in fact it had just that month appropriated upwards of $50 million for line-item construction projects that had not been assigned a high priority in the National Park Service's fiscal 1996 plan. Still, with the defeat of H.R. 260, it appeared to its detractors and to the American public that, for the moment at least, they had forestalled an ominous threat to our national patrimony.[24]

The reprieve was short-lived. Scarcely two months had elapsed since the defeat of H.R. 260 when the National Park Service faced yet another dilemma—one that threatened to touch off a national crisis between federal and state authorities. Failure of the Parks Closure Bill notwithstanding, the Republican-led Congress was still mindful of its pledge to balance the federal budget through strenuous cutbacks in annual appropriations. Democratic resistance to Republican parsimony, however, resulted in a seemingly irreconcilable budgetary impasse. Although partisan bickering adversely affected all federal agencies, the National Park Service seemed especially hard hit. On November 15, 1995, NPS director Roger Kennedy responded to the congressional stalemate with the temporary closure of all national parks. Congress countered with a continuing resolution, but the measure expired after only one month with no viable appropriations resolution. Frustrated NPS administrators furloughed most of their employees, resulting in a systemwide park closure during the Christmas holiday season.

State reaction to the first-ever national park shutdown was varied, but nowhere was the response more hostile than in the West. Informed that Grand Canyon National Park superintendent Rob Arnberger had announced the park's closure, Republican governor Fife Symington of Arizona called the action "unacceptable" and vowed to use "whatever power at his disposal to keep the park open." In a bold measure to champion states rights and rescue Arizona's tourism industry from economic calamity, Symington alerted the National Guard and the state police to resist the park's closure. On the morning of November 17, Symington and his thirteen-vehicle military convoy arrived at the entrance to the Grand Canyon. When Arnberger asked, "Would you like to visit the park?" The Arizona governor replied, "I'm not here to visit, I'm here to take over." After the initial crisis subsided, a Symington spokesperson admitted that a hostile takeover was never the intent. "We wanted them [the National Park Service] to take us very seriously," the aide explained.[25]

Whatever his intent, Symington's theatrics nearly caused what the *Salt Lake Tribune* labeled a "constitutional crisis." Not since 1962, when President Kennedy threatened to federalize the National Guard in response to Governor Ross Barnett's refusal to admit James Meredith to the University of Mississippi, had a state executive publicly challenged the federal government's authority. Although some criticized the National Park Service as having overreacted to the Arizona governor's antics, Interior Department officials were especially mindful of the tragedy that had befallen federal employees in Oklahoma City just one month earlier. The federal government, it seemed, could ill afford complacency. Although tensions were eventually resolved without serious confrontation, the incident at the Grand Canyon underscored the degree to which some states were prepared to assert their rights over the federal government's will. Perhaps more evident, the public's indignation at the temporary closure of the national park system, although for the most part not as hostile as that demonstrated in northern Arizona, underscored the economic importance of the national parks not only to local but to regional economies as well.[26]

CONCLUSION

Throughout the history of the West there has been a long and often contentious relationship between states rights proponents and the federal
government. Small wonder that the battle lines of the modern West have
been drawn in the breathtakingly scenic canyon country of southern Utah
and northern Arizona. For these reasons the venue for Clinton's pronouncement of the Grand Staircase–Escalante National Monument was
carefully chosen. First, the signing ceremony took place in the home state
of Secretary of the Interior Babbitt, to whom fell the principal responsibility to mediate the potential clash between the Park Service and the state
of Arizona. Second, when placed in historical context, the Grand Canyon
epitomizes the canon of federal executive privilege as executed on numerous occasions in the cause of environmental conservation. Finally, that
Clinton announced the nation's newest national monument nearly one
year to the day that Hansen's park closure bill had failed to pass the House
vote was, in my judgment, more than pure coincidence.

To the dismay of multiple-use advocates in general and the Utah congressional delegation in particular, 1.7 million acres of land once designated for coal mining has been removed from the public domain to be
preserved and protected for generations to come. In turn, this newest federal unit will anchor the billion-dollar Lands Legacy Initiative recently
enunciated by Clinton. In summer 1999 the national park system, which
nearly fell prey to conservative, antifederal legislation, will for the first
time reap the monetary benefits of the Recreational Fee Demonstration
Program. Eligible parks have submitted requests by the hundreds for long
overdue funding to address maintenance problems.

The Recreational Fee Demonstration Program provides the National
Park Service with some independent means to restructure itself financially. Conversely, the determination of Congress to downsize the federal
government to improve government effectiveness has left the nation's
parks hard pressed to satisfy the demands that have resulted from escalat-
ing visitations. There have been few new hires in the National Park Service since it emerged "reorganized" in October 1998. By the NPS's own
admission, the current ratio of park rangers to park visitors is one for every
eighty thousand campers and hikers. Recreational Fee Demonstration
money may provide some relief to this imbalance as well. It is hoped that

fees generated by the parks for expenditure in the parks will eventually make funds that are not specifically designated for maintenance and repair available for personnel recruitment.[27]

If the optimistic predictions of Clinton's Lands Legacy Initiative are a prelude to the conservation practices of the future, federal and state officials have little choice but to cooperate more like partners and to behave less like protesters. One recent example, which may illustrate the direction of parks management in the next century, is the manner in which the National Park Service collaborated with the Oklahoma State Historical Society and the Southern Cheyenne-Arapaho Tribe to recommend that Congress establish the Washita Battlefield National Historic Site. The Omnibus Bill that Clinton signed shortly after his reelection in November 1996 included the new federal park.[28] It appears that congressional reluctance to create additional parks can thus be mollified somewhat by the promise of state and federal cooperation in their management. Perhaps the example set in Cheyenne, Oklahoma, will serve as a model for Utah to work in consort with and not in opposition to the Bureau of Land Management and its implementation of Grand Staircase–Escalante National Monument.

NOTES

1. This new federal unit is more than double the size of the nation's next largest national monument, Alaska's six-hundred-thousand-acre Cape Krusenstern National Monument.

2. Richard Benedetto and Linda Kanamine, "President Protects Utah Lands," *Arizona Republic,* September 19, 1996, pp. A1, A3; Ben Moffett, "Grand Staircase–Escalante National Monument Created under Antiquities Authority," *Mountain Time,* National Park Service, Intermountain Field Area Newsletter, p. 1; Richard West Sellars, "The Roots of National Park Management: Evolving Perceptions of the Park Service's Mandate," *Journal of Forestry* 90 (January): 16–17.

3. Other existing parks outlined in the president's initiative include Big Bend, Crater Lake, Glacier, Grand Teton, Rocky Mountain, Yellowstone, Great Smoky Mountains, and Cumberland Gap National Parks, in addition to most of the country's national seashores and wildlife refuges.

4. President Bill Clinton, State of the Union Address, January 19, 1999; Roger Schlickeisen, "Reaction to the State of the Union Address by the Environmental Community," *Mountain Time*, National Park Service, January 20, 1999, p. 1.

5. Benedetto and Kanamine, "President Protects Utah Lands," p. A1.

6. Ibid.

7. Visitation statistics to national parks in the Southwest courtesy of the U.S. Department of the Interior, National Park Service, *Statistical Abstract, 1985–95*, in Colorado Plateau Forum Research Committee (CPFRC), *The Devil's Bargain: Community and Tourism on the Colorado Plateau* (Flagstaff: Northern Arizona University, Department of Tourism and Visitor Services, 1997); Benedetto and Kanamine, "President Protects Utah Lands," p. A3; Barbara J. Morehouse, *A Place Called Grand Canyon: Contested Geographies* (Tucson: University of Arizona Press, 1996), especially 39–48.

8. Typescript, Stewart L. Udall interview with W. W. Moses, April 7, 1970, John F. Kennedy Library, 90, 103 (hereafter cited as the Stewart Udall interview).

9. Udall's comments on the "golden circle" as cited in George B. Hartzog Jr., "The Golden Circle Concept," in Stewart L. Udall Papers, Box 156, File 4 (hereafter cited as the SLU Papers); Weldon F. Heald, "Bold Plan to Save the Canyonlands," *Desert Magazine*, April 1962, p. 17.

10. Arthur R. Gómez, *Quest for the Golden Circle: The Four Corners and the Metropolitan West* (1944; paperback rpt., Lawrence: University Press of Kansas, 2000), 119–21; Stewart L. Udall, "Scenic Circle Needs Regional Marketing," *Arizona Republic*, May 4, 1997, pp. C1-C3.

11. Governor Clyde's comments as cited in the *Moab Times Independent*, August 10, 1961, p. 1.

12. Gómez, *Quest for the Golden Circle*, 141–48; U.S. Congress, Senate Committee on Interior and Insular Affairs, *Proposed Canyonlands National Park in Utah*, 87th Cong., 2d sess., S. 2387, 1962,1–5; Clyde to Lowell D. Blanton, August 4, 1961; Udall to Clyde, December 1, 1961, in SLU Papers, Box 156, File 1.

13. Visitation statistics for Canyonlands National Park from 1985–95 in CPFRC, *Devil's Bargain*, 20; Udall's comments as cited in Udall interview with Moses, April 7, 1970, JFK Library, 104–5.

14. House Subcommittee on National Parks, *National Park System Reform Act of 1995: Hearings on H.R. 260*, 104th Cong., 1st sess.; House, Congressman Joel Hefley of Colorado speaking for the National Park System Reform Act of 1995 to

the Subcommittee on National Parks, *Congressional Record*, 104th Cong., 1st sess., January 4, 1995, H9084–9086.

15. Congressman Bill Richardson of New Mexico speaking against the National Park System Reform Act of 1995, *Congressional Record*, 104th Cong., 1st sess., January 4, 1995, H9087.

16. "Don't Close the National Parks," *Salt Lake Tribune*, May 6, 1995, pp. A1, A7.

17. "Parks in Peril," *New York Times*, July 4, 1995.

18. "America for Sale," *St. Louis Post-Dispatch*, July 17, 1995, p. A1; "Congressional Budget Cuts and Anti-Government Attitudes Threaten America's Heritage," *Miami Herald*, June 27, 1995, pp. A1-A3; for visitation projections to the national parks by the year 2000, see Bill Conrad, "National Park Service Attendance and U.S. Population Growth: A Brief History and Projections," paper presented at the George Wright Society Bi-annual Conference, Albuquerque, N.M., March 1997, 4–5.

19. "GOP Readies Land Grab of Our Parks," *Las Vegas Sun*, August 27, 1995, p. 1; "National Parks Deserve Help to Protect Nation's Heritage," *Wichita Eagle*, August 25, 1995, pp. B5-B6; Hefley, *Congressional Record*, H9084; "Parks in Peril," *New York Times*, July 4, 1995; Randal O'Toole, "The National Pork Service," *Forbes*, November 1995, 10–13; "Grand Canyon in Slump," *Arizona Republic*, July 18, 1996, pp. A1, A5.

20. Dissenting comments of Representative Bill Richardson in House Subcommittee on National Parks, *Reform Act of 1995 National Park System: Hearings on H.R. 260*, 104th Cong., 1st sess., June 7, 1995; "Parks in Peril," *New York Times*, July 4, 1995; "Preserving America's Past," *St. Louis Post-Dispatch*, August 14, 1995, pp. A1, A6.

21. "Parks in Peril," *New York Times*, July 4, 1995; "Preserving America's Past," *St. Louis Post-Dispatch*, August 14, 1995.

22. Secretary of the Interior Babbitt's comments as cited in "Statement on the Failure to Pass House Bill to Create a National Park Closure Commission," Department of the Interior, News Release, September 19, 1995.

23. Jeff Phillips, "Can We Save Our National Parks?" *Sunset Magazine*, June 1996, pp. 1–7; "Interior Department Announces Test Project to Fund Needed Improvements on Public Lands," Department of the Interior, Press Release, November 26, 1996. For the complete text of the Recreational Fee Demonstration Program, see *Omnibus Consolidated Rescissions and Appropriations Act of 1996*, Public Law 104–208.

24. "Americans Vote for Upkeep of Parks," *Maysville Advertiser*, September 16, 1996; "Commercial Tour Vehicles Fees to Increase Under 3-Year Recreation Fee Demonstration Program," Department of the Interior, Press Release, January 14, 1997.

25. Pat Flannery, Clint Williams, and Jeff Barker, "U.S. Feared Symington Coup to Keep Grand Canyon Open," *Arizona Republic*, February 12, 1996, pp. A1, A6; Christopher Smith, "White House Was Ready to Federalize Arizona Guard: Constitutional Crisis at the Canyon," *Salt Lake Tribune*, February 11, 1996, pp. A1, A12-A13.

26. Associated Press, "Report: Canyon Effort Courted National Crisis," *Scottsdale Progress Tribune*, February 11, 1996, pp. A1, A3, A5.

27. Phillips, "Can We Save Our National Parks?" 9; statement of Denis P. Galvin, Acting Director, National Park Service, before the Subcommittee on National Parks, Historic Preservation and Recreation, Senate Committee on Recreation Use Fees, Special Park Uses, and the Recreation Fee Demonstration Program Implemented by the National Park Service, as cited in *Mountain Time*, June 19, 1997, pp. 1–6.

28. The Washita Battlefield National Historic Site was established by Public Law 104–333 on November 12, 1996. The new federal unit is "a symbol of the struggle of the Southern Great Plains tribes to maintain control of their traditional use areas." A second objective in creating the park is to "provide opportunities for American Indian groups including the Cheyenne-Arapaho Tribe to be involved in the formulation of plans and educational programs for the national historic site," in Washita Battlefield National Historic Site Briefing Paper, Department of the Interior, National Park Service, Intermountain Support Office, Santa Fe, N.M.,1997, pp. 1–2.

Owning It All in Alaska

The Political Power of a Rhetorical Paradigm

STEPHEN HAYCOX

O n a warm summer night in 1958, civic leaders, businesspeople, and politicians took turns putting a torch to an enormous bonfire that workers had been assembling all day. At a park along the southern edge of downtown Anchorage, under a slightly overcast but near-daylight sky because of the "midnight sun," twenty-five thousand people (a third of the town's residents) stood about cheering and talking animatedly. The air was electric with energy and excitement. The flammables—warehouse pallets, cardboard boxes, and the like—rose nearly three stories before being ignited. Red, white, and blue bunting hung from office buildings adjacent to the park, and nearby a military band played snappy, martial music and some of the popular tunes of the day. Several portable concession stands sold hot dogs and Coke. A National Guard howitzer crew fired off forty-nine rounds, and forty-nine civilian aircraft flew over as the fire burned. Fireworks boomed late into the night.[1] But it was not the Fourth of July these Alaskans were celebrating. It was June 30, and these elated Alaskans were celebrating passage of the Alaska statehood bill in the U.S. Senate; Alaska would become the forty-ninth state in the union.

THE PARADIGM

Alaskan statehood was the culmination of a long and difficult struggle. Alaskans had overcome immense odds; their hard-won victory had never been assured.[2] As in many western territories before Congress enabled their statehood, in Alaska the issue was the people's right to free access to the fruits of economic exploitation of the region's natural resources. Those contesting that right were considered the enemy. Both the federal government and the canned-salmon industry earned that label during the territorial period, but the federal government surpassed private enterprise as the more egregious, for its history in the area was longer and its power greater. Not only did the public lands agencies seek to retain jurisdiction over as much acreage as possible, but even the military opposed statehood, viewing the territory as critical in Cold War defense.[3] The conservative Congresses of the 1950s would have happily turned over large sections of the territory to residents and investors, but the question of financing the new state constituted a significant impediment, one for which statehood advocates had no satisfactory answer. Traditional extractive industries in Alaska—primarily fish, some gold, and pulp timber—would not generate sufficient tax revenues. Nor would oil, which had recently been discovered along the shore of Cook Inlet, but not in quantities that could pay for statehood.

To overcome these obstacles, Alaskans needed a strategy, a battle plan that could unify territorial residents and at the same time mobilize national public opinion. Several years before the vote in Congress, a particularly astute politician had worked out such a plan, a clever if perhaps obvious one. He was Ernest Gruening, an old Progressive, a liberal Democrat who served as Alaska's appointed territorial governor from 1939 to 1953.[4] A graduate of Harvard Medical School, Gruening had become managing editor of the liberal weekly *The Nation*. Brought to Washington, D.C., by Franklin Roosevelt in 1933, he had been exiled by Secretary of the Interior Harold Ickes to Alaska in 1939 because he was viewed as too independent and thus unreliable as a team player. Once there, he became an ardent supporter of statehood.[5]

Gruening began constructing his plan by asking what would be the value of statehood. Aside from tracing to completion the familiar pattern for new communities in the American West, fulfilling a traditional ritual, the obvious benefit would be independence. From the time there had been any appreciable number of non-Native immigrants in the territory (that is, since the Klondike gold rush), Alaska residents had resented regulation and had chafed at the federal government's heavy hand and the monopolistic power of absentee corporate control over the extraction of their natural resources. In the 1910s the Guggenheim Corporation's Alaska Syndicate had developed the only viable railroad in the territory, on which transportation to the interior was highly dependent. In the political rhetoric of the time, this monopoly was seen as an example of corporate "interests" who held the "little guy" hostage to whatever freight rates they wished to charge.[6]

The Guggenheims soon were followed by a government "lord," the conservationist Gifford Pinchot. Pinchot had inspired Theodore Roosevelt to withdraw Alaska coal lands from public entry, thereby, Alaskans were convinced, increasing substantially the cost of residence and development. The famous Ballinger-Pinchot controversy that grew out of the coal dispute made Alaska momentarily visible during the 1912 presidential election.[7] But, despite this visibility, Alaskans continued to pay higher coal prices. Then Congress passed the Jones Act, the Maritime Act of 1920. This legislation mandated that ships carrying goods between Alaska and the contiguous states must be of American registry, which was much more expensive than using Canadian or Panamanian carriers.[8] In a test of the act in 1922, the U.S. Supreme Court found that although Maine could be exempted from the act to trade with Nova Scotia, Alaska could not have an exemption to trade with British Columbia. The reasoning was that Alaska was only a territory, and the Constitution does not bar congressional discrimination against territories, only states.[9]

The principal nemesis for Alaskans, however, was the canned-salmon industry, with its notorious fish traps, another monopolization of an extractive enterprise by private, absentee corporate power. Industry appetite for Alaska salmon threatened to exhaust and destroy the resource, and Alaskans seemed powerless to prevent it. The 1924 White Act somewhat mitigated this exploitation by guaranteeing a 50 percent escapement from the fishery and setting in place an enforcement mechanism.[10] But residents believed that the industry continued to rape the territory through government collusion with the packers, manifested in limited enforcement budgets and fish agents who were willing to do favors for their corporate clients.[11]

There were other instances of regulation and restriction, and in all of them the federal government played some role. During World War II, for example, when Alaska became an active theater of war, residents learned that they had to apply for identification cards ("green cards") from the Immigration and Naturalization Service when they left the territory for Seattle, Corvallis, or elsewhere.[12] The regulation persisted until several years after the war. In typical western fashion the Alaskans resented and railed against federal power while at the same time demanding money, succor, services, exceptions, and privileges. Perhaps the most significant example of this was the financially hopeless Alaska Railroad, which was built by the federal government and operated as an alternative to the Guggenheim railroad, the only such example of full federal largesse in the American West.[13] The Alaskan residents' relationship with industry had always been tempered by a realization of direct economic dependence; if the industry were to shut down, residents would be unable to sustain themselves without the corporate jobs and tax base.

So Gruening's battle plan was to focus the statehood struggle wholly on the federal government's villainy and to raise that villain to such visibility that no one could miss it. Gruening followed the grand western tradition of laying all of Alaska's ills, real and imagined, at the federal government's door. Alaskans were thwarted in achieving their full potential, he declared, frustrated in creating a productive, democratic, responsible society by the restrictive, overweening, and arrogant power of the federal government. Gruening titled his keynote address to the Alaska constitutional convention, held on November 9, 1955, "Let Us End American Colonialism." The Alaska Statehood Committee printed his remarks for statewide distribution.

In cataloging Alaska's grievances in this address, Gruening mimicked the Declaration of Independence. "For the purpose of 1955," Gruening wrote, "he" in the Declaration, meaning the reference to King George III, could be changed to "it," meaning the federal government. Topping his list of complaints, Gruening wrote that "it" had refused "for some forty years assent to the following most wholesome and necessary laws," and then he appended ten pages of abuses. Gruening concluded that Alaska was "no less a colony than were those thirteen colonies along the Atlantic seaboard in 1775."[14] His comparison represented the creative rhetoric familiar in western history. To drive home his point, Gruening wrote a marvelous polemic on the theme of federal villainy in Alaska. Called *The State of Alaska*, it was published by Random House in 1954, four years before statehood passed in Congress; the book purported to be an analytical, objective history of the territory.[15] Calling on federal legislative history, Gruening included a myriad of data on territorial political and economic development. But federal culpability was the organizing and interpretive principle throughout. The section headings alone convey the comprehensive character of his approach: "The Era of Total Neglect" (1867–84), "The Era of Flagrant Neglect" (1884–98), "The Era of Mild but Unenlightened Interest" (1898–1912), "The Era of Indifference and Unconcern" (1912–33), and finally "The Era of Growing Awareness" (1933–54).[16]

The book was a stunning achievement. It authenticated the case for villainy and called for independence as the antidote. Of course, it was a politician's history. Gruening omitted the fact that a federal presence had been established from the beginning of Alaska's territorial history, immediately following the purchase, as the army and navy, customs agents, special investigators for the Indian Office and the Treasury Department, surveyors for the Coastal Survey, and a host of annual visitors from other agencies combed the territory for information.[17] He repeated the canard about the unpopularity of the purchase, the Alaska Treaty having passed the Senate despite a few newspaper editors labeling it "Seward's Folly" and "Walrussia."[18]

Gruening also missed the pattern of federal response to each substantial increase in non-Native population, and he minimized the Progressive initiative to mitigate the power of absentee capital investment.[19] Though he wrote at length of the salmon fishery's exploitation by Seattle and California packers, Gruening included virtually nothing of the infusion of federal aid during the Great Depression, which protected both the Native and immigrant populations from economic peril.[20] And although he wrote of the censorship and other burdens visited on the territory's residents during World War II, Gruening wrote little of the period's massive economic impact and the ensuing Cold War.[21] The book *State of Alaska*, therefore, was a rhetorical paradigm that grossly misrepresented the Alaskan past, using a highly selective rendering of the historical record to bolster a specific agenda.

But because few Alaskans actually knew much about their history, perhaps because of the high rate of transience among the immigrant population and poor education in Native communities, the book became the bible of the statehood movement. It provided a unifying principle around which all statehood advocates could rally, an argument to which all apparently could relate. The Alaskans put together a successful national campaign around the book's theme. This was especially useful in a Republican era, with the national leadership emphasizing the need to diminish the federal government's role in American life. Indeed, the Alaskans eventually overcame great odds, persuading Congress to vote for Alaska statehood in the summer of 1958.

STATEHOOD REALITIES

Strangely, there was not much discussion during the statehood campaign about what Alaska statehood would actually mean. Independence, of course, but independence to do what? Only two ideas emerge from the literature: to design and administer an efficient and just state government, and to free Alaska's resources for development.[22] A meeting in Fairbanks during the winter of 1955–56 provided a glimpse of the autonomy the Alaskans hoped statehood would bring. At the meeting, where they benefited from the advice of consultants from across the nation, fifty-five delegates drafted a progressive state constitution, which was approved by a two-to-one margin in a territory-wide election in April 1956.[23] In the same election, voters approved a proposition calling for the abolition of fish traps by a margin of five to one.[24] Although the vote was only advisory, the Interior Department soon implemented the proposition.

Gruening knew how difficult economic development would be in Alaska because there were so few resources: fish, minerals (excluding oil), and forest products. This understanding led him to suppress Native land rights in the 1940s, despite his commitment to Native justice, by opening the eighteen-million-acre Tongass National Forest to timber sales and pulp production.[25] State land title would be critical to resource development, Gruening believed, for it would provide the power both to nurture resource development and then to tax it. Title was an integral part of Gruening's paradigm, which became the ruling political rhetoric of Alaska. Almost all of Alaska politics since statehood has been cast in these terms, no matter how strange the fit.

The Alaska Statehood Act provided a grant of 103.35 million acres from the unappropriated territorial public domain (28 percent of the total land area, but larger than the total land area of California) in state lands.[26]

There was no stipulation regarding land use. The state constitution, however, provided that state resources should be managed in such a way as to benefit all citizens equally. The resources article declared that it was the policy of the state "to encourage settlement of its land and the development of its resources by making them available for maximum use consistent with the public interest.[27] The statehood act officially created the state on January 3, 1959, and state resource officers immediately set about selecting those lands to which the state wanted title. The act addressed the problem of financing state administration by stipulating that 90 percent of all federal mineral lease revenue be returned directly to the state.[28] The framers anticipated that this would be sufficient for the purpose. The act also included a provision dealing with Native lands, which had yet to be identified. Alaskan residents explicitly disclaimed any right or title to lands that might be held in Native title.[29]

The act also provided for a territory-wide plebiscite on whether citizens accepted the act as written. On August 26, 1958, voters overwhelmingly approved the proposition, six to one.[30] With statehood, then, Alaska was ostensibly independent, or at least autonomous, and apparently poised for development, whatever that might mean in practice. Initially, events following statehood seemed to bear out Gruening's proposition that statehood would free Alaska from federal power. By the 1950s several Native villages in southeast Alaska operated their own fish traps, which the Interior Department had permitted to continue to function when it banned all non-Native-owned traps in 1956. Soon after statehood became official, the state attorney general moved against the Native traps. Unsuccessful in lower courts, the state eventually prevailed in the U.S. Supreme Court.[31]

Alaskans soon learned that such victories would be rare, however. The disclaimer to Native lands and the grant of 103.35 million acres to the state represented a contradiction that threw Alaska into turmoil. This confusion had not been anticipated: not only had Native lands not yet been identified, but there were no traditional Indian reservations in the territory, and there were few recognized tribes.[32] In January 1959 the state began to make its land selections. One of the first parcels was two million acres on the Arctic Coast in the vicinity of Prudhoe Bay, between the naval petroleum reserve and the newly created Arctic National Wildlife Range, lands that seemed geologically promising for oil exploration.[33]

To facilitate the new state's hopes for economic development, the Interior Department moved quickly to convey title to selected lands. The result was chaos. Natives immediately began to protest that the lands being selected were lands subject to Native title, based not only on current occupation but on the basis of aboriginal title, which was inherent in all lands that had once been used by Natives, even if currently abandoned, unless such title had been explicitly extinguished by Congress.[34] The legal division of the Bureau of Indian Affairs and the newly established Alaska Legal Services agency provided research and legal assistance. Meanwhile, proceeding with its own agenda, the state began the process of selling oil leases on the North Slope, arguing that the absence of Native villages in the area of the sales made moot the issue of Native title. By 1966 the total acreage in Alaska under Native protest exceeded the total acreage in the state, due to overlapping claims.[35] Native claims threatened resource development everywhere in Alaska outside of the southeast panhandle.[36]

Acknowledging the growing confusion in Alaska, and seeking to protect Native interests, Secretary of the Interior Stewart Udall in 1966 imposed an executive injunction on the land selection process, effectively freezing all further applications for title to the public domain in Alaska.[37] The "freeze" would continue until a resolution to the claims conundrum was forthcoming. In an attempt to force a resolution, Senator Henry M. Jackson of Washington charged a presidential committee formed after the 1964 great Alaska earthquake, its work on reconstruction then virtually complete, to study the claims question and recommend a solution. In 1968 the committee published its report, *Alaska Natives and the Land*, which advanced a "framework for decision."[38] Native title should be confirmed in forty million acres of traditionally occupied land, and compensation should be paid for extinguishment of title to the remainder of Alaska. With the addition of a corporate structure for investment and distribution of the compensatory funds, this would be the pattern for the 1971 Alaska Native Claims Settlement Act. It is noteworthy that the framework did not envision the development of much Native land. Instead, the reason for the land grant was protection of the Native way of life. Residents of many of the 208 Native villages identified in the act still lived primarily by subsistence (and still do today), though in a modern context.[39]

Then, in January 1968, Atlantic Richfield Oil Company made the first commercial oil strike on state-leased land at Prudhoe Bay. Geologists estimated the field to contain fifteen billion barrels, the largest find in the history of North America. The formidable yet environmentally delicate nature of Arctic ice mandated construction of a hot oil, overland pipeline to transport the oil to a warm-water port. Early in 1969 a loose consortium of oil companies involved in Alaska announced plans to build a 798-mile line from Prudhoe Bay to the warm-water port of Valdez on Prince William Sound. But a pipeline through Alaska would have to cross hundreds of miles of land under Native title protest. Settlement of the Native claims therefore became an urgent necessity.[40]

At this point, Walter J. Hickel, a follower of Gruening's rhetorical paradigm, entered Alaskan resource development history. Hickel had come to Alaska in 1940 with only a few borrowed dollars in his pocket, but by the 1960s he had made millions from construction (and bartending) and later real estate and hotels.[41] He thought of himself as a self-made man in the mold of the classic Alaskan, that is, in the mold of the mythical American frontier. Unafraid of conflict, Hickel had clashed with the state's biggest banker and wealthiest man in the territory, Elmer Rasmuson, and by 1966 he was ready for a gubernatorial bid. Hickel had bought Gruening's paradigm in full; in fact, he built his campaign on it: The federal government must not be allowed to push Alaska around. The state's first governor, William Egan, had been too willing to appease Washington, D.C., thus compromising the independence of the new state and squandering its opportunities for progress. Alaska must stand up to the "feds" and demand a lifting of the injunction that prevented the state's land selections.[42] Elected governor in 1966 on this vigorous anti-federal government, pro-development platform, Hickel's first act as governor was to institute a suit against Udall, the secretary of the interior, over the land freeze.[43]

Soon after the 1968 election, however, newly elected President Richard Nixon selected Hickel as *his* secretary of the interior, an opportunity Hickel relished. Where better to attack federal interference in Alaska than from a position of power within the federal government itself? Eschewing subtlety, Hickel announced before his confirmation hearing that what Udall had done with a pen, Hickel could undo. But the Senate gave Hickel a lesson in the realities of national politics. Members of the Interior Committee did not share Hickel's cavalier attitude toward Native claims; as a cost of his confirmation, they extracted from him a pledge that he would not lift the land transfer injunction until the Native claims matter had been resolved. Reflecting on the hearings several years later, Hickel called them "an inquisition."[44]

Both the oil companies and Alaska politicians grew restless with the delay in pipeline construction. Soon after his confirmation, Hickel announced his intention to grant a permit for a haul road along the proposed pipeline route. The federal government had jurisdiction within the pipeline corridor. Fearing this opening wedge, five Native villages along the Yukon River filed suit to block the permit on the grounds that Native claims needed to be settled first. Several weeks later three environmental groups filed a suit of their own. The Wilderness Society, Friends of the Earth, and the Environmental Defense Fund charged that the line as proposed violated provisions of the 1920 Mineral Leasing Act regarding rights of way; they also cited a section of the National Environmental Policy Act of 1969, which mandated the consideration of alternative proposals for environmental impacts for large projects. The environmental community regarded these as the strongest grounds for protest. Their deeper agenda was to halt the line or, failing that, to erect environmental safeguards. In response, a federal judge in Washington, D.C., George Hart, granted a restraining order. Alaskans immediately protested, the press howling hysterically about a conspiracy against the state's rights of environmentalists in league with eastern elitists, supported by a willing tool, the judge, whom they castigated as uninformed and inept.[45]

The oil companies went to work with a coalition of Native leaders and produced a claims settlement in 1971, probably many years earlier than without the oil incentive. In exchange for the extinguishment of Native title to 330 million acres in Alaska and the extinguishment of Indian country, Natives received title to 44 million acres (12 percent of the total state land area) and $1 billion to capitalize twelve regional economic development corporations. All Natives would be stockholders in at least one of these corporations.[46] Half the capitalization would be paid from royalties on oil production. Though the framers acted to protect Native culture through preservation of the land base, Native corporations have developed resources through which they have found it economically feasible to do so. Alaskans accepted the forty-four million acres because the resolution of Native claims paved the way for economic development, through, for example, the pipeline and Prudhoe Bay production. Still, there was a certain amount of grumbling about all that land going to Natives, being placed off-limits to non-Native residents. The state had initially suggested ten million acres. There was also a lot of criticism of the fact that Native selections were made ahead of the state's selections promised in the statehood act, even though the Native selections were almost all in traditionally Native-used areas and for the most part did not include significant economic resources.

By the time Congress passed the claims settlement, however, Hickel was no longer secretary of the interior; he had been fired after November 1970, for outspoken criticism of Nixon's hard-line stance against anti-Vietnam protests. Hickel believed that communication could solve nearly all problems; this falling out with Nixon came over Hickel's conviction that the nation's youth had as much right to express their opinions and to inform public policy, including foreign policy, as did their elders. Hickel did not meaningfully address the problem of conflict resolution, however. In a defense of his policies (titled *Who Owns America*), which he published shortly after leaving office, Hickel emphasized the universality of resource ownership, making a distinction between owners and stewards. He was unclear regarding the uses of ownership, however. The ownership itself seemed to be more important an idea than what it might lead to. It was always the amorphous "economic development."

Hickel saw no conflict between wilderness protection and sustained yield development.[47] All the people should benefit from development through using resources for beneficial products. Government should monitor the satisfactory protection of the environment during production and its restoration afterward, acting as steward for the owners. Hickel thought scenic wonders should be left undisturbed, but undeveloped resources offended him. They constituted a waste of the people's assets, he thought. Yet even though they were the people's resources, their development by corporate wealth constituted no crime, provided such development was environmentally sensitive. During his two-year tenure as interior secretary, regulation enforcement absorbed much of Hickel's time. As secretary he set out to protect the country's resources by enforcing environmental legislation, which he interpreted as an expression of the people's will. Hickel thought of himself as a doer, and as secretary he apparently was much led by circumstance. The paradigm he used to organize his thinking on resource development was populism, the people rather than the government. It was a false but familiar paradigm, for Alaskans had always thought of themselves as the common people pitted in battle against the insensitive forces of arrogant power, the power of federal government.

Alaskans were soon to find themselves assaulted by government power yet again, for the Native claims settlement act,[48] itself a manifestation of the great social change in America represented by the civil rights revolution, contained a truly dramatic environmental provision representing still another revolution. It called for eighty million acres of Alaska's land to be set aside by the U.S. Congress within ten years in four conservation categories: national forests, parks, fish and wildlife refuges, and a relatively new category, wilderness. This provision was remarkable as a kind of culmination of a decade that had witnessed federal clean air and water legislation, migratory mammal and waterfowl protection, the significant 1964 wilderness act, and finally, the National Environmental Policy Act (NEPA) of 1969.

The wilderness act had called for setting aside only fifty million acres. The eighty million acres in the Native claims settlement act were to be chosen on the basis of whole ecosystems, rather than piecemeal selections, as had usually been the case with the fifty-four million acres that already had been reserved in Alaska as Mount McKinley National Park, Katmai National Monument, Glacier Bay National Monument, Tongass and Chugach National Forests, Naval Petroleum Reserve No. 4, and an assortment of oddments.[49] Alaskan political leaders put the Congress on a schedule that, working with a joint federal-state study commission that had been established in the settlement act, would lead to a vote on the conservation reserves to be set aside by 1979.[50] The legislation would have to be completed before the state would be permitted to resume its own selection process.

Just as Alaskan residents were celebrating the achievement of a Native claims settlement, and looking forward to the billions in anticipated income represented by pipeline construction and oil production, they saw on the immediate horizon the environmental suit (still pending). Furthermore, they saw in the claims settlement act the taking not only of Native lands but also a huge withdrawal for environmental protection. The Alaskans, of course, went ballistic. On the environmental integrity of the pipeline, even industry analysts agreed that the consortium of companies involved had not produced sufficient studies. In addition, the Environmental Protection Agency, the U.S. Department of Transportation's Office of Pipeline Safety, and even the U.S. Army Corps of Engineers registered their lack of confidence in the industry. Before being fired, Hickel had produced a short draft environmental impact statement (EIS), but his predecessor, Rogers C. B. Morton, promptly disowned the statement upon taking over the office.[51]

After two years of industry redesign and furious attacks on environmentalism in the Alaskan press and legislature, the Department of the Interior produced a comprehensive 3,500-page EIS. Morton prepared to issue the construction permits. At the same time, the federal district court dissolved the environmental suit, arguing that its concerns had been met by the EIS. However, an appellate court found that the question of the width of the right-of-way had not been satisfied, and the court warned that the permits would be in violation of the law.[52] In the meantime, the Arab oil embargo following the 1971 Arab-Israeli war led to a crisis in delivering gasoline across the country. The U.S. Congress decided to step in to amend the right-of-way provision and to declare that the NEPA requirements had been met by the Interior Department so construction could proceed. Debate on the bill came down to a critical vote on the NEPA requirement in the Senate: The solons divided on the issue, 49 to 49. It was July 17, 1973; the vice president was Spiro Agnew.[53]

In their celebration, Alaskans began to flail environmentalists over the conservation withdrawal provisions in the claims settlement act. The subcommittee marking up the House bill held hearings in Alaska. Press criticism was particularly strident and aggressive.[54] Staffers worked out a compromise bill, but riding the crest of a wave of environmental sentiment, environmentalists in Congress refused to accept it. As the deadline approached, Senator Mike Gravel, Alaska's junior senator, announced that he would filibuster the Senate bill beyond Congress's self-imposed deadline.[55] This prompted Secretary of the Interior Cecil Andrus to recommend that President Jimmy Carter use the 1906 Antiquities Act to withdraw the areas under discussion as national monuments. This Carter did in 1978, setting aside 154 million acres from the public domain with a stroke of his pen. The largest withdrawals previously made under the Antiquities Act barely exceeded one million acres. The Carter-Andrus withdrawals in Alaska were a tactical move to force Congress to pass a bill, and to show that he was serious, Andrus sent out rangers and administrators to work up regulations for management of the monuments. In some areas signs appeared on trees and fence posts warning that Alaskans could not be responsible for the safety of government personnel. Alaskans saw the withdrawal as federal power run amok, protesting again in terms of the Gruening paradigm.[56]

Manifesting the pervasive power of the paradigm and its use in such circumstances, the state legislature created and funded a statehood commission to review "the status of the people of Alaska within the United States, and to make recommendations on that relationship."[57] This was the first time since the Civil War that citizens of a state had "by their vote indicated unease with the federal union." After two years of study, the commission duly produced reports saying effectively that it was true: Federal sovereignty exists, there is a U.S. Constitution, and Alaska is a state. In fact, the commission concluded that of all the options available, statehood was preferable to any other.[58]

In November 1980 the American electorate abruptly turned to the political right with the election of a Republican president and Senate. Seeing the political writing on the wall, Representative Morris Udall of Arizona, leader of the environmental forces in Congress, capitulated, and the Alaska lands bill known as the Alaska National Interest Lands Conservation Act passed the Congress on what was understood in environmental circles as "Black Tuesday."[59] Set aside were 104 million acres of Alaska's lands for conservation in three categories: forests, parks, and refuges; and 54 million of these acres were designated as wilderness.[60]

CONSTITUTIONAL REALITIES

There was no celebration in Alaska this time, as residents talked of locked up lands and the broken promises of the statehood act that had authorized the state's selection of 103 million acres back in 1958.[61] Still, Senator Ted Stevens, Alaska's powerful senior senator, asserted that no economically viable lands had been affected by the bill. Stevens was right; they had all been exempted: a world-class lead and zinc mine on the northwest Bering coast, access to the Ambler mining district in the northern interior, a valuable molybdenum deposit in the southeast, a promising gold mine on Lynn Canal. The bill even included a $40 million annual subsidy ($25 million for operations; $15 million to service existing fifty-year pulp contracts) to the Alaska Region of the U.S. Forest Service to guarantee sufficient timber lease sales in the Tongass National Forest, to maintain the two pulp mills that had been built there after the 1947 Tongass Timber Act.[62] The Tongass subsidy permitted the Forest Service to sell a five-hundred-year-old western hemlock or western red cedar tree to logging companies for about the cost of a MacDonald's "Big Mac."[63] Now, smarting with resentment after waiting for the Native entitlement to be identified and conveyed and watching American conservation interests set aside Alaska's environmental "crown jewels," the state was permitted to resume selecting its 103 million acres. By 1990 that process was about 97 percent complete.

But the rather hysterical protests about land selection within the state had not completely submerged the voice of environmental responsibility. In 1960 the Bureau of Land Management (BLM) set aside the five-hundred-thousand-acre Chugach State Park behind urban Anchorage, the largest state park in the United States.[64] In 1974 Alaskans elected former wilderness guide Jay S. Hammond as governor. Hammond had run on a moderate environmental platform. But by this time, newly flowing oil money drowned out discussion of the hard questions. The Hammond administration poured millions into agricultural initiatives in dairy and barley production, a nodding obeisance to the powerful ideal of pioneer self-sufficiency. Economies of scale defeated both projects, leaving scores of embittered would-be farmers cursing the "field of dreams" syndrome.[65] In 1976 an Anchorage physician launched an initiative drive to compel the state to open to homestead entry 30 million acres of the state's 103-million-acre entitlement, when it should finally be conveyed; any resident would qualify for 160 acres. Though voters passed the initiative handily, the state Supreme Court struck it down on a technicality, much to the relief of most state planners.

Oil revenue in unanticipated amounts from Prudhoe Bay production stilled most protests over federal power in the 1980s, particularly following adoption of the state's permanent fund and the related dividend distribution program.[66] But the Gruening paradigm was not dead, just momentarily dormant. In 1990, responding to environmental pressure over the loss of old-growth trees, Congress passed the Tongass Timber Reform Act, which among other things reduced the annual Forest Service subsidy from $40 million to $4 million.[67] Since that time, both pulp mills in the forest have closed, as has the largest sawmill.[68]

Also in 1990, Walter Hickel decided to reenter politics. Going back to his 1971 book and resurrecting that paradigm, he declared during the campaign that Alaska must become an "owner state," by which he meant that Alaskans, rather than the American people in general, should own Alaska's natural resources. The resources could then be used for development, he argued. "Owner state" became the mantra of the campaign.[69] That the federally owned areas were not economically viable was information that got lost in the rhetoric. Raging again against the villainy of the federal government, Hickel charged that the Congress had violated a solemn contract with the people of Alaska, the statehood compact, in passing the Native Claims Settlement Act of 1971 and the Alaska National Interest Lands Conservation Act of 1980 (ANILCA). The compact had been solemnized, he said, by the territory-wide plebiscite after the act was passed but before it went into effect. Basing his claim on the statehood act provision that 90 percent of federal mineral royalty would go to the state to pay for state government, Hickel argued that the 1971 and 1980 withdrawals represented lost mineral royalties that would have come to the state if the lands had remained productive. He directed his accountants to calculate the amount of the lost revenue, which they told him it was $29 billion. With great fanfare, a long-time Hickel aide published a campaign polemic called *Going Up in Flames: The Promises and Pledges of Alaska Statehood under Attack.*[70] On the cover was a photograph of the Anchorage statehood celebration bonfire from 1958.

Hickel won the election and promptly filed suit against the federal government for the $29 billion, perhaps the ultimate compensation suit, but in the context of states' rights rather than private property. Constitutional lawyers around the country laughed at the prospect of such a suit actually being tried in court, but Hickel kept up the drumbeat of federal villainy, and the territorial legislature responded by endorsing the cause.[71] Hickel directed the state public information office to produce a video about the suit, titled *Broken Promises*, at a cost of $30,000, which was distributed to schools statewide.[72]

In 1996 Alaska and the United States duly presented their arguments in court, and in May a federal judge dismissed the suit, asserting that there is no such thing as a binding statehood compact. Only those parts of such an act are irrevocable which the parties explicitly state are such upon passage of the act. The royalty provisions of the act were not so identified in 1958, the judge ruled, nor were they singled out in the plebiscite. "Ultimately," the judge wrote, the subject matter of the statehood act—entry into a union of states—is sui generis and cannot be strictly compressed into a contractual or legislative mode. The statehood debate thus cannot be analogized to the normal negotiations between parties to commercial contracts.[73] Moreover, the judge noted, this issue had been argued in the courts many times before. The Alaska case did not contribute any new understanding on the issue.

CONCLUSION

Gruening's villainy paradigm lives on. Alaskans elected a new governor in 1994, Tony Knowles, a Democrat and ostensibly a liberal. Yet, upon taking office, he directed his attorney general to continue the suit, and after the lower court decision, he directed that it should be appealed.[74] In 1997 the circuit court upheld the district judge's decision, and in 1998 the U.S. Supreme Court declined to hear the further appeal, thus killing the case.[75] Perhaps in a different environment the Supreme Court's refusal to hear the appeal would put an end to arguments based on the state's presumed ability to limit federal authority within its borders. But Alaskan political leaders have so embraced the notion that within a few days of the opening of the 1998 annual legislative session in Juneau, nine members of the Legislative Council filed yet another suit in federal district court challenging a federal directive regarding Alaska, this time a congressional mandate to provide a rural preference for subsistence hunting and fishing in Alaska.[76] The theory of the new suit, written by the same attorney who wrote the failed compact suit, is that based on the "equal footing" doctrine and the Alaska statehood compact, the Congress had no authority to enact the subsistence provisions of ANILCA.[77] The plaintiffs have responded to criticism of this new effort with the traditional victimization rhetoric, arguing that Alaskans must not surrender the state's "birthright."[78] Such sloganeering continues to be a common element in the platforms of a number of state politicians. It helped to inspire a protest march in Anchorage on May 7, 1998, with more than four thousand Natives complaining of "racism" in the legislature.

The Gruening "victimization" paradigm, then, has crowded out much serious discussion of land use in Alaska. There is a viable environmental community in the state, and not everyone is hell bent on owning all the land, as the response to the homestead initiative demonstrates. But in large measure, these are still voices in the wilderness. There has been no serious discussion of public-lands historian Paul Wallace Gates's idea that private land possession must be stewardship or his reminder that there have always been conditions on private land ownership.[79] Alaskans simply are not positioned to debate such sophisticated ideas to any substantive degree. Alaska is too close yet to the imagined West of popular culture. It is too close to the imagined western freedom from restraint and to the democratic impulses that Frederick Jackson Turner thought defined the frontier, and that popular culture, particularly Alaskan popular culture, takes for granted to be an essential part of western history. The Gruening paradigm is also dangerous, for it has made the population susceptible to manipulation by politicians who have no other context for conceiving the past, a susceptibility exacerbated by the population's high rate of transience. It is also exacerbated by Alaska's geographic remove from the contiguous states: Remoteness encourages notions of exceptionality, which in turn encourage a sense of persecution.

In essence, this is not much different from the same ignorance and confusion that occur in other western states and occurred in the territories as they became states. Alaskans share the sincere and patriotic impulses of those public land protesters who got themselves elected county commissioners in Catron County, New Mexico, and Nye County, Nevada, and have undertaken such acts of civil disobedience as bulldozing closed access roads to federal areas in their region; in other words, they have taken the law into their own hands.[80] But in Alaska the paradigm's effect seems more pervasive. Alaskans have yet to develop a coherent, strategic view of their state and its future. They still are fighting for statehood, that is, for what they consider their rightful autonomy, using the same rhetoric that worked in 1958. Though raised consciousness on Native rights and environment have created new circumstances, and the state's population has nearly tripled, from 225,000 to 650,000, the state's politics seem locked in time back in the mid-1950s, when the enemy could be easily identified, and voters could be rallied at a moment's notice with cries of "tyranny" and "oppression." Astonishingly, it seems they still can be today.

The continuing strength of Gruening's villainy paradigm in Alaska represents a lamentable, perhaps tragic, failure of education. The people of the state do not know much about their history, as few in America know much about the history of the individual states in which they reside, especially the history of the American West, as thinkers from Richard White and William Cronon to William Kittredge have pointed out for some time now.[81] It is not only the manipulated but also the manipulators who are thus disadvantaged. The sincerity of Walter Hickel is evident, as is the sincerity of those state legislators who see only federal power when they look toward the horizon. The only antidote is continuing scholarly and public elucidation and debate. In time, the bonfire will surely burn itself out, and the lay of the land will be revealed in its true, complex grandeur.

NOTES

1. Gerald E. Bowkett, *Reaching for a Star: The Final Campaign for Alaska Statehood* (Fairbanks, Alas.: Epicenter Press, 1989), 97.

2. The story of the statehood movement is told in Claus-M. Naske, *An Interpretive History of Alaska Statehood* (Anchorage: Alaska Northwest Publishing, 1973).

3. Jonathan M. Nielson, *Armed Forces on a Northern Frontier: The Military in Alaska's History, 1867–1987* (Westport, Conn.: Greenwood Press, 1988), 191–92; Naske, *An Interpretive History*, 119, 126, 151–53. President Dwight Eisenhower opposed statehood for the same reason, refusing to endorse the Republican party statehood plank in 1952 and 1956.

4. Claus-M. Naske, "Governor Ernest Gruening's Struggle for Territorial Status: Personal or Political," *Journal of the West* 20 (1981): 32–40.

5. Robert David Johnson, *Ernest Gruening and the American Dissenting Tradition* (Cambridge: Harvard University Press, 1998), 171.

6. Claus-M. Naske, *Alaska: A History of the Forty-Ninth State* (Grand Rapids, Mich.: William Eerdmans, 1979); William R. Hunt, *Alaska: A Bicentennial History* (New York: W. W. Norton, 1976), 62, 97–102.

7. Herman Slotnick, "The Ballinger-Pinchot Controversy in Alaska," *Journal of the West* 10 (1971): 337–47.

8. 41 U.S. Stat. 999; Ralph Rivers, "The Jones Act," *Alaska Life,* January 1947, p. 6; Charles McKetta, "Deregulating the Jones Act in Alaska," *Journal of Forest History* 86 (1988): 32–36.

9. *Territory of Alaska v Troy*, 5 Alaska Fed. Reports 104 (1922).

10. 43 U.S. Stat. 464.

11. Richard A. Cooley, *Politics and Conservation: The Decline of Alaska Salmon* (New York: Harper and Row, 1963), 82, 145.

12. Nielson, *Armed Forces,* 130–31; author's interview with U.S. District Court Judge James Fitzgerald, November 10, 1995, Anchorage, Alaska.

13. William H. Wilson, *Railroad in the Clouds: The Alaska Railroad in the Age of Steam* (Boulder, Colo.: Pruett, 1977), 8–9. On western reactions to federal largesse, see Patricia Nelson Limerick, *The Legacy of Conquest: The Unbroken Past of the American West* (New York: W. W. Norton, 1987), 78–96, especially the chapter "Denial and Dependence."

14. Ernest Gruening, "Let Us End American Colonialism," Alaska Constitutional Convention, held in Fairbanks, November 9, 1955, pp. 3 and throughout.

15. See particularly Robert A. Frederick's preface and Gruening's foreword in the revised edition of *The State of Alaska,* published by Random House in 1968.

16. Gruening, *State of Alaska,* 31, 45, 101, 155, 295, respectively.

17. Morgan Sherwood, *Exploration of Alaska 1865–1900* (New Haven, Conn.: Yale University Press, 1967); Bobby Dave Lane, "North of 53: Army, Navy and Treasury Department Administration of Alaska, 1867–1877," Ph.D. dissertation, University of Texas, 1974; Ted C. Hinckley, *The Americanization of Alaska* (Palo Alto, Calif.: Basic Books, 1972).

18. Scholar Richard Welch discovered some years ago that all but four or five of the fifty major urban papers in the United States in the summer of 1867 editorially supported the purchase: Welch, "American Public Opinion and the Purchase of Russian America," *American Slavic and East European Review* 17 (1958): 481–94; see also Stephen Haycox, "Unmasking the Dead Hero: Myth in Alaskan History," in *Society: An Alaskan Perspective,* ed. Sharon Araji (Dubuque, Iowa: Kendall-Hunt, 1994), 53–64.

19. Ken Coates, "Controlling the Periphery: The Territorial Administration of the Yukon and Alaska, 1867–1959," *Pacific Northwest Quarterly* 78 (1987): 141–51; Evangeline Atwood, *Frontier Politics: Alaska's James Wickersham* (Portland, Oreg.: Binford and Mort, 1979).

20. Orlando W. Miller, *The Frontier in Alaska and the Matanuska Colony* (New Haven, Conn.: Yale University Press, 1975); Mary Childers Mangusso, "Anthony J. Dimond," Ph.D. dissertation, Texas Tech University, 1974; Richard L. Neuberger, "Anthony J. Dimond, of Alaska," *Alaska Life*, September 1948, pp. 5–8; Virgil Heath, "Alaska's CCC Days," *Alaska Journal* 2 (1972): 51–56; Kenneth Philp, "The New Deal and Alaskan Natives, 1936–1945," *Pacific Historical Review* 50 (1981): 309–27.

21. Stephen Haycox, "Mining the Federal Government: The War and the All-America City," in *Alaska at War, 1941–1945: The Forgotten War Remembered*, ed. Fern Chandonnet (Anchorage: Alaska at War Committee, 1995), 203–10; Nielson, *Armed Forces*, 125–220.

22. Claus-M. Naske and Stephen Haycox, "A New Face: Bringing Law to the New State of Alaska," *Western Legal History* 1 (winter/spring 1998): 1–22.

23. The vote was 17,447 to 8,180, as reported in Naske, *An Interpretive History*, 146.

24. The vote was 21,285 to 4,004, in Naske, *An Interpretive History*, 146.

25. Stephen Haycox, "Economic Development and Indian Land Rights in Modern Alaska: The 1947 Tongass Timber Act," *Western Historical Quarterly* 21 (February 1990): 20–46.

26. 72 U.S. Stat. 339; 800,000 acres were to come from existing federal reserves; these were superseded by the Alaska National Interest Lands Conservation Act in 1980, reducing the state's actual entitlement to 102.55 million acres. Alaska's total land area is more than 375 million acres. By comparison, Oregon's total land area is just over 62 million, and Washington's is just over 43.5 million.

27. Alaska State Constitution, art. 8, Natural Resources.

28. 72 U.S. Stat. 339 (1958). By the Mineral Leasing Act of 1920, states received 37.5 percent of federal mineral lease receipts; 52.5 percent went into a federal reclamation fund, created by the Reclamation Act of 1902; 32 U.S. Stat. 388; Alaska had begun receiving 37.5 percent even as a territory when the Reclamation Act was amended in 1947. The Bureau of Reclamation undertook to spend within a state monies collected from federal leases within that state, whenever possible; the remaining 10 percent of lease revenue was used to administer federal lands within the states. See 30 U.S. Code, art. 181–287.

29. Section VI of the Alaska Statehood Act, 41 U.S. Code, sec. 103.

30. Naske, *An Interpretive History*, 167. There were in fact three propositions: Should the state be immediately admitted to the union, should the external boundaries of the state be approved, and should existing federal withdrawals be

approved; about fifty-four million acres had been withdrawn in conservation reserves (Mount McKinley National Park, Glacier Bay and Katmai National Monuments, Tongass and Chugach National Forests, and several U.S. Fish and Wildlife reserves) and military reservations (particularly the twenty-three-million acre National Petroleum Reserve No. 4 on the North Slope); the numbers were essentially the same on each proposition, 40,000 to 7,500.

31. *Organized Village of Kake v Egan*, 369 U.S. 60 (1959); *Metlakatla Indian Community, Annette Island Reserve v Egan*, 369 U.S. 45 (1959). Kake was not on a reservation; before the 1940s there had been only one traditional Indian reservation in Alaska, the Annette Island Reserve, where the village of New Metlakatla was located. The court found that the Interior Department had the authority to permit traps only on reservation land, but because the department had never promulgated regulations for Metlakatla, its trap was also subject to state law.

32. The Annette Island Reserve was the sole exception before the 1940s, and the only reserve located in a salmon fishery. It had been created by Congress in 1891 for a group of Coast Tsimshean Indians from British Columbia, who, along with their missionary patriarch William Duncan, had petitioned to move to Alaska to escape the negative influences of white settlement. In 1855 they had established their village of New Metlakatla in Alaska. After Congress amended the Indian Reorganization Act to apply to Alaska in 1936, the Bureau of Indian Affairs (BIA) urged the formation of Indian Reorganization Act councils in Native villages; four organized in the 1930s, forty in the 1940s, five in the 1950s, and two in 1971, a total of 71. See David Case, *Alaska Natives and American Laws* (Fairbanks: University of Alaska, 1984), 339.

33. Redesignated the Arctic National Wildlife Refuge in the Alaska lands legislation of 1980.

34. Case, *Alaska Natives*, 47–70.

35. Robert Arnold, *Alaska Native Land Claims* (Anchorage: Alaska Native Foundation, 1976).

36. In 1959 the Tlingit and Haida Indians of southeast Alaska had won a judgment before the U.S. Court of Federal Claims confirming their title to most of the eighteen-million-acre Tongass National Forest in the southeast panhandle at the time of the U.S. purchase of Alaska, and recommending compensation for the 1905 taking of the forest by congressional action.

37. Even the Alaska Congressional delegation in Washington, D.C., was surprised by Udall's action. The language of the statehood act authorized selections from "vacant, unappropriated, and unreserved" lands; the secretary justified his

action on the grounds that the land being selected was not unappropriated, asserting, on behalf of Alaska Natives, that selected lands were subject to Native title "on the basis of aboriginal use, occupancy, and continued possession." See *State of Alaska v Udall*, 420 F.2d 938 (Ninth Circuit, 1969); cert. denied, 397 U.S. 1076, 90 S.Ct. 1522 (1970). Udall's action is Public Order No. 4582, 34 Fed. Reg. 1025 (January 23, 1969).

38. Federal Field Committee for Development Planning in Alaska, *Alaska Natives and the Land* (Washington, D.C.: Government Printing Office, 1968).

39. Tom Kizzia provides a sensitive and comprehensive description of village Alaska in *In the Wake of the Unseen Object: Native Cultures of Alaska* (New York: Henry Holt, 1991).

40. Peter Coates, "The Crude and the Pure: Oil and Environmental Politics in Alaska," in *Politics in the Postwar American West*, ed. Richard Lowitt (Norman: University of Oklahoma Press, 1995), 3–21.

41. Walter J. Hickel, *Who Owns America* (Englewood Cliffs, N.J.: Prentice Hall, 1971).

42. "Egan-Hickel Race Down to the Wire," *Anchorage Times*, November 7, 1966, p. A1.

43. *Alaska v Udall*.

44. Hickel, *Who Owns America*, 21–22, 32.

45. Peter Coates, *The Trans-Alaska Pipeline Controversy: Technology, Conservation, and the Frontier* (Bethlehem, Pa.: Lehigh University Press, 1991), 220.

46. The actual compensatory award was $962.5 million, a compromise between the House and Senate bills. The 208 Native villages also were permitted to form corporations; as of 1996, 172 had done so. The capitalization was to be evenly divided between the regional corporation and all the village corporations in a region. The regional corporation received title to the subsurface estate throughout the region, but village corporations received surface title to the village.

47. Hickel, *Who Owns America*, 308–28 and throughout.

48. 85 U.S. Stat. 689 (1971).

49. Coates, *Trans-Alaska Pipeline Controversy*, 308; G. Frank Williss, *"Do Things Right the First Time": The National Park Service and the Alaska National Interest Lands Conservation Act of 1980* (Washington, D.C.: National Park Service, 1985), 114.

50. Williss, *Do Things Right*, 159.

51. Coates, "Crude and the Pure," 12, 15. Hickel's environmental impact statement was 246 pages.

52. *Wilderness Society v Morton*, 479 F.2nd, D.C. Cir. (1973), pp. 842 and thereafter.

53. Coates, "Crude and Pure," 18.

54. "Environmental Protests Stifle State Development," *Anchorage Times*, April 21, 1977, p.1; *Anchorage Times*, July 5, 1977, p. 5. See analysis in *Congressional Quarterly Almanac*, 1977, 673 and thereafter.

55. Williss, *Do Things Right*, 212.

56. Stephen Haycox, "On the Politics of Environment: Cecil Andrus and the Alaska Lands Act," *Idaho Yesterdays* (fall 1992): 17–28; *Congressional Quarterly Almanac*, 1978, 724–42; "Federal Agents Threatened," *Anchorage Times*, December 2, 1978, pp. 1, 5.

57. Alaska Statehood Commission, *More Perfect Union: A Plan for Action*, Final Report (Anchorage: Alaska Statehood Commission, 1983), 1.

58. Alaska Statehood Commission, *More Perfect Union*, 2; Harold A. Hovey, *Shifting Power from the Federal Government to the State of Alaska*, Final Report (Anchorage: Alaska Statehood Commission, 1982), 3.

59. Williss, *Do Things Right*, 237.

60. See editorials in the *New York Times*, November 12, 1980, p. 30, and November 14, 1980, p. 30. *Alaska National Interest Lands Conservation Act*, 94 Stat. 2371 (1980). When added to previous federal withdrawals, ANILCA brought the total federal lands in Alaska to 257 million acres (68.5 percent); this includes 23 million acres in National Petroleum Reserve–Alaska and 74 million acres of unallocated public domain managed by the Bureau of Land Management (BLM). Most previous conservation reserves were enlarged, and Mount McKinley National Park was renamed Denali National Park, though the name of the mountain remains the same.

61. Williss, *Do Things Right*, 223.

62. Stephen Haycox, "Economic Development and Indian Land Rights in Modern Alaska: The 1947 Tongass Timber Act," *Western Historical Quarterly* (1990): 21–46; "ANILCA Guarantees Timber Supply," *Anchorage Times*, November 15, 1980, p. 5.

63. Timothy Egan, "Fighting for Control of America's Hinterlands," *New York Times*, November 11, 1990, p. IV18; *Congressional Quarterly Almanac*, 1990, 294–95.

64. "BLM Conveys Anchorage Park," *Anchorage Daily News*, November 4, 1994, p. F2.

65. Gerald A. McBeath and Thomas A. Morehouse, *Alaska Politics and Government* (Lincoln: University of Nebraska Press, 1994), 15, 67, 173; Jay S. Hammond, *Alaska Journal of Commerce*, February 26, 1996, p. 1.

66. The Alaska Permanent Fund invests about 10 percent of annual oil tax receipts; in 1996 the principal was about $20 billion. About half the earnings each year are distributed equally to all qualifying Alaska residents; in 1996 the individual checks were just under $1,000. When voters approved creation of the fund by constitutional amendment in 1982, they also repealed the state income tax.

67. 104 U.S. Stat. 4426; *Congressional Quarterly Almanac*, 1990, 294–95.

68. "Wrangell Mill Closes," *Anchorage Daily News*, October 20, 1996, p. F2.

69. "Hickel Pushes Owner State," *Anchorage Times*, November 7, 1990, pp. A1, A10.

70. Commonwealth North, *Going Up in Flames: The Promises and Pledges of Alaska Statehood under Attack*, ed. Malcolm Roberts (Anchorage: Alaska Pacific University Press, 1990).

71. Michael Carey, "Outside Experts Offer Perspectives on Hickel Suit," *Anchorage Daily News*, August 29, 1993, p. M6; Charlie Cole, "Lawsuit Is Rooted in History of Alaska Statehood," *Anchorage Daily News*, September 30, 1993, p. B4; Walter Hickel, "Lawsuits Will Define Alaska Rights with U.S. Government," *Anchorage Daily News*, January 4, 1994, p. B8; Senator Ted Stevens, "Compact Lawsuit Critical to Alaska's Future," *Anchorage Daily News*, January 2, 1995, p. B3; Lew Williams, "Feds Not Laughing Now about Alaska Suit," in "Voice of The Times," *Anchorage Daily News*, November 28, 1995, p. B5.

72. The case was filed in the U.S. Court of Federal Claims in Washington, D.C., Judge Bruggink, Case No. 93–454L; the finding was filed on May 31, 1996.

73. *Alaska v U.S.*, p. 26 of the decision.

74. Hickel continued to justify the suit even after the decision: "Decisions Made in 1959 Should Stand Forever," *Anchorage Daily News*, June 29, 1996, p. B6.

75. The appellate court upheld the finding of the district court judge in the following words: "Judge Bruggink's opinion is thoroughly supported with cited and quoted authority and record evidence. Nothing more need be said." *Anchorage Daily News*, November 2, 1997, p. B3. See Michael Carey, "Hickel's Fight Lost before It Was Begun," *Anchorage Daily News*, March 11, 1998, p. B6.

76. The Alaska lands act (ANILCA) of 1980 mandates the rural preference. In 1989 the Alaska Supreme Court struck down a state legislative rural preference guarantee on the grounds that it violated a natural resources "common use" provision in the Alaska constitution. The federal government took over management of game on federal lands in Alaska in 1990 and took over fishing management at the end of 1998; *McDowell v State*, 785 P.2d 1 (1990).

77. Donald Craig Mitchell, "Legislative Council Off on 'Dumb' Legal Pursuit," *Anchorage Daily News*, January 13, 1998, p. B6.

78. Bob Tkacz, "Subsistence Struggling under Deadline," *Alaska Fisherman's Journal* 20 (August): 6–7.

79. Paul Wallace Gates, "An Overview of American Land Policy," *Agricultural History* 50 (1976): 213–29. See also William Kittredge, *Owning It All* (St. Paul, Minn.: Graywolf Press, 1987).

80. *Outside Magazine* devoted a full issue to public lands protest in October 1995; see also "Sagebrush II" in "Voice of *The Times*," *Anchorage Daily News*, April 13, 1995, p. B7.

81. In 1990 the Alaska Board of Education rejected the state legislature's appeal to require an Alaska history course as a secondary school graduation requirement on the grounds that the board should not mandate specific courses in the curriculum. In the Anchorage School District, which enrolls just fewer than half of the state's school population, the only Alaska history requirement is a six-week exposure in the seventh grade (though some secondary schools offer aspects of Alaska history as an intermittent elective); *Session Laws of Alaska*, 1988, HCR SCR 39; author communication with Douglas Phillips, Social Studies Curriculum Specialist, Anchorage School District, January 20, 1997.

Contested Terrain

The Business of Land in the American West

RICHARD WHITE

When I was a graduate student in the early 1970s, the history of the public lands was at the heart of the training for a western historian. Paul Wallace Gates and Vernon Carstensen in particular built on the work of the pioneering historians in the field, Thomas Donaldson, Benjamin Hibbard, Roy Robbins, Fred Shannon, and others. These historians did not just write books, they created tomes: at three hundred pages they were just hitting their stride. They created a body of scholarship so grand, so sweeping, so detailed that it finally came to a halt by its own accumulated weight. For nearly a generation there seemed little else left to say; historians, at least, went on to other things. Only recently have some talented younger historians, such as Karen Merrell, again made land policy and the public lands a topic of much scholarly interest.

The theme that emerged from the older scholarship was less that American land policy had become a contradictory mess than that it had *always* been a contradictory mess. Land policy was considered an ad hoc hodgepodge better explained historically by looking at the particular considerations that had prompted the passage of various acts than by trying to see how the laws conformed to some overarching principles. To be sure, there *were* overarching principles; it was just that they were ignored whenever they became inconvenient.

By the late 1950s and early 1960s, this history of American land policy had become vaguely celebratory. In those years—when there was still a rough consensus by experts on management of public lands, on multiple use, and on the limits of the market—this contradictory history could be seen as yielding a muddled triumph of sorts. Things seemed to have worked out well, and the lessons learned on the public lands seemed clear. In 1964, as part of the compromise that produced the Wilderness Act, Congress established the U.S. Public Land Law Review Commission to recommend changes in public land law. At this time the task seemed largely one of codification and making explicit what had long been implicit in the law. The commission hired Paul Wallace Gates, the well-known public lands historian, to produce his *History of Public Land Law Development*. In what remains a magisterial work, Gates concluded that pride in the public ownership of parks, forests, and dams seemed to have displaced earlier policies of putting public lands into private hands.[1]

It seemed that a corner had been turned. The commission proved Gates both right and wrong. Partly the brainchild of Wayne Aspinall, the Colorado congressman who for so long dominated public land politics, the commission and its report, *One Third of the Nation's Lands*, attempted to bring the letter of the law into correspondence with what had over the years become the spirit of the law. A rough consensus on public ownership, multiple use, and environmental protection dominated much of the report. The commission sought direct legislative sanction that would end disposal as the principle behind U.S. land policy. In this way the report thus echoed Gates.

In practice, however, the commission's legacy was more complicated, because it also recommended the disposal of significant amounts of public lands. It would allow alienation so that cities could expand and new cities could be established. Perhaps more significant, the report recommended the sale of a substantial portion of federal lands, primarily those useful for grazing. In making these recommendations, the commission took into account future population growth, but it overestimated that growth. It predicted that between 1965 and 2000, population would grow by one hundred million. In 1965 population was estimated at 194,303,000, so estimated growth of one hundred million would supposedly yield a population of 294,000,000 in 2000. At the beginning of 1997, however, the estimated population was 266,581,648. The estimate for 2000 is 276,241,000. The commission therefore overestimated growth by almost twenty million people.[2] The commission thus managed to recommend enshrining the public lands as a permanent facet of American life, even as it moved to diminish the extent of those lands. The report became another shot in a battle over public lands that had been raging since World War II and has continued to rage in one form or another ever since (for example, the Sagebrush Rebellion, the New Resource Economics, Reagan's asset management program, and various bills introduced in the 1995 Congress).[3]

In the years since the commission's report, their conclusion that there should continue to be extensive public lands managed by a federal bureaucracy has come under increasingly bitter attacks. Environmentalists have criticized the actual management of these lands. The credibility of foresters and other experts and the success of multiple use—all of which were accepted by the commission—have come under heavy challenge. But an even more serious assault has come from the Right, which opposes not only existing management strategies but the very existence of much of the public domain. Twenty-five years after the commission's report, there is no longer a consensus about the public lands. For example, the Forest Service has written off a century of management in the Blue Mountains of Oregon and Washington as an unfortunate mistake. The great land management agencies—the National Park Service, the Bureau of Land Management, and the National Forest Service—all battle demoralization as well as congressional and public attacks. And two of the great fundamentalisms of American life—the market knows best, and nature knows best—both demand control of the public lands. Gates's consensus has thus crumbled, and it is time to take another look at the public lands.

Interestingly enough, such a reexamination comes almost exactly on the schedule established by the Public Land Law Review Commission. In making its recommendations for the "foreseeable future," the commission defined that future as terminating in the year 2000. Periodic reexaminations are useful in any case, because changes in the present mean that there is a constantly changing perspective on the past. Different contexts demand different questions, and different questions yield different histories. My own questions about the public lands are quite purposefully broad. First, I question Gates's assumption of a progressive history in which a policy of the public lands' alienation gradually leads to public management. At least potentially, public management could end up being an odd interlude in a longer history of turning public lands into private property. Connected with this is the question of what "public" and "private" mean regarding the public lands and how these concepts might determine the country's use of the land.

Such questions cannot be answered by a narrow history of public land law. The public lands are not simply a feature of either land law or environmental management, because so many of America's social hopes and cultural ambitions are wrapped up in them. It is useless to talk of public lands as if they were just a managerial problem that had nothing to do with an array of other social programs and the broader political scene. Gates knew this. He carefully detailed ways in which, from the beginning, public lands were tied to other issues. From a distance some of these issues—tariffs, federal debt, the power of federal government, slavery, internal improvements, the equality of the states—still seem understandably critical, but it is hard to imagine that other issues ever influenced the politics of the public domain.[4] Any successful attempt to manage the public lands therefore has to recognize the shifting cultural, social, and political baggage these lands carry as well as the environmental relations that they embody. This is, in a sense, what any reasonably perceptive public land bureaucrat knows on the day-to-day level.

I begin this brief examination of the big questions by going to what seems the heart of the matter: how we interpret such words as "public" and "private." Historians refuse to give these words—public, private, commons, nature—a life of their own outside of history. Instead, we recognize that these concepts must be historicized and interpreted in context. Over time people have fought over and changed the meanings of these terms. These words, so important for understanding the public lands, are deeply ideological. They all carry baggage, and historians specialize in baggage. What is and should be public, and what is and should be private—that is, what is public business and what is none of the public's business—is one of the great elemental contests of the Republic. In the past two centuries, the categories of public and private and what they contain have repeatedly shifted, and the meaning of the public lands has accordingly shifted with them. What it means to have public lands is therefore a historical question. But why do past answers matter when confronting today's problems? The answer is analogous to the situation one faces when one moves into a house. Each past owner has shaped the house: painted it, decorated it, kept it up, allowed it to fall into disrepair, added to it, subtracted from it. When one makes a repair, one confronts the past: the idiot who bundled the wires with electric tape instead of using a junction box; the fool who punched a hole in the foundation figuring groundwater would never rise this high. The past is constantly there. As houses exist in neighborhoods, history also has to extend further to include the relationship established between public lands and their neighbors, the equivalents of neighborhood compacts, covenants, and zoning. To complete the analogy, in many ways the past owners of a house have not fully moved out; others still possess use rights to parts of the house; and still others are suing for repossession.

The concept of the public has rarely been at a lower ebb than today. Richard Fox's recent and wonderful *A Companion to American Thought* contains entries on "privacy" and "publicity," but not one on "public." Among politicians and activists, "public" is a word in considerable disrepute. A couple of years ago I attended a series of meetings of some of the authors represented in *Uncommon Ground,* the collection of essays edited by the historian William Cronon, and the leaders of several environmental groups. Most environmental leaders hate *Uncommon Ground* for needlessly muddying the line between nature and culture. These meetings were not notable for consensus, but there was one point that most people on both sides agreed on: that the word "public" weakens the appeal of whatever idea it is attached to. Because I like the word, I've wondered about this ever since. Americans can hardly hope to get a clear idea of what to do with the public lands when we are abandoning the very concept of public.[5]

What has happened to the word "public"? Comparing the use of the word in the report of the Public Land Law Review Commission with some of its present uses provides a sense of this. It is striking how consistently the commission used the word "public" and how readily its members referred to "the public good" as the overarching goal of land management. They did not use the term simplistically. Rather, they recognized that the phrase "the public good" was hardly self-evident and that what was good for some parts of the public was not necessarily good for others. The commission recognized that there were competing public goods in land management, and that there were competing publics. They sought to define the general public by making it a collection of several smaller and often conflicting publics: the national public, the regional public, the federal government as sovereign, the federal government as proprietor, the state and local government, and the users of public lands and resources.[6]

When compared to current discussions, this is a remarkably nuanced approach. Politics have moved considerably to the right since 1964, and "public" has become a word associated with an oppressive federal presence: the federal government as proprietor and sovereign. As a result, on the public lands the word "public" seems at times to be in the process of being redefined as simply the sum of privates. To illustrate, here is an admittedly extreme example. My stepdaughter works for the Bureau of Land Management in Prineville, Oregon. Two years ago a citizen decided that indeed he knew what the term "public" meant. He took the total federal land in Oregon, divided it by the total adult population, and claimed his proportional share. Then he posted boundaries and claimed the right to shoot trespassers. He has since moved on to Idaho. Perhaps he was less confused than premature, or maybe he had simply read the New Resource Economics too literally.

Strictly speaking, Karl Hess, the author of *Visions upon the Land: Man and Nature on the Western Range,* is not a representative of the New Resource Economics (what might be called laissez-faire environmentalism of the Gallatin Institute).[7] Like these Gallatin environmentalists, however, Hess believes in the market *and* nature. Usually, one has to choose, but the New Resource Economics embodies what I call the "Doublemint of fundamentalisms": that is, the market knows best and nature knows best. Hess adds to the mix what he calls "landscape visions." In practice, however, he wants to allow the market free play on western range lands— which are heavily public lands—and he relies on nature to sort out the best uses. It is an interesting proposition. By this logic, the eastern United States should be an environmental paradise because it has relatively little public land compared with the West and has long allowed the market to work its magic. Hess does not hold the East up as an environmental example, however. Rather, he believes in big principles more than actual histories. His history is less one of "on the ground" history than of his landscape visions.

Given Hess's emphasis on the market and private choices, he has little place for the public lands. His diversity of landscape visions amounts to the wholesale divestiture of the public lands.[8] Hess lives in the wonderful world where the auctioning off of common resources into the hands of those with enough money to buy can be seen as an attack on elitism. He claims, of course, that divestiture would not amount to an auction of the lands. His plan imagines giving every holder of a social security number a share that would have market value.[9] This, however, does not make his sale less of an auction, nor does it curtail the ability of those with money to reap the bargains; it is just a method for dividing up the proceeds.

There is a precedent to Hess's scheme. In the nineteenth century, Congress often voted shares of the public land to deserving members of the public, such as veterans, in the form of land scrip, or pieces of paper entitling the bearer to a certain amount of land in the public domain. Congress also issued land scrip to create land-grant universities and to fund other public projects. This scrip became floating shares in the public domain, much as Hess's shares would be. Speculators purchased scrip and used it to acquire land. Land scrip became a leading tool for land speculators on the public lands and a constant source of fraud. The results were hardly egalitarian or democratic. Public land flowed toward those with the greatest means to acquire it. Hess's system is therefore only a slightly more sophisticated version of the methods of the squatter near Prineville. Hess is only one of a long line of economists, politicians, ranchers, and others arguing for divestiture of one kind of another. Ever since the Sagebrush Rebellion, no sooner does one group fail than another appears.

On one level all of these plans seem to be a journey into Wonderland in which "public" merely becomes a synonym for "private." But on another level these various plans can, at least on the surface, appeal to strong historical precedent. For much of this country's history, after all, the public domain was a way station on the road to complete privatization. The current passion among some in Congress to dispose of essentially all the public lands simply mimics the common wisdom of the nineteenth century, a wisdom that persisted well into the twentieth century. Recent arguments for liquidating the public lands do have historical lineage, but they are a resurrected corpse from the nineteenth century brought back to life without the nuance, subtlety, and context of the nineteenth-century debates that created them.

Still, it is unwise simply to denounce and dismiss today's ideas about privatization as extreme. The Right's current dominance shows that charges of extremism do not forestall eventual political success. And at times, extreme ideas are even useful and practical. Virtue does not necessarily lie in the middle of the road. As Jim Hightower, the former agricultural commissioner of Texas, is fond of saying, the only things in the middle of the road are yellow lines and dead armadillos. The public lands thus need to be defended on the same level on which they are attacked: as an ideal attached to a larger social vision. If history matters, and if privatization can plausibly claim long historical precedent, it is time to examine that history.

Today, understandably, one thinks of the public lands as a western phenomenon. The presence of large areas of federal lands is one of the things that sets off the West from the East. But at one time, essentially everything west of the Appalachians (except Texas and parts of other regions that were acquired from Mexico, Spain, and France) was part of the public domain. The East as well as the West is a product of federal land laws and practices. Americans need to look at public lands as palimpsest. Just beneath today's current uses and ideas are the older uses and ideas that have shaped the land and its present options.

To understand public lands, it is necessary to do a little intellectual archaeology. The following points, while admittedly overgeneralizations, are both useful and true. Intellectual archaeology, unlike the real thing, does not have to begin at the top layer. Strip away historical layers and at the bottom there is a fundamental assumption operating at the beginning of the Republic: Land would be property. Over much of North America, this had not been the case before. Vernon Carstensen, one of the greatest historians of public lands, liked to quote Pee-o-pee-o-mox-a-mox (Peu-peu-mox-mox) at the Walla Walla treaty council of 1855: "Goods and the Earth are not equal: goods are for using on the Earth. I do not know where they have given land for goods." [10] By 1855, however, Americans had for generations given land for goods and established their equivalence over most of the continent.

This idea of turning land into property was coupled with a second idea: Lands ceded by the original states and acquired by purchase from Indian peoples were to become public lands, public property owned by the people of the entire United States. This public domain was, however, only to be a preliminary stage; the land, with only a few exceptions, would be turned into private property. General agreement on this principle was basic to the early land system, but how the land would be distributed and the purposes this distribution would serve would remain a matter of considerable dispute. This idea of making public lands into private lands was not, however, the equivalent of current belief in the magic of market. The goal was to achieve social purposes, public purposes. Land was to produce revenue for government. Land was to provide for growth of new communities. Land was to reward veterans. Land was to provide for education, internal improvements, and more.[11]

Current advocates of divestiture would surely counter by arguing that putting land in private hands serves public purposes by providing for more efficient use and higher productivity, thus similarly serving public purposes. This misses the crux of the issue, however. Such claims reduce to economics the much broader social criteria of the early system. As the land system evolved in the early and mid-nineteenth century and as a Jeffersonian agrarianism triumphed over a Hamiltonian desire for maximum revenue, economic criteria had yielded to social criteria in shaping the purpose of the public domain. The goal was not simply efficiency and wealth. It was to create a certain kind of society: an egalitarian society of small-scale producers.

Laissez-faire was at this time a means, not an end. Economic liberalism was the doctrine of American radicals such as Thomas Paine and Thomas Jefferson; it is now the doctrine of American conservatives. Private property and minimal government interference in the economy were embraced in reaction to European hierarchical societies in order to spawn a democratic and egalitarian society. Jefferson feared elite governments rewarding their favorites. He wanted a general equality of condition, and he believed that widespread distribution of property and limits on government were the best ways to achieve egalitarian ends. The goal was not privatization per se. One of Jefferson's best-known quotes demonstrates how little regard he had for property rights in the abstract: "Whenever there is in any country uncultivated lands and unemployed poor, it is clear that the laws of property have been so far extended as to violate natural right. The small land holders are the most precious part of the state."[12]

In the twentieth century the context has changed: Minimal government regulation and privatization are not tools for egalitarian ends. These things have become an end in and of themselves. Modern conservatives rarely argue for equality of condition, and they certainly have not been talking lately of the redistribution of private property. The economic content of the idea has pretty much remained the same, but its social content has changed. The basic point is that originally divestiture was less an economic end in itself than a social measure that was designed to produce a certain kind of society that for now we refer to as "agrarian." The goal was not simple divestiture of land to allow the market to work its magic, but creation of small productive units run by the labor of owner and family. The Homestead Act eventually became the symbolic centerpiece of the system. Later divestitures that would hardly seem to be agrarian at all—railroad grants—were justified as serving the agrarian idea of small farmers. Without railroads, there would be no way for farmers to get crops to market, and therefore there would be no farmers; the market alone was incapable of producing railroads in the West. The government, which lacked cash but had land, stepped in to subsidize development. When the railroad grants failed to achieve these purposes, they came under attack and ceased.

This policy of alienation, encouragement of small farms, and use of land as capital for public purposes suffered from fraud and abuses, but it also achieved what early in the twentieth century appeared to be great success. Eugene Davenport, dean of the College of Agriculture of Illinois, admitted waste and abuse, "but we have these farms, these cities, these railroads, and this civilization to show for it, and they are worth what they cost." [13] But even as Davenport spoke, these policies were in the midst of yet another transformation. Piecemeal—through creations of national forests and then explicitly through Theodore Roosevelt's Public Land Commission—the idea of national management of resources on the federal domain began to gain ascendancy.

The general program of divestiture lost its dominance at a certain time and in a certain place. The time was the late nineteenth and early twentieth centuries; the place was the West. But to understand this change, and the western landscape it produced, it is necessary to clarify how and why this happened. The reservation first of national parks and forests and then of larger tracts of the public domain was an achievement of the early conservation movement. Gifford Pinchot, the head of the National Forest Service under Roosevelt, was a critical figure in this transformation. Pinchot's utilitarianism was an appeal to the greatest good for the greatest number over the longest period. Part of this good was undeniably measured by the economic productivity of the public lands, but simple productivity existed alongside other social purposes.

Progressive reform is under a historical cloud today. This cloud arose largely from work on the academic left, including that by environmental historians Samuel Hays and Donald Worster. There are, I have come to realize, certain books that are too good, too persuasive. One of them is Hays's *Conservation and the Gospel of Efficiency*.[14] He outlined the emergence of rational, bureaucratic management by experts with such skilled persuasiveness and brilliance that his interpretation has dominated conservation literature for nearly half a century. The book is brilliant, but like any work that successfully promotes a single idea, it tends to make competing ideas seem like historical losers. Hays was perfectly correct in showing how Forest Service management indeed strove for efficiency and how this led to cooperation among bureaucrats, corporations, and large landowners, but what was lost in this was the democratic and egalitarian tendencies that were also at work. Later environmentalist evaluations of Pinchot go even further. Pinchot's appeals to a common good, to the greatest good for the greatest number, are often made to seem self-serving, tactical, or hypocritical.

As recent literature is beginning to point out, however, the older, now largely discredited, interpretation of Pinchot and the Forest Service as democratic reformers (rather than as bureaucratic managers) was not totally incorrect. The lingering strength of the older agrarian ideal and its core fear of privilege could easily attach itself to utilitarian arguments of the greatest good for the greatest number. Roosevelt's Public Land's Commission of 1903, for example, accepted the idea that the ideal use of the public lands was for homemaking. The commission argued that current laws governing the disposal of these lands did not achieve that purpose, while retaining large amounts of land in the federal ownership would do so by protecting grazing and watersheds.[15] Appeals to private property were not always winning arguments. Property alone could always be trumped if it was associated with privilege.

By the early twentieth century the fear of privilege and dominance by the wealthy elite and the old desire for rural independence could justify both continued alienation of the public domain and retention of the public lands by the federal government. The former governor of Colorado, Alva Adams, argued at the 1911 Dry Farming Conference that "the best way to conserve the land is to use it, and it will be a fortunate day for state and nation when there are no great reservations and no public land; but when every quarter section will be the home of an industrious, producing American citizen." [16]

But the same appeal to agrarian ideals could buttress arguments for national forests in mountains that provided water for irrigation and for retention of grazing lands for the use of small farmers and ranchers. Historian Karen Merrill cites a Pinchot speech to the National Livestock Association in 1904 as "a sort of text" for President Theodore Roosevelt's policy of forest reserves: "He was talking about the policy of home-making and he said that it was the primary object of our Government; that everything else is secondary; and that the object of the forest reserves . . . is absolutely the making of homes. . . . The way to keep a home prosperous is to keep the forest yielding wood, water and grass, and keep them at it permanently." [17]

In practice, progressive reform abandoned the old agrarian technique of disposing of the entire public domain in small lots and sometimes grafted the ideal of homes and small holdings onto the government's efforts to break up what were regarded as monopolies of public resources. Historian Michael Reese, in looking at Forest Service grazing policies in eastern Oregon in the early twentieth century, makes a strong case for how the Forest Service drives large grazers and itinerant herders out of business to open up more opportunities for small herders operating out of homesteaded lands. [18] Agrarianism, as rhetoric and practice, remained quite vital in the early twentieth century. [19] Western ranchers recognized the continuing strength of this ideal and set out quite consciously to transform their image from that of land barons, isolate males, and armed capitalists to the closest equivalent of family farmers available to them: home builders. What is significant in this agrarian rhetoric of homes and small holdings is that ideologically the appeal was not to economic efficiency or property rights but instead to a just and desirable social order.

The idea of using the public domain to support an agrarian, egalitarian social order survived late into the twentieth century alongside a growing managerial ethos; together, these two things created today's idea of a permanent public domain. This is a relatively new idea, one that emerged only piecemeal in the early twentieth century and became de facto policy during the New Deal. Although the Taylor Grazing Act of 1934 closed much of the West to homesteading and other withdrawals, homesteading did not disappear. People filed small numbers of claims in the lower forty-eight states into the 1960s, with larger numbers of claims filed in Alaska.[20] Distribution of the public domain went into eclipse, but it periodically reemerged for what, so far, have been failed crusades.[21] Congress proclaimed retention of the public domain in federal hands as official policy only in 1970.

The last layer of this intellectual archaeology is so current, it is hardly an archaeological layer at all. It is the late-twentieth-century idea of nature. In this era, claims based on nature, along with those based on the market, have largely replaced social claims based on public purposes—the achievement of an agreed-on just society—as the rationale for managing public lands. This is at the root of many of today's difficulties. As agrarianism as a realistic social vision has faded in an increasingly corporate, urban, and industrial society, no compelling social vision for public lands has replaced it. The early and mid-twentieth-century public power crusade tried to articulate public purposes for public resources, but these never achieved the cultural power of agrarianism. The vacuum left by the loss of a compelling social vision—the kind of society the public lands should be used to produce—has given the bureaucratic and corporate vision of market-driven productivity a dominance greater than it ever achieved in the Progressive Era. The only effective counter to the market has been nature. Relatively marginal attempts at preservation in the late nineteenth and early twentieth centuries have grown into something much grander. Preserving nature on the public lands stirs many Americans in the same way that the belief in a just agrarian society produced by the public lands stirred Americans in the nineteenth century.

There are, however, several problems with using nature as guide to policy on the public lands. The first, at least for a historian, is that preserving nature cannot serve as a policy goal because there is no such thing as a static nature that can be preserved. Nature changes. One needs to specify the nature one is after and then intervene to produce it. Biodiversity, preserving or restoring the environment as it was at contact, and letting "natural processes" proceed are all quite different goals that will yield quite different natures. David M. Graber, a government-employed ecologist, has recently written an article about the difficulties and futility of managing what he calls the organizing myth of American national parks: wilderness.[22] Because managing for condition at contact, biodiversity, the free play of native and existing species, and the cultural ideal of wilderness all yield radically different landscapes, Graber contends, it is necessary to specify which phenomenon an ecologist or bureaucrat wants to manage for. One cannot have them all, and given the pervasiveness of human impact, one may not get a pure form of any of them.

If nature conformed to Clementian models with its self-correcting system of succession and its climax, if it was a balanced system with stable ecosystems perfectly adjusted to soil and climate, one could conceivably use nature as an ideal for management. But natural systems are far more complicated. Nature is contingent in its own right—it has a history of change and disruption—and what we see now is a product of that contingent history. But the natural history of the public lands has long been doubly contingent: Human uses and influences have affected them. Humans are part of nature and have shaped natural change. White settlers and explorers did not find "wilderness" or pure nature. By and large, they found a nature shaped by Indian use, primarily by fire but also by grazing, hunting, and agriculture.

As if this contingency did not complicate things enough, nature is also a social construction. This does not mean that there are not "really" plants and trees and animals out there, but rather that humans understand them in terms of larger ideas. Wilderness, for example, as William Cronon has argued, "far from being the one place on earth that stands apart from humanity, . . . is quite profoundly a human creation—indeed, the creation of very particular human cultures at very particular moments in human history . . . it is the product of [a particular] civilization."[23] An appeal to nature is always an appeal to a certain *kind* of nature, but it masks this choice by making it appear that humans are not making a choice about which nature—but rather that we are letting nature itself choose and nature always knows best. Therefore, humans mask and obfuscate the social elements involved.

Appeals to nature disguise social purposes in the sense that certain groups claim to speak for nature. In doing so, their own interests become intermingled with and inseparable from nonhuman populations. Samuel Hays's still underappreciated *Beauty, Health, and Permanence*, which ties environmentalism to consumerism, makes this case.[24] Nature does not speak; only humans' constructions of nature do. This confusion of human interests and natural interests contributes the kind of arrogance that sometimes shows up in environmentalists. Secure in their own virtue, they are outraged when opponents argue that environmentalists also seek selfish purposes—leisure, increased property values, recreation—under the rubric of environmental protection. Opponents of environmentalism will continue to use such arguments as long as they are effective, and these points will be effective until environmentalism has more of a realistic and acknowledged social vision. I am not arguing here that environmentalism involves social interests in order to discredit it—human beings inevitably act from complicated motives—but only to get at the question of nature and the public lands. In laying claim to nature, environmentalists have introduced a second fundamentalism onto the public lands: Nature knows best. I know that in private many environmentalists hold more complicated ideas, but publicly this is the stance they take. And on public lands, it is public visions that matter.

At the end of the twentieth century, without a clear consensus on how public lands should serve public interests and with the loss of a compelling social vision, the public has retreated to sometimes battling, sometimes cooperating, fundamentalisms: Nature knows best *and* the market knows best. But these fundamentalisms will fail as adequate guides because neither has a destination. Both mistake process for purpose. Whatever happens in the market or in the natural world is for the best. The critical thing is that the workings of market and the workings of nature are not interfered with. But humans are deeply involved in both, of course; the prescription is therefore impossible, and the processes it purports to describe are, in part, illusory. Unfortunately, history is unable to supply a social purpose when existing ideologies fail. History is useful, however, for setting out problems and for gauging the claims people make about the cause and origins of these problems. The environmental, social, and economic problems that Americans face on the public lands are pressing and severe, but they will not be adequately confronted—nor will public lands be preserved in any meaningful form—unless Ameri-cans forthrightly face the issue of resurrecting "public" as a meaningful category.

NOTES

1. Paul Wallace Gates, *History of Public Land Law Development* (Washington, D.C.: Government Printing Office, 1968), 32.

2. U.S. Public Land Law Review Commission, *One Third of the Nation's Land: A Report to the President and the Congress by the Public Land Law Review Commission* (Washington, D.C.: Government Printing Office, 1970), 115.

3. Christopher McGrory Klyza, *Who Controls Public Lands: Mining Forestry and Grazing Policies, 1870–1990* (Chapel Hill: University of North Carolina Press, 1996), provides a summary of some of the recent battles.

4. Gates, *History of Public Land Law Development*, 1–32.

5. Richard W. Fox and James T. Klappenberg, *A Companion to American Thought* (Cambridge, Mass.: Blackwell, 1995); William Cronon, ed., *Uncommon Ground: Toward Reinventing Nature* (New York: W. W. Norton, 1995).

6. U.S. Public Land Law Review Commission, *One Third of the Nation's Land*, 6–7.

7. Karl Hess Jr., *Visions upon the Land: Man and Nature on the Western Range* (Washington, D.C.: Island Press, 1992), 224–25.

8. Ibid.

9. Ibid., 234–35.

10. Vernon Carstensen, *The Public Lands* (Madison: University of Wisconsin Press, 1968), xiii.

11. Gates, *History of Public Land Law Development*, 765–66.

12. Quoted in Gates, *History of Public Land Law Development*, 62. Jefferson to Edmund Pendleton, August 13, 1776; Julian Boyd, ed., *The Papers of Thomas Jefferson* (Princeton, N.J.: Princeton University Press, 1950), 1: 492.

13. Carstensen, *Public Lands*, xxvi.

14. Samuel Hays, *Conservation and the Gospel of Efficiency: The Progressive Conservation Movement, 1890–1920* (Cambridge: Harvard University Press, 1959); Donald Worster, *Rivers of Empire: Water, Aridity, and the Growth of the American West* (New York: Pantheon, 1985).

15. Gates, *History of Public Land Law Development*, 488–91.

16. Cited in Karen Merrill, "Whose Home on the Range?" *Western Historical Quarterly* 27 (1996): 437.

17. Merrill, "Whose Home on the Range," 447.

18. Michael Reese, "Dividing the Range: Progressive Conservation, Anti-Monopolism, and Sheep Raising in Central Oregon, 1890–1925." Unpublished paper, copy in author's possession.

19. Merrill, "Whose Home on the Range," 434–46.

20. Gates, *History of Public Land Law Development*, 613.

21. Ibid., 622–27.

22. David M. Graber, "Resolute Biocentrism: The Dilemma of Wilderness in National Parks," in *Reinventing Nature: Responses to Postmodern Deconstruction*, ed. Michael E. Soule and Gary Lease (Washington, D.C.: Island Press, 1995), 123–35.

23. William Cronon, "The Trouble with Wilderness, or Getting Back to the Wrong Nature," in Cronon, ed., *Uncommon Ground*, 69.

24. Samuel Hays, *Beauty, Health, and Permanence: Environmental Politics in the United States, 1955–85* (New York: Cambridge University Press, 1987).

Contributors

CARL ABBOTT is professor of urban studies at Portland State University and the author of several books on the urban West, including *The New Urban America: Metropolitan Growth and Politics in Sunbelt Cities* (1981) and *The Metropolitan Frontier: Cities in the Modern American West* (1993).

DANIEL W. BROMLEY, editor of *Land Economics* since 1974, is Anderson-Bascom Professor of Applied Economics at the University of Wisconsin, Madison. His most recent book is *Environment and Economy: Property Rights and Public Policy* (1991).

JAMES C. FOSTER is chair and professor of political science at Oregon State University and the author of several books, including (with Susan M. Leeson) *Constitutional Law: Cases in Context* (2 vols.; second edition, 1998).

ARTHUR R. GÓMEZ, a National Park employee, is supervisory historian of the Intermountain Cultural Resource Center in Santa Fe. He holds degrees in history from the University of New Mexico; his most recent book is *Quest for the Golden Circle: The Four Corners and the Metropolitan West, 1945–1970* (1994; paperback 2000).

STEPHEN W. HAYCOX is professor of history at the University of Alaska Anchorage, where his research and publications have focused on Natives, environment, law, and politics in Alaska. His history of Alaska will be published in 2001.

MICHAEL W. MCCANN is chair and professor of political science at the University of Washington and the author of several books and articles, including *Rights at Work: Pay Equity Reform and the Politics of Legal Mobilization* (1994)

MARÍA E. MONTOYA holds a Ph.D. in history from Yale University and teaches at the University of Michigan. She is the author of *Children of the Land: Power, Property, and Identity on the Maxwell Land Grant* (2000).

SARAH PRALLE is a Ph.D. candidate in political science at the University of Washington where she teaches environmental politics. She has researched and written about the property rights movement and the globalization of environmental issues.

WILLIAM G. ROBBINS is Distinguished Professor of History at Oregon State University and the author of several books, including *Landscapes of Promise: The Oregon Story, 1800–1940* (1997; paperback 1999).

WILLIAM D. ROWLEY is professor of history at the University of Nevada, Reno, and the author of several books on western range and reclamation policy. His most recent book is *Reclaiming the Arid West: The Career of Francis G. Newlands* (1996).

RICHARD WHITE is professor of history at Stanford University and the author of several award-winning books and articles. His most recent book is *Remembering Ahanagran: A History of Stories* (1997).

BRUCE YANDLE is Alumni Professor and Southern National Bank Scholar at Clemson University, and the author of numerous books, including *The Political Limits of Environmental Regulation*, and editor of *The Land Rights Rebellion*.

Index

Index